REACHING PORT

Reaching Port

A Montana Couple
Sails Around the World

KEITH JONES

St. Martin's Press
New York

REACHING PORT: A MONTANA COUPLE SAILS AROUND THE WORLD.
Copyright © 1983 by Keith Jones. All rights reserved. Printed in
the United States of America. No part of this book may be used
or reproduced in any manner whatsoever without written permission except in the case of brief quotations embodied in
critical articles or reviews. For information, address St. Martin's
Press, 175 Fifth Avenue, New York, N.Y. 10010.

Design by Kingsley Parker

Library of Congress Cataloging in Publication Data

Jones, Keith.
    Reaching port.

    1. Jones, Keith.   2. Mustang (Yacht)   3. Voyages
around the world—1951–   . I. Title.
G440.J7125   1983   910.4'1   83-2988
ISBN 0-312-66431-1

First Edition

10   9   8   7   6   5   4   3   2   1

Contents

Preface

Leaning back in the cockpit of our thirty-two-foot sailboat, gazing at the beautiful little island three hundred feet away, the thought went through my head that, in the wildest dreams we had ever had, never had we thought that we would ever be this close to heaven. Raiatéa, which has to be the most idyllic spot on this earth, was stretched out before us. Beautiful scenery, beautiful people, beautiful weather. How in the world did it ever happen?

Ports of Call

1 Seattle
2 Portland
3 San Francisco
4 San Diego
5 Ensenada, Mexico
6 Puerto Vallarta
7 Acapulco
8 Panama
9 Cartagena, Colombia
10 Panama
11 Galapagos
12 Marquesas Islands
13 Tahiti
14 Raiatéa
15 Rarotonga
16 Pago Pago

17 Suva, Fiji
18 Nouma
19 Gladstone, Australia
20 Cairns, Australia
21 Port Moresby, New Guinea
22 Thursday Island
23 Tanimbar Island
24 Jakarta, Indonesia
25 Singapore
26 Pula We, Sumatra
27 Sri Lanka
28 Maldives
29 Berbera, Somali
30 Djibouti, French Somali
31 Jidda, Saudia Arabia

32 Egypt
33 Rhodes
34 Italy
35 Sardinia
36 Spain
37 Gibraltar
38 Tangier
39 Casablanca
40 Canary Islands
41 Cape Verde
42 Barbados
43 Windward Islands
44 Bahamas
45 Fort Lauderdale

The Mustang's Six-Year Voyage

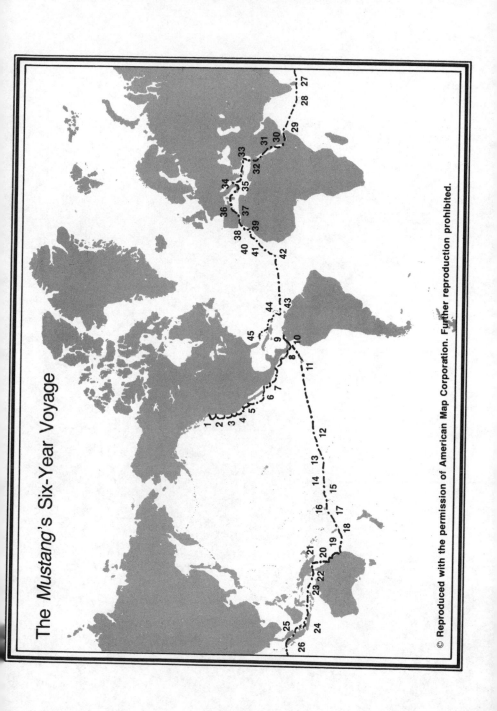

1 MUSTANG

1

No Queen Mary

Rosemary says the adventure started the day I came home from work and asked if she would like to take a trip around the world. She immediately had visions of the *Queen Mary* tied to a New York dock with colored ticker tape billowing out in a light breeze coming in gently from the sea. She imagined bon-voyage flowers and cards filling the stateroom, our friends sipping champagne, giggling and laughing, and finally the call, "All ashore that's going ashore."

Thus, I couldn't understand her look of surprise and dismay when I told her of my plan to spend my spare time for the next ten years building a sailboat about thirty-six feet long. By the time it was finished, our four children would be out of college and we would be able to take off from work to tackle the world.

Women are funny. It surprised me then how much sweet talk, hugs, squeezes, and that sort of thing it took to get her to realize what a wonderful way of life I had planned for us. But she's pretty smart; she came around to my way of thinking in about six months.

Sometimes it surprises me that I dared to think of it. Neither of us were deep-water sailors. I had been born and reared on a Wyoming ranch and left it at age seventeen to go into construction in Alaska. The closest I'd been to the ocean had been as a Seabee during World War II, and I'd spent all that time at a base in Hawaii. Rosemary hadn't been that close. Born and reared in Montana, mostly in the Billings area, she hadn't spent any time out of the state. I had returned to Thermopolis after the war and we met when I moved with my two children to Billings after my first wife died. Rosemary also had two children from a previous marriage. In 1950 we merged our two families, and after her father died we took over the family mobile-home business in 1961.

First, I had to find a marine architect with a set of plans we could afford for a boat capable of going around the world. We wanted one that would be comfortable, yet small enough so that I could handle the sails, pull up the anchor, and do the hundred other things that need to be done when your life depends on you and your boat's performance.

For an architect we found Edwin Monk of Seattle, Washington. As time went by I could see that he had more common sense in his little finger than some men have in their head.

Next, I needed a place to build the boat. Montana is cold in winter and I needed a building. An old garden space on the back of our lot provided the place, and by scrounging up "cull" two-by-fours from small sawmills, I built a shed twenty-four by thirty-eight feet from stacked two-by-fours. Since it was barely large enough, I had to put a big window at each end where planks could be run through before being cut off. Eventually the bowsprit protruded out the front window. The building looked like an old barn, but the neighbors were a kindly group and didn't raise any objections. The city fathers also waived a few building restrictions when I promised to keep the area cleaned up and to turn it back to a garden within ten years.

Rosemary is an income tax accountant. Each tax season, I would wheedle as much money as possible to buy lumber. It is hard to comprehend the amount of lumber that goes into a thirty-six-foot sailboat. It is even harder to come up with the money to pay for it.

I used Monk's recommendation of vertical-grained fir for all the deadwood, fore and aft timbers, keelson, stem, and whatnot. The planking was of Alaskan yellow cedar. The ribs were of white oak and the masts of Sitka spruce. What beautiful timbers, all straight grained. When a plank was lying flat, I could sight along the grain from one end to the other for all twenty-four feet, then turn the plank on edge and again follow the grain end to end.

My only qualifications were five years in construction in Alaska and three in the Seabees. When I stopped to think, I wondered if I had not been somewhat insane to think I could carry out this project. I found the answer to my qualms was simple: Don't think about it. Work. Work. Work. Don't think.

The next nine years became one of life's small bonuses. I would come home from the mobile-home lot, eat supper, go out to the boathouse, pat the boat a couple of times, and go to work. Talk about relaxation. Of course, many times I did not know the next step. I was completely in the dark, for instance, on how to bend eighty-eight two-by-two oak ribs, some of which were supposed to wind up looking something like a piece of spaghetti.

Once again luck was with me. I drove by a dry-cleaning establishment and saw an old upright boiler in the alley. The proprietor was glad to have me haul the old one away for a ten-dollar bill. Then, I found an old road culvert eighteen inches in diameter in which to put the ribs. I had a fairly good wood steaming plant, but what I did not have was any experience bending ribs. My good friend Stewart Cousins informed me that he had bent thousands of ribs while working in his father's boatbuilding yard in East Bluehill, Maine. With him as supervisor, and four other friends as helpers, we completed the rib-bending in three evenings. Total cost to me for labor— six cases of beer. Pounding, driving, and kicking that many ribs into place is not an easy job under a tough taskmaster like Stewart, so I figured we laborers earned the beer.

With the ribs in place I began to put on the planks. What a pleasure it was to work that Alaska yellow cedar into planks. There were thirteen planks to a side, not counting the garboard, the plank that fits on top of the keel. As each plank went into place, I felt as an artist must at each successful stroke of the brush. I caulked the hull with red cedar strips, glued and driven into place between the planks with a wood mallet.

The planks were held in place by three thousand Monel nails, two and a half inches long. Three-eighths-inch wood

5

plugs were glued and driven into place on top of the nails so that the grain of the plugs ran with that of the planks. To determine which way the grain ran in those little wood plugs, I went through them first and marked the grain direction with a pen. Then Rosie dipped them in glue and handed each one to me and I would drive it into place.

Next, it was "pick up that plane, boy, and get to work." Hard, warming work was welcome that winter. I could drive the plane diagonally away from the shear line for hours and never sweat. On the finishing strokes some two months later, a beautifully contoured hull emerged in place of a stack of nailed-up boards. My boat might even float. Oh, what a beautiful thing—as pretty as a mermaid with all the bulges in the right places.

By then I was really enthusiastic. I was neglecting my business to work on the boat for an hour or two each morning as well as each evening. All the neighborhood boys hung around, wanting to assist. To keep the little devils occupied, I gave them nails and a board and told them I needed the board pounded full of nails. They had a great time, but always forgot to take home the hammer, and I accumulated quite an assortment.

One job I worried about was building the masts. Because the boat was a ketch, it needed a mainmast in the middle and a mizzenmast toward the stern. The plans called for a mainmast fifty-six feet tall and a mizzen of thirty-four feet. The masts were to go through the deck and stand on the keel. Each mast was a rectangular hollow tube. The main was eight by six inches at the butt and five by three inches at the top. Both masts were of Sitka spruce, one and a quarter inches thick, glued into place—no nails to rust at the touch of salt water.

I cut two holes in the roof of the boathouse so that I could put the masts in place. Then I gathered friends and relatives, male and female, to help with the gluing. The main took sixty clamps when we glued it together. The glue, clamps, boards, everything had to go into place at one time. As far as I know, no one got glued up inside. Later, when the masts were planed and sanded, painted, and the sheaves put on at the top, I called a crane. Up went each mast to be lowered through the hole in the roof, through the deck of the boat and into place. I swear they reached clear to the sky. I could not sleep that night just thinking about it.

I hated the interior work. I would spend all day on three board feet of lumber, building a cabinet or locker and not even get it into place. It is said that the hull is only 25 percent of a boat, and it is true. When you put on a plank thirty-some feet long, you can see that you have done something. But after working a month on a table or a cabinet, you have not moved two feet from where you started.

At last, almost ten years after the first nail was driven, the *Mustang* was finished. When the building was torn down, my little ship looked so magnificent, I thought it might try to fly away. She had a running horse's head for a figurehead. Her masts were so tall and straight, her curves so beautiful, I stared at her like a lover.

Then the great hassle began. We had to sell our home, sell our business, and wind up hundreds of details from twenty-five years of living in Billings. It seemed we knew everyone in the town of fifty thousand and they all came by to shake hands. There were plenty of skeptics, too, when they heard we were planning to sail around the world. We ignored them, but the going-away parties every night certainly slowed up work the next day. Visitors from all over the West stopped to have a look at the boat, the phone rang constantly, and the local newspaper had to make a visit.

I called a boat hauler in California who had agreed to arrive June 1. I had also arranged for a crane to lift the boat onto the truck. About two days before loading time, the trucking company called me to say the truck could not be there for another two weeks. Either the wire burned out or they hung up because I was unable to finish calling them all the names I thought of. Within two hours I found a trucking company unloading a boat in Cody, Wyoming, one hundred miles away. They had their truck in Billings the next day. By the time we arrived in Seattle, a thousand miles away, the trucker was our friend as well as our driver. I sent Rosie to town from Shilshole

Marina to buy brushes so that we could paint the last coat of bottom paint. The driver told her to get three brushes because he would help. He did, too.

The painting done, we brought a crane over to lift the *Mustang* off the truck and delicately set her down into the water of Puget Sound. I thought I should step aboard and get the feel of her. I stepped over to the companionway and looked below. Yikes! Someone had poured water in her—quite a lot of water. It was rushing over the supplies and floating the new carpets. I ran over to the new bilge pump to pump the water over the side. The pump couldn't keep up and the ship settled deeper into the water. I told the crane operator to lift her up again.

My heart was in my stomach. I couldn't believe my beautiful little ship leaked because I couldn't see even a hairline crack.

After some thought and some long conferences with just about all of the dockside superintendents, I gathered my wits and realized my ship had been drying for nearly ten years in a dry climate and would probably swell. At least, I hoped so. After more conferences with crane operator, truck driver, and several of the "superintendents," I sent Rosie uptown to rent an electric pump, or perhaps two small ones. She rented one one-and-a-half-inch pump and a one-inch one. Keeping the slings around her, we put the *Mustang* back into the water and began pumping. We baby-sat those pumps day and night while I wondered if the adventure was ending before it started. Some thirty hours later, when we changed watches in the night, Rosie said, "It may be my imagination, but I think, just maybe, we are gaining on it."

Sure enough, in another twenty-four hours, my *Mustang* had swelled enough that our own pump could keep up with the water. It was a lesson learned—one of hundreds in the next few years—and a big blow to my ego.

We cruised the Puget Sound area and its islands for about three months. Those pine-covered islands are a joy to the cruising man, with quaint little harbors, steepled churches, and clapboard buildings. Our good friends Bob and Hattie

Martin, as well as several other friends, joined us for some cruising.

What a way to live! Every day a holiday! One night we would anchor in a quiet little cove and go ashore to dig clams and oysters; the next night we would find a small village.

One day in the shipping lanes we were enveloped in fog. From all directions we heard the eerie *ooh-wah* of foghorns, but we could see nothing. It was foolhardy to go forward, but with tides and currents we could not stay in one place. I realized we had no radar reflector, so I grabbed a galvanized pail, hooked it to the mizzen halyard, and hauled it up the mast. Then, with our little foghorn, we tried to answer the honking of the large ships. One ship came so close we heard the big engines thumping. They were almost as loud as my heart. Such a helpless feeling, not knowing which way to go, or if to stay. Then, we could tell that he was going around us. What a relief when the fog lifted and we were in bright sunshine again.

I felt pretty foolish when I realized I had hauled the bucket up the mast but had no way to haul it down. Another lesson learned.

In all our sailing in Puget Sound, entering Bellingham Harbor was possibly the most satisfying. After leaving the ranch in my teens, I had lived for a while in Bellingham before going to Alaska. I had seen the beautiful sailboats at anchor in that bay and had looked at them with envy, knowing I would never be able to set foot on one. They were for the rich; in fact, for the very rich. What a wonder that one day Rosie and I sailed right into the harbor among them just like we knew what we were doing.

We were soon to learn that we did not.

2

First Storm

The honeymoon was over. A few days later, in early October, we sailed through the Juan de Fuca Strait, around Cape Flattery, and turned south. The fishermen and experienced cruising people had warned us that we were starting south too late in the year. Some had told us that in October this coastline would compare to the dreaded seas of Cape Horn. We were determined to get south into balmier country, however, and thought we could handle some bad weather.

About two hours after we reached the sea, all hell broke loose. The wind, after a short calm, switched to the south-southwest, so we were trying to beat into it. The skies darkened, and black clouds raced overhead. The waves continued to rise, first lifting the boat into a fearsome, awe-inspiring view of dark gray water, then dropping us down into the trough until there was a wall of that same gray water twenty-five feet above us on every side. Spray blew almost horizontally from the breaking waves.

We closed the companionway door and sat huddled in the open cockpit. I tried to get Rosie to go below, but she said, "It's worse down there, not knowing what's going on." Between intermittent rain and the breaking waves, we were soaked and shivering. By four in the afternoon, it was nearly dark. A long night lay ahead. Reefing the sail, taking it in, was long past due. It had to be done before dark. What had seemed so easy in practice on calm seas now looked nearly impossible.

As we came into the wind, the sails cracked and flapped with a racket. The boom jerked crazily, swinging back and forth with tremendous force. I could barely hang on to tie the reef knots. My hands were so cold and stiff that every knot took an endless time. Every so often a giant wave came from a new direction and washed a wall of water over the boat. It took all my strength to hang on. Like a fool I had gone on deck without a safety harness, never realizing the force of wind and ocean. Rosie stood up, wanted to help, but I yelled crossly at her, "Don't be an idiot. Stay in the cockpit!"

It must have taken an hour to get the miserable job done. Finally, we could "fall off" and fill the sails. Just to cut down the racket of flapping was a relief.

When I returned to the cockpit, Rosie was crying and shivering violently. I asked, "What's wrong?"

"I'm j—j—just so darned sc—scared! How can the boat hold up under this terrible beating?"

"You don't have a thing to worry about," I tried to reassure her. "This boat can take it. It's designed for it and it's strong. I know, because I built it strong. Right now, it's important to get into dry clothes and to get a little food in us." I had been feeling squeamish all day. Perhaps some hot soup would help.

"Will you be all right while I go below and change?" I asked her. I hated to leave her alone in the cockpit, but this was going to be a long, rough night. We had to conserve our energy. "Then you can go below and change and maybe put together something to eat."

"I—I think so," she said.

Below I found a mess. Several items Rosie had thought secure had tipped over, including a canister of flour. Flour was everywhere. Rose would be horrified, but there was nothing to do about it then. Shivering violently, I found dry clothes and oilskins, braced myself against the bulkhead, and finally got out of the wet clothes and into the dry ones. I put on insulated underwear, two pairs of slacks, two sweaters, a jacket, and, over all, the oilskins. I felt myself warming a little.

Outside the mountainous waves were an overwhelming sight as they bore down on the boat, their breaking crests the only white in a pitch-black night sea. In the distance shone the lights of a freighter. It looked so secure that we could not help envying the crew.

"Go below now," I told Rosie, "and don't worry about the mess. We'll clean it up later."

Quite a while later she handed up some hot canned stew, which we ate while huddled in the cockpit taking turns at the tiller. We decided on one-hour watches, although even an hour can seem like a long time alone in the cockpit.

About three in the morning, when we were not doing much more than hanging on, we had a near-miss with what I thought was a four-story house floating around. It came out of the dark, a sudden ghostly shadow looming out of the sea so close alongside that I could have practically reached out and touched it.

Later, we found that it had been a big oil barge that had broken in two in the middle and sort of folded up like a big strap hinge. The tug pulling it had put out the word that about forty feet of it was sticking up out of the water. According to later reports, the tug still had a line on it, but we never saw the tug, only the terrible shape of the barge bearing down on us and sliding by. It was a weird—and frightening—experience.

The next day was more of the same. I wondered how long we could stand up to it. We were making very poor time, perhaps only a knot. When night came again, we could see lights on the land, but by then we were so disoriented we could not locate the entrance into Westport, which has a bad bar in front of it. After reading the sailing directions about the thing, we were more frightened than ever: "Small craft should exercise extreme caution entering this harbor when the bar is breaking."

It seemed essential, however, that we get into harbor and rest up. I decided to call the Coast Guard to see if they could set us straight. We contacted them, our first experience using our ship-to-shore radio. By asking us what we saw on the shore in front of us, they determined we were not in front of the approach at all. They advised us to throw out the anchor and stay where we were while they sent a boat to locate us and lead us over the bar. So, for the first time, out went the hook—

into only thirty feet of water. The *Mustang* pitched and rolled, jerking crazily on the anchor line. We kept peering for the Coast Guard boat. In about a half an hour a boat flashed a light at us and the big red stripe on the bow of that white Coast Guard boat loomed up. It certainly looked good!

They told us on the ship radio to start our engine and follow them. As we started the iron mainsail, all twenty horsepower, their boat was disappearing into the high seas and rollers. We took out after them at full speed. They kept urging us to speed up so that both ships would have more steerageway. I told them our rpm's were higher now than I had been told to run the engine and I could hear them over the radio doing a lot of muttering.

Our motor quit. Oh, boy! There were clamshells, rocks, mud, and whatnot rolling around in the tops of those big seas. I went out to put up some sail and Rosie told them on the phone what had happened.

They said, "Forget the sail. We'll circle and throw you a line and tow you across the bar. A breaking bar is no place to start sailing."

Rosie overheard the skipper of the boat leading us in talking to his commanding officer ashore: "Their engine has quit. We are going to get a towline to them and tow them across the bar."

"Where are you now?" asked the commander.

"About one hundred feet off the bar."

"Can you make it?"

"We'll sure give it a good try."

The Coast Guard helmsman did a tremendous job of controlling his boat, bringing it close enough for a sailor to heave us a line, but not close enough to knock against our boat. Both boats were pitching up and down. I grabbed their inch-and-a-half-diameter line and secured it. At what seemed to us a breakneck speed they towed us across the bar.

All at once it was quiet. We were inside. We were in that beautiful, peaceful harbor. My God! What a wonderful feeling!

In the morning we could see boats everywhere: fishing boats, sailboats, small freighters, and charter boats (locally often called pukey boats because the landlubbers they take out are hanging over the side before they get across the bar). We were told that one thousand boats were inside waiting out the storm. No one could believe we had been out in it in a sailboat.

Mornings, skippers would get up and walk out to look at the breakers crashing on the breakwater sending spray fifty feet into the air. They would shake their heads, look at one another, and say, "Not me. I'm not going out over that bar today. No sir. Not me!"

It was ten days before we could leave for the Columbia River and Astoria, Oregon.

3

Getting Our Sea Legs

In company with another sailboat, we finally left Westport—in the middle of the night because the tide was right. The treacherous Columbia River bar proved to be tranquil, smooth water compared to Westport. With a favorable wind and an ingoing tide, we sailed right up to Astoria. That turned out to be a pleasant and interesting stay.

Going out a week later, however, was anything but pleasant. Twice we had to turn around and go the nine miles back up the river because the bar was so rough. On the third try, we had no choice. The motor quit again, so in spite of the bar being rough, we could not turn around and had to sail on out.

Someone told me when I bought the little diesel that nothing could go wrong with a diesel. Well, maybe nothing could go wrong, but the darned thing would not run when we needed it most.

Our next stop was Newport, Oregon, a nice little town in a

good harbor with a bad bar out in front. We got in with no great problems. I spent the next few days working on the engine. Rosie insisted on a motel for a couple of nights. She maintained that a hot bath was the only thing that would remove the salt. Such luxury.

As we were leaving the harbor a few days later, Rosie said, "Keith, I think the gale warnings are up—two red flags flying. I'm sure."

"Naw," I said. "That's just the small-craft warnings and we are not a small craft. Look, it's a beautiful day."

The sun was just coming up and it did look like a good day. It did not last long. Within an hour the wind was blowing fifty knots. It was Cape Flattery all over again. All day we pitched and rolled, and tacked back and forth. We were not making any time and the seas were rising. I wanted to get offshore, but we could still see land after eight hours. Suddenly, there was a loud crack like a gunshot and down fell the reefed mainsail, about to go overboard, while the steel halyard flew up the mast and whipped in the wind.

I crawled forward as fast as possible to gather up the mainsail. By the time I had the mainsail tied down, Rosie was pointing to the top of the mast. The steel halyard had whipped around the jib. Quickly, I tried to get the jib down, but it would not budge. I yelled at her to loosen the jib sheet, but still the sail would not come down.

"Start the engine and bring it into the wind," I yelled at her. Without steerageway we were really out of control. While she started the engine, I tugged at the jib. With a sharp tearing sound, the jib sail tore completely across. The engine gave a couple of coughs and quit. It took a minute for me to realize that the jib sheet, the line that holds the sail taut, had gone over the side and was in the propeller. We were in a hell of a shape: no mainsail, no jib, no engine, and the rocky shore still in sight.

I got the sails somewhat under control and went back into the cockpit to figure out the next move. The mizzen only brought us into the wind. Without momentum, we could not steer.

"Please, please, Keith, let's call the Coast Guard," Rosie said.

"My God, not again." But I could see the stricken look on her face and I knew it was the sensible thing to do. "This is the last time," I said to myself as I put the call through.

The Coast Guard came through again, and at midnight we were going under the bridge at the entrance to Newport. Two commercial fishermen who had heard our distress call were waiting to receive our lines.

After a few days of repair work, we sailed on down the coast, heading for San Francisco, passed ill-tempered Cape Mendocino easily, and had no problems until, outside the Golden Gate Bridge, we got into a dead calm. The engine then quit again. We were drifting right into the paths of freighters, barges, tugs, and fishing boats, helpless to do anything about it. The boat rolled constantly, slapping the sails back and forth.

Someone must have called the Coast Guard and told them there was a boat adrift in the entrance because one of their boats came alongside. The officer said we would have to get out of the road. I asked them how they expected me to do that with no wind and no motor. Once again, a line was put aboard, and the Coast Guard towed us under the Golden Gate Bridge to Berkeley Marina. It was a terribly humiliating way to enter a harbor. I really had looked forward to sailing through the Golden Gate.

Here Rosie gave one of her numerous ultimatums: "I'm not moving another foot in this boat until the engine is fixed!" Ah, women! I had fixed it ten times. What was she complaining about? But, I called a diesel mechanic who was supposed to know what he was doing. He could not find the trouble. It took much head scratching, hemming, and hawing, but the solution was simple when I figured it out. I had to buy a new engine, a two-thousand-dollar remedy.

Only when the boat was hauled out to install the new engine did I find the problem with the old one. When I bought the first engine, a used one, I was told it had a two-to-one reduction gear, and I bought a propeller on that basis. Instead, the reduction was closer to one to one. When we really needed the engine and revved it up to full power, it became overloaded, could not turn the propeller, and stopped. It was that simple.

By now the old engine had been ruined, so we purchased a new Swedish diesel and had it installed by the company selling them. That company was right on Fisherman's Wharf, and so for two weeks we were in the center of that unique atmosphere. First thing every morning we smelled the sourdough bread baking and the crabs boiling, and we could hear the vendors hawking their wares. It was really something to see Rosie head up Market Street to the post office on our Honda 90. Gramaw on a motorcycle.

After our new engine was installed, we motored out under the Golden Gate and headed south. Again, it was dark when we entered Newport Beach, went around the breakwater, and up the channel. Suddenly, a ferry pulled out in front of us. I threw the engine into reverse while we were still going forward. Nothing happened. We did not stop. We did not slow down. We did not go in reverse. We just continued coasting along on a collision course with the ferry. He did not change course one degree. The skipper was cussing me. I was cussing him. But ferries do have right-of-way. Finally, we turned left, to port, to glide by his stern. I think we had the clearance of only a coat of paint between us.

The engine was still running, but we were going nowhere. It was dark, there was no wind, and we were in the middle of a busy channel. I threw out the anchor. I then crawled down into the engine room and looked things over. I told Rosie to put the motor into reverse then into forward. The engine and transmission seemed to be working okay, but the shaft was not turning. By hanging by my heels from the cockpit floor with my head down in the lowest part of the bilge, I could see that the propeller shaft had pulled out from the socket in the transmission. Fishing around in the bilge, I found the key, put it in the keyway on the shaft. I strained, I grunted. I cussed the damned mechanic who had not tightened the setscrew. I pushed. I hammered and swore some more, and finally, we were mobile again.

We found a buoy to tie to. It took three rums and a lot of

sweet talk to calm that Rosie down. Mad? Gracious! Rosie wanted me to go back to 'Frisco and beat up that mechanic, but I got out of that one by telling her we had to get south as soon as possible.

Three days later, while Rosie was shopping, I took the boat for a sail alone. As I was approaching the wharf, I grabbed a line, jumped off, and attempted to whip the line around a cleat. But the boat was moving forward faster than I realized. The line tightened instantly and tore the end of my middle finger off. I looked down in shock. I could not believe it had happened so quickly.

A friend took me to the emergency room of a nearby hospital. The doctor who was called would not operate until they had checked my credit rating. They gave me a pail of soapy water in which to hang my hand while I sat there waiting for four hours. Of course, the pail kept about a gallon of blood from getting on their cussed hospital floor. That doctor was one of the most obnoxious men I have ever met. When he did operate, he cut off about three-quarters of an inch more of the finger and sewed it up. He did a miserable job, too. He wanted to cut off the one next to it also, but Rosie told them that if he did, she would raise more hell around there than they had seen in a while. During that conversation, I was waiting in the operating room under some kind of dope. They didn't cut that finger off, but I left the hospital the next day with heavy bandages on both fingers.

A sailor with the use of only one hand is a pretty sorry sight, and I wondered how I would cope. By fumbling around with one hand and trying to keep the bandaged one out of the way, I managed the hundred miles to San Diego. After a week there, making final arrangements to leave the United States, stocking up and getting the necessary permits for Mexico, my hand was better.

Away from San Diego we sailed for Mexico. In Ensenada, we had our first experience with foreign port authorities, our first taste of Mexican food, and our first time anchoring out and taking the dinghy ashore. To get the anchor down in the right place and in the right way when there are dozens of boats in a harbor is one of the hardest things to do on a boat, and I never fully got used to it. You have to anchor so that when the boat swings on a change of wind you don't hit another boat. If we anchored after they did, it was our responsibility to clear everyone.

When a boat enters a foreign port, it must fly the Q flag, yellow in the sail alphabet. Then officials such as customs, doctors, immigration, port captain come out to examine the boat's papers, the crew's passports and medical clearance. They usually ask, "Has anyone died between here and your last port?"

Sailing down the coast of Baja was a real delight. It seemed as if the adventure had really begun. The land, though barren, was beautiful from the sea, sometimes as dark blue, very rugged hills, sometimes as red and orange flatland. Some bays would have no other yachts in them, and in some we would meet other cruising people. At least a dozen boats were anchored in Turtle Bay.

From there it was on to Mazatlán, Puerto Vallarta, Manzanillo, and Zihuatanejo. Beautiful little Zihuatanejo, undoubtedly one of the best anchorages we had been in, was a small bay with a small village on its shores. Friendly people, little restaurantes, and Mexico's high, dry hills coming down to white sandy beaches made it pretty close to heaven.

We anchored offshore about three hundred yards and had to row in. They had a short, concrete dock. The method of tying the dinghy to the dock was to drop a stern anchor, then stretch a bowline to the dock. One day an outboard came in fast and cut my anchor line. As anchors are hard to come by in that part of the world, I decided to get my snorkel to dive down and get my anchor. What did I see? Fish. Nothing but fish. It was impossible to see the bottom through them—even though it was only about twelve feet down.

I am a strong man who weighs about 170 pounds. The largest fish down there did not weigh ten pounds. But could I fight ten thousand fish? I answered myself: No!

I was back on the dock looking discouraged when a little

Mexican boy about eight years old came along. I think he had been watching all the time. He said, "Anchor, *señor*? Anchor?" He pointed down.

"*Sí, sí*," I said, about to cry because of losing the thing. The kid dove off the dock, and so help me, he was underwater (and fish) for at least five minutes. When he came up my anchor was in one hand, a seashell in the other, and a big grin was on his face.

I sheepishly looked around to see who else was watching. I wanted to step on the kid's head and see if he could spend ten minutes underwater. Instead, I took the anchor and him out to our boat, treated him to a Coke, and gave him a couple of bucks.

Zihuatanejo (pronounced *Zee-what-an-nay-ho*) to Acapulco was about 117 miles. It was the best sailing we'd had. A good offshore breeze blew about twenty knots, the day was warm, and the night balmy. On a southeast course, we met no reefs or offshore dangers. We could stay between one-half and one mile offshore in twenty fathoms and watch the palm trees go by. That was the life.

About noon, we were sailing through the entrance into Acapulco. What a jewel! A good harbor, a good anchorage, and flowers, flowers everywhere.

Shipwrecked

In Acapulco Rosemary and I decided we were ready to sail our boat around the world. I knew the boat was seaworthy. For ten years I had shaped every plank and sanded every board in her. She'd proved her ability in the ten months since we'd put her into Puget Sound after the haul from dry-land Montana. Now we thought we knew the *Mustang* well enough to tackle the world. First, however, we decided to go back up the coast to San Diego, do some work on the boat, and then start out around the world via Hawaii.

We knew it would be a hard beat back up the coast—the wind, currents, and weather were against us—but it seemed the thing to do. So we retraced the route we'd come down. It was beat, beat, beat, tacking against the wind, hard work, and wet all the time. By May 3 we were leaving Capo San Lucas, the southern tip of Baja California. Six days later we had made only another three hundred miles, and the weather was turning worse.

For two days the wind had been rising, eventually to about forty-five knots. Since we were taking such a pounding and were both so dead tired, I decided we would go into a slight indentation north of Abreojos to anchor and rest for a day or two. From midnight until 6:00 A.M., I worked the boat around Punta Abreojos while Rosemary tried to sleep. When daylight came, I called down to ask Rosie if she would take over for a couple of hours while I took my turn trying to sleep. She said, "Sure."

Fifteen minutes later I was sound asleep despite the boat's rolling and pitching all over the place. A half hour after that I was wakened by Rosemary screaming my name. Just then we struck something hard. The boat jarred and boomed like a drum.

We were in bad shape, about two miles offshore. All around us water boiled over reefs. The wind blew a gale directly toward shore. A big roller lifted the boat and dropped it hard onto one side, throwing the boom to the opposite side. With every big swell we were lifted about twenty feet and then dropped into the bottom of the trough between waves with a terrible crash. The boat rattled and creaked and groaned. As we hit bottom, a wall of water poured over the transom, into the cockpit, and down into the cabin. I threw out the stern anchor, hoping it would hold until I could do something right. I climbed forward and tried to get the sails down. Waves broke over the top of us, getting higher all the time, and I had to give up. The sea turned us broadside and water poured over the side, bouncing and rolling us from side to side. The force of the water was tremendous. The engine was worthless against it. I thought one of the large waves might roll us clear over as we hit on one side; then, the water turned us and we hit on the other.

I was scared. I cut the lashings on the partially inflated rubber dinghy and started pumping it up. The shore looked forbidding and desolate. I could see nothing but sand dunes. Nothing! I thought, Even if we get ashore, can we survive?

Rosemary was below, wading in water over her knees to get blankets and food together. She handed up some blankets. I put them into the dinghy, but the wind carried them away. Then the boom crashed across the cabin and into my head. It must have knocked me out for a moment. I came to hanging on. When I brushed at the stuff stinging my eyes, my hand came away bloody. My nose was broken, I learned later. I clung to the boat until I could see again.

I had been naked all this time and suddenly realized it as I shivered with cold—or was it fright? Naked or not, I thought we'd better get out of there before the boat rolled over and trapped one or both of us under it. With every wave, the dinghy bucked wildly, trying to capsize. Rosie brought up water and a few cans of food, which, when I could function again, I lashed in a sack to the dinghy. I could see that we would have to get into the water to hold the dinghy from capsizing as we went through the surf. I knew there were sharks and that they were attracted to blood. As I was still bleeding, I could only hope that they didn't find us. With a last look at the havoc on my wonderful boat, we got into the water, one on each side of the dinghy, and started the long swim toward shore.

Every wave crashed over our heads. We caught our breath between them. When we were about halfway to shore, a man appeared on the beach and waved at us. I had never been so glad to see a human being. By the time we climbed out of the water, a dozen people were pulling and hauling on our dinghy—all talking Spanish at ninety miles an hour. I put on a soggy pair of pants Rosie had thrown into the dinghy and looked up at the beach.

Various items of gear were floating ashore. I looked at Rosie and only then realized that we had not bothered to put on life preservers, had not even thought about them.

Now that we were safe, the impact of what had happened hit me in the solar plexus. I think that if I had had a gun, I would have shot myself right then. Ten years of work gone! Twenty-five thousand dollars or so, no insurance, and all of our personal gear gone!

I was too sick to care that the whole population of Abreojos, fifty-some people, was running up and down the beach, scrambling for our gear as it washed ashore. I did notice that among them were several big, young, husky fishermen. With Rosie ashore and with the knowledge that I could swim that far in the surf, I decided to try to hire two or three to go back to the yacht with me to see if we could reposition the anchor and possibly save my boat. They agreed—for five dollars a day—and one went to his home and got a sixteen-foot boat with an outboard motor.

For the next ten hours we worked, never stopped pumping. We even pumped out through the head. We tried to take the anchor out but had to give up after several attempts—no small boat could stay upright in the breaking waves.

It was surprising that the boat held together under the pounding. The steel shrouds had snapped and were lashing back and forth. The sails trailed over the sides into the water. The engine still ran—to no effect. I hoped we could keep the boat pumped out and that a rising tide would give us enough water to sail out. But by the end of the afternoon, I was just too tired to go on. My nose and head hurt like hell. I shivered with cold. When I looked down along the side and saw pieces of the boat breaking away, I knew it was hopeless. I told the fellows we might as well quit. They nodded. I think they had known for some time that it was useless, but did not have the heart to tell me.

Halfway in I looked back and noticed the motorcycle still tied on deck. I talked the fellows into going back after it. I was too done in to join them and swam on to shore.

Luckily, they had put a line on the motorcycle, for they dropped it into the sea getting it into the rubber dinghy. As they approached the beach, the dinghy capsized, and again the cycle was dumped into the ocean. But they recovered it and landed it on the beach where everyone was laughing and talking, having a great time collecting whatever they took a fancy to and taking it home.

As I came out of the water, Rosie had just returned. She had gone up the beach about twenty miles where she had been told there was a larger boat that might be able to pull us out to sea.

"The boat left about an hour before we got there," she said. "Such rotten luck."

She was crying and so was I. I could not look out at my brave little boat taking such a beating. I could not help her. That was that! The end of everything, of all our plans and dreams, of everything!

5

Up the Baja

One of the older men, Pedro Zunigo, asked us to get into his pickup and go up to his house to eat and sleep. We loaded the motorcycle into his pickup and started toward his house. What a country! We were stuck three times in about a mile.

Over the hill and about two miles away was a little cluster of houses. Zunigo took us into his house, and the first thing he did was to give us both a big glass of tequila. Gad, it burned going down, but it also caused me to stop shivering. His wife cooked up a good, hot meal of *langosta* (lobster), bread, and potatoes. She felt so badly about our losing the boat that she was crying along with Rosemary.

The next morning we went back out to the beach, but it was just as hopeless as before. The boat was still there, underwater. We could see the masts flopping back and forth. I could not stand to look at it. We began to look for a way home.

There was no way out of the village unless we waited a month or so, when a DC-3 would come in to fly their fish and lobster out to Ensenada, about five hundred miles north. Since there was nothing to do, no newspapers or books, no radios, and no one who spoke English, I decided to try to start the Honda. I took everything off that I could and dried it out. I got the water out of the gas tank and Pedro took the battery someplace to get it charged and new water put into it. Two days later, in the evening, I got the doggone cycle started. Oh, were we happy. I took all the children in the village for a ride to charge the battery and further dry the thing out.

When we said we were going to ride it to Ensenada, the people told us, *"No vayan on moto,"* "Don't go on the motor." *"Malo camino, señor, malo camino,"* bad road.

We had taken our valuable papers and about four hundred dollars off the boat. Two hundred remained after we paid the people who had helped us. I do not know why, but in the first trip ashore I had taken the sextant, a good Plath. We'd been there a day or so when I realized it was missing. I inquired and found someone who had seen the man who'd taken it. We went to this Mexican's house to claim it, and, of course, he denied having it. He acted as if he did not know what we meant.

We were not in a very good position to be fighting with anyone or, for that matter, to be accusing them of stealing, so we just waited around outside his miserable shack. Finally, his wife started berating him and he reached under his board bed and produced it. Then he wanted a reward for returning it. Pedro had told me he was not too much trusted in the village, so I told him what I thought of him. Since I didn't know any cuss words in Spanish, about the worst I could come up with was *"Muy malo hombre,"* very bad man.

We had to leave! Finally, Mr. Zunigo drew us a map on a piece of brown sack paper. Mrs. Zunigo cooked enough food to last us three days, wrapped it in a cloth flour sack, dampened it, and told us to dampen it whenever we could.

We hated to say good-bye to them. We had never met such kind, unselfish people. But we felt that perhaps a little action would rid us of the sunken feeling.

They gave us a double wool blanket, a rubberized tarp, a plastic jug for water, clothes, gasoline, and everything they thought we would need to travel the five hundred miles. We left them our rubber dinghy, about all we had salvaged except the sextant.

So, four days after our calamity, we started north. Let me here say one thing: If a Mexican ever tells you *"Malo camino,"* believe him. His idea of a good road seems bad to us. That first day, we had to get off the cycle many times and wade through the sand, pushing the cycle in gear. At one point we came across a Mexican in a pickup who had been stuck in the sand for two days. He was just sitting there patiently waiting for someone to come along and help him. He apparently thought there was no use getting excited. In the back of his pickup, an old one, was a barrel of water, about thirty gallons. On the seat beside him were two bottles of tequila. Outside the pickup were three empty bottles. He indicated that they had really helped to steady his nerves while he was waiting for help.

We gave him what help we could and he finally got going in the opposite direction. When we finally got out of the sand ourselves, we got into barren, rocky terrain. It looked like the moon.

Late in the afternoon we reached San Ignacio. Here there was a small hotel, or according to the nice lady who ran it, "a leetle otel." It was full. Two Americans in a plane had been forced to land nearby, and two college boys were roughing it on 350-cc motorcycles complete with camping gear. They told us we couldn't make it through the Baja on the Honda. The nice lady proprietor must have seen the dismayed look on Rosie's face when she said she was full, because she said we could have her bed. She would stay next door with a friend. She also told us to help ourselves to cold beer in the refrigerator, keep track of what we drank, and pay her in the morning. There was a delightfully green, enclosed garden and a shower of water heated on the stove. That was one of the best hotels we have ever been in: water, food, beer, and a bed. What more could any human being desire out of life. I wanted to settle down right there, but Rosie said no.

We were told that about fifty miles north there was a rancho where we could stay under cover and where we could get food and gasoline. We found it, and others, all the way to Ensenada. They were crude houses, usually fenced off a bit, with some sort of water supply close at hand. They looked like stage stations on today's television or in western movies.

What a desolate desert the center of Baja is. I could understand why the two boys on the two 350-cc motorcycles had predicted that it was impossible for us to make the trip riding double on a small Honda 90. Actually, the road was a jeep trail: sometimes sand six inches deep, and sometimes nothing but rocks. Every so often we would come to a fork in the trail. Which one should we take? It was no place to get lost: too hot in the daytime and too cold at night. The method we used at all the forks was to stop and count the tracks and then take the most traveled one. Occasionally the damn road went off in three different directions. That called for plenty of conjecture and talk. Fortunately, we managed to stay on the right trail.

The second night out, our destination was the village of El Arco, at, I think, about three thousand feet elevation. On the edge of the village was an old, weather-beaten, sun-bleached board on a gnarled, crooked post stuck catawampus between some rocks. On the board in shaky letters was the word *motel*. Off to the left a couple of hundred yards were three shacks, two goats, a half-dozen chickens, and four barking dogs.

I said to Rosie, "I think this is the local Hilton. Does it suit your fancy this evening?"

"If they just have shade and water, it will be heaven," she

said. We were filthy dirty and about done in.

They had shade and water. They also had a bed, which the children scurried around and made up with clean sheets and everything. It came pretty close to heaven, or so it seemed to us. Supper was tortillas, frijoles, goat meat, and coffee. After breakfast, I paid the bill: two dollars. The proprietor said he could make money at that. He also had a little silver mine about one quarter of a mile from his house. The mine shaft had been driven back into the base of a cliff. He would mine about one hundred pounds of ore by hand, bring it up to his house, and crush it by hand in a big dish-shaped tub about three feet in diameter. He sat patiently in the evenings crushing the ore he had extracted that day. For those efforts, he told me, he made about five dollars a day.

The third day we traveled until we found a pretty good-looking rancho. "Yes," the owner said, "I can feed you and put you up for the night."

We had to wait until later, however, until after the Mexican cowboys were through drinking at the bar. So we had dinner and waited at the eating table at the other end of the room. The more the cowboys drank, the uglier they got. Every so often they would look over at us, seemingly discussing us with some crude laughter thrown in. About ten o'clock I decided we'd better depart the premises for our own safety. After all, we were "rich Americanos" and a long way from any kind of law and order.

So we gathered up our things and went out and the dang motorcycle would not start. I put Rosie on it and started pushing. I think I must have pushed her a mile up that dusty road in the dark before the cycle finally started. We drove a couple of more miles and then we saw car lights behind us. We took off from the road and got behind some big cacti. A few minutes later a big truck went roaring by with several laughing Mexicans in it. Whether it was the same group or not, I could not be sure, but we were darned glad they did not spot us. That night we slept right there. It was bitter cold, but we slept, very glad we had our tarp.

The next morning a tire was flat. It took me about an hour to fix it by hand, as my old hand pump would barely pump it up. The tires remained a nagging worry. If they gave out, we would be through.

We had been told that about fifty miles farther on there was a modern rancho run by a Mexican lady named Josephine. It was supposed to be the best rancho in interior Baja. It was off the main trail, but one man told us that there was usually an airplane visible from the main trail.

Sure enough, early in the afternoon, off to the right, we saw an airplane. The road leading off to the rancho then was easy to find. The man at El Arco had told us that this delightful lady even had a hot shower, bunk beds, and beer. Oh, how we needed that shower. By then the dust was caked to our eyelids and face, and our hair was too dirty to comb.

About five minutes after turning down toward the hacienda, we crossed the airstrip and parked beside a pickup loaded with all kinds of goodies—canned peaches, corn, beans, pineapple, jam, and beer. A truck close by had drums of diesel fuel and gasoline. We could hear a light plant running and see a water tank and a tall radio antenna up on a hill. Two Holstein milk cows chewed their cuds in the corral. The sprawling, one-story stucco house was surrounded by trees and flowers. Rosie said, "I think maybe we're dreaming. I think I'll just stay here the rest of my life."

Before knocking on the door we tried to brush some of the dust and grime off ourselves. We were afraid they would take one look at us and slam the door. More or less timidly, I knocked on the door and it was opened by a beautiful lady of Spanish descent. I could not say a word. Finally, Rosie said, "We're looking for a bed and meals until tomorrow. Would you have anything like that?"

That gracious lady said with as much courtesy as though she were talking to a queen, "Come in, my child, out of the sun. Would you care for a cold drink of water?" It was too much for Rosie. She broke into tears. I guess a word of kindness in English was more than she could stand.

In less time than it takes to write this, Josephine and an American lady there had Rosie in the bathroom with hot water and some clean clothes. A bed was made up if she wanted to rest and a lunch was put on the table with some delicious canned peaches and homemade bread and butter. By then, of course, they had heard the story of our shipwreck from Rosie, and the place was ours. Ah, those wonderful people. The next morning dawned after a beautiful night's sleep. The first thing Rosie said, even before getting out of bed, was, "Can we stay another day?"

"Heck, no," I said. But during breakfast, of bacon, hot cakes, and fried potatoes, Miss Josephine said to me, "You're going to stay one more day, you know, because Rosemary wants to." I tell you, you can't resist woman power. So we stayed another day.

Miss Josephine had word that there would be ten or twelve Americans coming in that night to stay overnight. So everyone, Rosie and me included, jumped into preparations. Rosie helped the most. I sort of stood around and watched that Señora Josephine give orders and organize things. She was in her early seventies, but a beauty and a queen for sure. The next morning, when we were ready to depart, I went to her to pay the bill, but she would not take one cent, even though I argued with her for some time. We later sent her a guest book, as she had said she had a hard time remembering all her guests. I will bet none of them ever forgot her.

When I tried to start the cycle, it would not fire. Two big Americans from Escondido who were sort of partners of Josephine pushed us almost the length of the landing strip and the thing finally started. It was in really bad shape and we still had about 250 miles to go. I determined to stop only on top of a hill, if possible, so the cycle could be started again by coasting down the hill.

We left Josephine St. Ynes's feeling almost human again. In fact, we felt jolly. The boys at Josephine's said it was only 220 miles to Ensenada with the town of Rosario in between.

We only stopped the motor once on the way to Rosario. That

was to eat a lunch of turtle stew at a rancho that had several trucks parked by it. While we were eating, someone stole our tire pump, so from then on a flat would finish the trip.

We made pretty good time that day and got to Rosario just before dark. The motel was almost stateside except it had outside plumbing. We slept very well that night, for we felt we had Baja almost conquered with only 172 miles to Ensenada, 80 miles of which were oiled road. The next day we headed out, hoping the tires and the cycle would hold out. We didn't shut the motor off all day, as the sounds coming from the various parts of it were not good. One man said he thought the pistons were going up and down sideways.

I wanted to ride the cycle to San Diego just to do it, but in Ensenada it quit and refused to start, period. Even with a hired boy to help push, it wouldn't fire once. But by then we were back in civilization for sure and could rent a car. With the help of credit cards and our remaining cash, we bought some clothes and spent a luxurious night in a good motel with a bathtub with plenty of hot water.

The next day we drove on to San Diego in the car with the cycle in the trunk. The first place we stopped was the Honda repair shop. The foreman stepped on the start pedal several times and turned to me to ask, "Has this cycle been in Mexico?"

2 ACROSS AN OCEAN

6

Another Boat

After we delivered the Honda to the repair shop, we were lost sheep. We did not know what to do or where to go. We had started out for a three-year world cruise and less than a year later we were on the beach. We had lost our boat, sold our home and business, and wished all our friends good-bye. It seemed rather humiliating to return to Billings and rent an apartment. I could already see the sly looks of those who had said we would never make it. We did not have a great deal of money, since we'd had no insurance on the boat nor any of our possessions in it. I don't think I have ever been so depressed. I could not bear to look out at San Diego Bay with all the beautiful sailboats on it.

Finally, after some deliberation, we decided to drive up the California coast in our rented car and, maybe, look for a place to settle. We had been in Morro Bay before and liked the little town, so we thought that might be the place. After signing in at a motel, we naturally headed for the marina. The port captain there told me he had been shipwrecked not too far from where we had, and had been on a sand island with four other men for ten days before being rescued by a fishing boat. That sealed our friendship immediately.

He said, "I know of one boat here that I think is a good buy. It is a gaff-rigged cutter owned by an old fellow seventy-two years old. To my knowledge, it has never been outside the harbor, but he works on it all the time."

We walked over with him to look at it. Unlike the *Mustang*, this Heritage cutter, which we later named *Mustang II*, had

35

only one mast, with a topmast and sail. The gaff was a long pole, something like a boom, which when raised up the mast held the top of the mainsail. The gaff allowed the boat to carry a larger mainsail than it would otherwise have been able to. Later, that gaff was to scare the hell out of me. The boat was well constructed, of mahogany strip planks, edge-nailed. Although four feet shorter and a foot narrower than the *Mustang*, it seemed as if it might be a good, seaworthy boat. My new-found friend the harbormaster called the owner on the phone and made a date for the following morning.

Bill, the cutter's owner, showed up on time the next morning. He told us his boat was the best one in Morro Bay, the best sailor, the best in a rough sea, and could sleep seven people. He said it had a wood stove, as no one with any sense would go to sea with anything else. Rosie said, "Why, Bill, we heard that you have never been outside the breakwater with it." Bill colored a bit and stammered that he had worked around ships all his life and did not need to sail them to know what they would do. He could tell by just looking at them.

The inside was sort of a surprise. It could sleep seven people all right, as it had fold-down canvas bunks, pop-up plywood bunks, slide-out bunks, and hideaway bunks. The old wood stove was forty inches long and about twenty-eight inches wide. You had to suck in your tummy to slide sideways between it and the double sink on the other side of the cabin.

Rosie said, "Gee, I've never seen so many bunks in such a small boat."

Bill said, "Oh, I'm an inventor."

The table folded up at an odd angle. I could see the sink would not drain and the head was only six inches above the floor. He told us of some scheme to make the head disappear when not in use. All in all, however, the boat seemed to have possibilities and I made him an offer which he took.

We had bought a boat—now someway or another we would have to pay for it. That made a trip to Pocatello, Idaho, and Billings, Montana, necessary. In the rented car we took off for Pocatello where we had at one time owned a trailer lot. We also had some money in the bank there. From there up to Billings, four hundred miles over the continental divide, seemed a short trip.

I hated going to Billings under these circumstances, but there was no way out of it now.

Friends and relatives started to bring us various items to help stock and to buy the boat we had found in Morro Bay. One couple gave us everything we needed to stock the galley: pots, pans, stainless-steel silverware, the works. The largest gift of all, however, was from Rosemary's brother, a sizeable check. That helped with the teetering state of our finances.

Our income—all from investments—came in by the month from interest-bearing accounts and from dividends from stocks purchased over the past twenty years. This all came into our account in the bank—at the rate of about $600 a month. Our friendly banker, Bob Spannagel, arranged to procure an American Express letter of credit for five thousand dollars. Then all I had to do was keep five thousand in the bank all the time.

This enabled us to go to any one of twenty-some hundred correspondent banks all around the world and draw up to five thousand dollars. It was the best system of carrying money I have ever seen. We had absolutely no trouble getting either local currency or American dollars. There was also another side to that letter. It helped make friends. Just by itself it seemed to be a recommendation or an introduction to people of the business world.

At any rate, we were boat owners again. The *Mustang II* was ours. The diesel in our new boat had frozen or rusted, from salt water entering through the exhaust, a weakness that was to give us trouble for the next five years. After we broke a piston trying to get the pistons out, we finally decided the best solution was to buy a new diesel. I decided on a two-cylinder Swedish Albin. I also bought a new diesel stove and pulled up under the electric overhead crane at Red Doyl's Union 76 Marina at Morro Bay.

Red, the owner of the marina, didn't like yachts very much but consented to pull out that big old wood stove and lift out the old engine and lower the new one into place. We stayed at Red's for three months.

In that three months of hard work on the boat we came to like the people of Morro Bay. We bought two new Hondas, and we met another couple there who also had motorbikes. With the Haislips we rode all over that part of California.

In the latter part of August 1970, we started south once more. We had not previously taken the *Mustang II* out of the harbor, but it didn't take us long to find out it wasn't the boat the other had been. Still, it seemed good to be afloat again and took some of the sting out of losing my little ship.

We were in such a hurry to move south that we decided not to wait for Christmas. Bright and early December 16 we departed San Diego for the second time: a beautiful sail out past Ballast Point, Point Loma. "Ensenada, here we come for another try." The boat was leaking a bit and had some other kinks, but we decided to worry later.

Clearing into Mexico takes a day at least, as you need five copies of this and four copies of something else. Perhaps your passport is stamped wrong, so you go back to immigration where they stamp it someplace else. Then immigration gets mad and stamps it in three different places. After that hassle, we got back to the boat to find a fishing boat had dragged its anchor and was bumping against our bow. I raised the anchor from under him and moved.

Four days was plenty at Ensenada and we headed further south. On December 24 we were trailing a line and caught a two-foot tuna. Rosie already had a canned turkey cooking for Christmas, so she started seviche, a delicious Mexican dish of raw fish mixed with lime juice, onions, and peppers, and flavored to taste with hot sauce, and put the rest in the refrigerator. Christmas Eve was a beautiful night and we rolled along under twin jibs.

Turtle Bay held eight anchored sailboats, so we all had Christmas all over again. The party went on for days, extending into a New Year's Eve party.

While we were there a young Mexican doctor had us to his house for lunch. He said he wanted to practice English. When these people have guests, the wife never says a word. In fact, usually she never comes into the same room except to serve food. Men are supreme. We invited several local people to our boat, but the women never came along. The husbands say, "She is sick," or "Our baby is sick," or some such excuse. You rarely see man and wife together in public. Man is all. Ah me, would it had been so on the *Mustang*.

7

Abreojos Revisited

We left Turtle Bay on New Year's Day 1971. This had to be a better year. We planned on arriving at Abreojos in about thirty hours to deliver some presents to Pedro and his family who had helped us so much that we felt we could not do enough for them. We anchored around behind the point with a strong wind blowing from the northwest. That first day we decided not to go ashore, since there was a big surf. We did not want to leave our boat there alone with the seas so high and the wind blowing thirty-five knots. The morning of the second day was a little better, so we put out the dinghy and made it to shore.

Pedro's family welcomed us with open arms. They, of course, had not known it was us anchored out there. His wife immediately cooked up a lunch of crushed lobster cakes and coffee. Pedro told us we were not in the best place to anchor, so he and his boy went out to the boat with us to move it to a place between some reefs. He said that with this wind it would be a much safer place—even though it didn't look too good to me. He also told us it would soon blow harder. A person has to trust local knowledge. As he was leaving he pointed to a trail going up the small hill through the sagebrush behind us and said, "When you leave, watch behind you and keep in line with that trail. That is a clear passage through these rocks." He then invited us ashore tomorrow for a fiesta with much company and a big party.

All night long the wind picked up. From about midnight on I had the motor going on idle in forward gear. We did not know how the anchor would hold in this unfamiliar anchorage. Besides, we were uneasy about this whole locality. The three-quarter-inch nylon anchor line stretched like a fiddle string and groaned as the boat swung back and forth. The wind shifted until it blew directly toward shore. We took turns at anchor watch all night. I don't know why, since we could not see anything nor could we have moved the boat anywhere in the pitch-darkness. We could hear waves crashing downwind of us.

By daylight it was a full-fledged gale, but we were still at anchor. Immediately behind us were rocks as big as houses. Things did not look good. Rosie said, "If we lose another boat on this point, I'm going to shoot myself." I figured I'd better hide the pistol, as the chances of losing the boat looked pretty good to me.

When there was sufficient light to see the trail up the hill, we decided to try to raise the anchor and move out. Anchors are not easy to pull up by any sort of power, but with our hand-powered winch and by running up on it, we broke free. Had I known how well it was dug in, I don't think I would have moved. Hindsight is always good. Rosie never leaves the cockpit; so, she had to maneuver the boat into a heading with the trail up the hill directly astern while I raised the anchor and secured it to the deck.

Regretting that we'd miss Pedro's fiesta, we headed southeast down the coastline with the trail directly astern. It was right down toward the area where my friend in Morro Bay had been shipwrecked. Pedro had said we should follow this course for two miles and then turn out to sea. By the time we could head out to sea, I had the jib up and we were making good time more or less downwind. After a half hour, we tacked and put the boat on a heading straight out to sea, away from land. The more sailing I did, the more I liked deep water.

All hell was breaking loose outside, with fifteen to twenty-foot waves under a wind of probably forty-five knots. I took the jib down and put up a smaller one. We were going along pretty easy until about noon when the wind worsened. Rosie was below fixing hot soup for lunch when there was a loud explosion.

She bolted out of the cabin thinking a fuel tank had blown up. "My God, what's happened?"

I couldn't tell her. I just pointed. I had been looking right at the mast, trying to make myself go forward on the rolling, pitching boat to take down the jib and put up a storm sail. The mast had just snapped. I finally said, "The mast broke." I could hardly believe it.

The boat turned into the troughs of the sea, more or less across the wind with the bow slightly up.

"Oh, dear, what will we do now?" Rosie cried out to me.

"First thing, let's eat that lunch. I'm so hungry I could eat a skunk." Really, I wanted some time to think because I did not know exactly what to do. I had heard many things, such as getting an ax and chopping everything away. The piece of mast with the jib sail still attached was, of course, trailing in the water, and every so often the mast gave a great knock against the hull. Everywhere I looked lay tangled lines and wires. I had heard you should cut everything with bolt cutters, but I had none aboard. There are many theories, but I never discussed it with anyone who had actually been in that shape. Since the boat was lying fairly quiet for the conditions, I decided a little thinking might pay off. Maybe I was just hungry.

It was a good lunch: tomato soup, cheese and crackers. By the time I had finished I had decided the first step was to try and get the jib back aboard. What a mess! Rope cables, sail, and turnbuckles were tangled around the gear stored on deck. It looked like a can of worms. I hadn't realized until then how many different lines a boat had. It looked as if someone had dropped ten miles of rope on board from up in the sky.

It took me about a half-hour to get the jib aboard. Next problem was the engine, which refused to run. With that, Rosie was fit to be tied. I told her she had a nice even temper, always bad. We had a small gas-driven generator, and after I ran it two hours directly into the batteries, the Albin fired and we were on our way again.

We were not sure how far we had drifted, so we started taking sun shots, but it was almost dark and they did not turn out well. Later, we tried for a moon shot, or star shots, anything to establish our position. I thought that by staying on our original course we would pick up the light on Cabo San Lázaro early the following night, and if the coast was not too hazy, perhaps we would see the cape itself before dark.

By the next morning the wind and seas had abated somewhat and we hoped the violent storm had blown itself out. We chugged along all day, but before dark we saw no sign of Cabo San Lázaro. We thought that surely after dark the light would be flashing merrily away so that by taking bearings, we could find our exact position. Since we had not done much celestial navigation, we were not too sure of ourselves on that score.

We sailed all night without a sign of the light. According to our shots, we should have been in easy view of the sixteen-mile light. I put the motor in neutral, since I was afraid to shut it off in case we were close to shore and it would not start again. So we spent the night keeping an uneasy lookout and straining to hear the surf on the shore or see some sign of land.

When the sun rose we could see no shoreline or cape, just a thick haze in that direction, so we went east very cautiously. In about two hours we spotted land. We crept inshore, and sure as the dickens, there was a lighthouse. It had to be the Lázaro light, so we could safely turn south. I was as ill-tempered as Rosie by then. That light had not blinked once all night or we would surely have seen it. My eyes were bloodshot from peering into the darkness and we still had to locate the entrance to Magdalena Bay, about ten miles southeast. Three hours later we were trying to get around Entrada Point and into the bay. The tide was coming out right at that time, so we would get up to the point and then just hold our own. An American fishing boat was doing the same thing. This seemed a little odd and I watched him for some time. He would get fairly close to us and then back off. We finally went in ahead of him and turned more southerly, headed for the navy base.

A mile or so inside I asked Rosie, "Did you ever see so many buoys in all your seagoing life?"

"No," she said. "They must be navy buoys."

A short time later one of the "buoys" close to us was going *chomp, chomp,* and all at once there were whales around us. They were big devils, too, forty feet long. The buoys we were seeing were the great gray whales diving down and coming up headfirst out of the water. Some were practically standing on their tails. We did not like this, having heard stories of whales bashing in boats larger than ours. They did come close but never touched us.

About four that afternoon we anchored in the navy area as close as we could get. An hour or so later it seemed the whole navy was around us wanting to know what we were doing there, since it was not an area in which American yachts were allowed to anchor. I pointed to our mast stub and said, *"Necessario nuevo mast."* I tried to ask, *"Aquí?"* Here?

They got the message and left, indicating that they would find out and let us know. In the meantime, we could not go ashore.

The next morning a shore boat came out and the officer wanted to look at our engine. He not only wanted to look at it but also to hear it run. By golly, it started. Then the officer said that since our motor would run, and since they could not make a new mast for us, we would have to leave the area at once. I told him our diesel supply was about exhausted.

He said, "One minute, please," and off they all went back to shore. Four hours later they were back and asked me how much diesel I would need.

"Twenty gallons would be enough," I told him.

He then told me that they could not haul diesel in that boat, but that if I would come ashore in my dinghy, they would sell me twenty gallons. This they did. They also gave me a cup of the strongest coffee I ever drank and told me that possibly at San Carlos in the northern end of the bay someone might be able to build a new mast for us. I asked if we could stay that night at anchor there, as I did not want to be running around in Magdalena Bay in the dark. It has more shallow spots than deep ones. Permission was given, and we spent the night there.

The next day we arrived, via a dogleg channel, thirty miles north in San Carlos. They have a high solid concrete dock, and the American fishing boat that had played footsie with us at the entrance was tied up there. The fisherman helped us tie up and we invited him aboard. He explained that after seeing our broken mast he had been planning to offer us a tow, but his oil filters kept plugging up due to dirty diesel oil bought in Turtle Bay, so his motor kept cutting out. He was good and mad at Gordo for selling him dirty oil. I think, possibly, the truth was that since he was in the same little storm we had been in, the rolling and pitching had stirred up dirt on the bottom of his tanks, which got into his filter system.

We were down in the cabin having coffee when we heard a thump on deck and the fisherman said, "That will be the port captain. He's a good fellow." I went up the companionway and there stood a young, good-looking Mexican. The first thing he said after shaking hands was, "We can build you a new mast."

"Great," says I. "How long will it take and how much will it cost?"

"Tomorrow morning early I will bring the carpenter and we will tell you."

He made me feel so good I shook his hand again and invited him below for a rum or coffee. He took both.

The feeling of being tied up to a good solid dock after being in trouble is hard to express, but it's a feeling of complete tranquility that comes over you when, after trouble at sea, you now have no worries. Rosie says trouble at sea is like being pregnant: After it's over, it doesn't seem so bad.

This town had about two hundred people in it and they were all down on the dock to look at the broken mast that evening. They would wave to us and say, "Muy malo," very bad.

44

Early the next morning the port captain and the carpenter showed up with a lift truck to lift the stub of the mast out of the boat. We put it up on the dock with the top half so that we could measure them. I was amazed at the way the wood was shattered. It reminded me of the way a tree or a telephone pole would look if blown up by a stick of dynamite or a grenade. I could find no defects in either piece of timber.

Well, the carpenter and I liked each other at once. We measured and remeasured the mast. Rosie says that he only knew two words of English—"Very good"—and that I knew only the same two words in Spanish, *"Muy bueno."* Actually, she was wrong. I was quite fluent in it, only the Mexicans couldn't understand me.

The carpenter said he would have to go inland to purchase the lumber. The mast would take four days to build after one day rounding up the wood. I told them we certainly had that much time to spare, but the big question was *"Cuánto dinero,"* how much money? The port captain and the carpenter went into a huddle and with many smiles and handshakes told me, "About two hundred dollars."

Since it was about one-fourth of what I had expected to pay, I asked again to be sure. They seemed to think that at that price I was about to back out. What I did was to ask how much they wanted in advance.

"None," the carpenter said.

I told Rosie to bring rum and coffee topside and we sealed the bargain then and there.

I asked the port captain if he thought it would be okay if we rode our cycles over to La Paz for a couple of days while they worked on the stick. He said to go right ahead and he would put a man on the wharf to guard the boat night and day.

The ride over to La Paz, about 130 miles, was a pleasant little cycle ride. The local people always turned to look at Rosie riding, as women don't do that sort of thing there. When we stopped they always ganged up around the motors and usually someone would want to buy one right there.

At the La Perla Hotel in La Paz we luxuriated in the pleasure of a hot bath and some good meals. I was carrying a credit card

45

and a letter of credit to get money. The bank officer said that they would only give me eighty dollars on the card per day. If I came back the next day I could get eighty dollars more, and so forth. I went back three days in a row to have enough to pay for the mast and for all the groceries we could haul back on the motorbikes.

We had another pleasant ride back to San Carlos with everyone waving as we went by. I liked those people. If we tried to talk their language, they were very patient at trying to teach us.

Back at the boat everything was okay. A small freighter had tied up to the outside of the wharf and a shrimp fishing boat was just astern of us. The captain of the fishing boat gave us about five pounds of shrimp and some cooked turtle. The skipper of the freighter, a Mexican, said they were going to load 150 tons of cotton and about 100 cattle.

Loading of the cattle proved quite exciting. Trucks hauled the animals onto the dock and pulled up close to the freighter. Then a one-inch-diameter rope was thrown around the cow's horns, not even tied. The eye of the rope was placed over the freighter winch hook and up went the steer, hanging by his horns, bellowing loud and clear. The boom on the boat swung over toward the center of the boat and lowered the steer to the deck. A man was all ready for him. The first rope was thrown off and another, smaller one attached to the horns. Quickly, the steer was pulled over to a rail and tied snugly to stay until unloaded in Ensenada.

One steer was on the fight in the truck and presented a little problem to the boys. After he was hoisted up and lowered to the deck, he was really mad, fighting mad. One quick look at the situation and he took a running jump at the rail and cleared it by at least a foot. He must have expected to land on old mother earth over there, but he was graceful enough to make a neat dive into the ocean. What a surprise that must have been to him. I'm sure he had never been in water over ankle-deep before, but he came up swimming—straight out to sea.

Instinct is strong, it seems, and about five hundred meters out he started to make a big turn and was finally headed back toward land, but not that ship. We were rooting for him to go free, but a ship's boat put out after him so that before the steer reached shore the men had another rope around his horns and were towing him back to the freighter, where they let the winch cable down and picked him up out of the water. All he got for his efforts was a bath.

The freighter was gone by the time our mast was brought to the dock, where I took over and put all the hardware on it. It was an easy job, as the old one was six feet away to use as a pattern. When I had all the pulleys and lines on, the carpenter and his gang would place it in the boat.

They planned to have twenty or more men stand on the side of my boat against the dock at low tide. This would tip the boat at a good angle toward the dock and the crew would lift the mast and sort of slide it through the hole in the deck until the butt rested on the keel. I had never seen this method before, but it seemed reasonable if sufficient manpower could be brought into play. Everyone in Mexico likes to get in with the group, be it pulling on a fishing net or pushing an old car to get it started.

They started the project just after lunch one day. It was some show. There must have been thirty men around, everyone a chief and shouting orders. I couldn't help but laugh. In fact, I laughed so hard tears came to my eyes. The men who were supposed to be tipping the boat toward the dock would leave their position to run up to the high side to eyeball the mast to see if it was straight. The old carpenter was supposed to be the boss, but a couple of fellows could outshout him and he lost out right there. After about an hour, the mast was back on the dock and everyone was tired. No one, of course, paid any attention to me at all.

Then the skipper of the fishing boat came over and said that if we would pull our boat alongside his, he would lift the mast up with his net winches This we did. It wasn't as much fun, but the mast was in place a half-hour later. I brought out a couple of bottles of rum and we all drank to the new mast.

The next day we went to the port captain's office to settle up for the various things we had acquired. The total bill was $187 U.S.—less than the estimate! That included the mast, one chart, ten gallons of diesel, six quarts of crankcase oil, a new whisker pole (which holds the rear of the jib sail out to catch more wind), and one week of the best entertainment.

With regrets we left that desolate, but grand, little village on January 18, 1971, passing through the shallow water and dogleg turns during daylight and anchoring in Man-o'-War Cove just inside Magdalena Bay. We promptly bought six large lobsters for one dollar and two candy bars. It is a good thing sailing is hard work or sailors would grow out of their clothes, at least in this area. Who could resist eating a big lobster when it costs less than twenty cents?

Early the next morning we crept out of there in a dense fog, sailing solely by the clock times speed. Visibility was less than one hundred feet. We had set a course for Sail Rock and damned near hit it before we saw it. With only about fifty feet to spare, we made a sharp turn to port and were in the swell again, so we knew we were in the entrance to the open Pacific. Rosie had been blowing our foghorn industriously and, probably, uselessly. It was supposed to be heard for two miles and perhaps would be if there was no other noise, but with a ship's engines going I think it highly unlikely the skipper of such a ship would have heard it if we were on his deck.

Inching through the fog, we arrived in Cabo San Lucas at four o'clock the next morning. The anchorage was crowded, so we had to anchor on the shelf. We went to bed and must have promptly dragged anchor because at daylight we had drifted out to sea past about thirty boats and the huge rocks of the cape. We were so far out that we just set a course for Mazatlán across the Gulf of California. Again, at Mazatlán, the anchor wouldn't hold, so I changed to the CQR, an English anchor shaped like two plow blades back to back, and it took hold.

We sailed on down the coast of Mexico—our third time there. The ports were full of Americans, including some from our home state. The sheepherders do get around. Many had come down in boats, but more had flown or driven.

We anchored off La Penita, which was rough; then Puerto Vallarta, in the marina; then Chamela Islands; and then Tennacatita. That is one of the most beautiful harbors on the west coast of Mexico, with hardly any people about. To find anyone it is necessary to go back into the brush, where you may stumble onto a thatched-roof hotel. If your urge is to get away from it all, this could be the spot. Of course, you would also be away from electricity, roads, sidewalks, good food, water, doctors, and good company.

Our next stop was Manzanillo, Mexico. When we got anchored, we saw four other American sailboats. One had a young couple aboard. The husband had been shot in the throat by a Mexican while they were anchored behind the Chamela Islands. The wife had been pretty spunky and had run the attackers off with a dinghy oar for a club. This kind of thing could be a problem in the isolated anchorages. The husband was not dead and they hid in the brush until morning when she got the help of a rich Mexican who lived nearby and who owned a small airplane. He flew the wounded fellow to a doctor in Manzanillo. The wife told us that while her husband was unconscious on the operating table, the doctor found he did not have sufficient tools to extract the bullet, so he told the wife to watch her husband while he got into his car and went across town to borrow some more tools. I guess he borrowed the proper tools because when we arrived the American was in good health but with sort of an ugly scar. He looked as if his throat had been cut.

After a couple of weeks in this pleasant locality, we decided to leave. Leaving meant stocking up on groceries, and this meant riding the motorcycles around to the various markets and hauling the purchases back to the dinghy. Several trips had to be made to get the various items aboard. This took two or three days and was all rather fun, as everything had to be bargained for at great length. Never, never pay the asking price. It was a terrible waste of time but great fun. I think most of the world practices this method for purchases except the United States.

On about our last trip out to the boat with a stalk of bananas, we noticed that one sailboat, a recent arrival, was acting oddly, making strange maneuvers, and narrowly missing other boats. I told Rosie the skipper was surely drunk, celebrating getting into port, no doubt. Then I saw a lot of disturbance in the water at his bow and the man on board was shouting for help. I rowed Rosie to a boat close by that had women aboard and went over to find out what the dickens was his problem.

A very large manta ray had become entangled in his anchor line. Four of us yachties went aboard to discuss how to get rid of said fish. One of the men had a big pistol back on his boat and he went after it. Then we all hoisted away on the line and by slow stages pulled the manta up near the surface. A few times he went under the boat and his wings would come up on opposite sides so that we judged him to be about twenty-two feet across. He had entangled our line with another sailboat's line and it was a mess. We buoyed the one line from the second entangled boat and got the manta practically on the surface where they shot him several times. I hated to see it, but there seemed no alternative. He was still active, but the water all around was bloody. By that time some young Mexicans had showed up in a dugout canoe and they managed to slip the rope off the manta. I urged them to take him ashore, but they said that type of fish was not good to eat. When he was cast loose the poor devil swam off slowly.

My fish book indicated mantas are harmless to man. They can only open their mouth about three inches and they use handlike fins to push small fish into their mouth. This one had a mouth about two feet wide, so these "hands" were about three feet apart. This manta had probably been swimming by, looking for food, when he hit the anchor line and tangled it with his "hand." The more he fought it, the tighter it became.

We have seen hundreds of mantas out at sea, although none as big as that one, jumping clear of the water to land with a loud slap. I was told they do this to stun small fish. Often, if the boat was among a school of mantas, two, three, or four would be out of the water at the same time. With their little piglike tails and their wings curled upward, they somewhat resemble a jet fighter.

Out of Manzanillo, as we headed southeast, the weather really warmed up. We made Zihuatanejo in two days, then Acapulco and ten thousand American tourists and fifty thousand Mexican tourists, since it was Easter week. We lingered long enough to stock up and then were off to Bahia Marquis and on to the Panama Canal. That is, we were off after getting the anchor unfouled from an old car engine. What people don't throw into the sea!

8

Awed Through the Canal

At the Panama City Club, a launch came out to assign us a buoy. What a relief to be tied up to something and not worried about the anchor dragging. Blow a horn and anytime within the next three hours the launch would stop by to take you ashore. It was a no-no to take your own dinghy, as the small club wharf didn't have room for many dinghies.

At the club there was good food, drink, and excellent company from a bar full of skippers and Panama Canal pilots. Oh boy, the stories everyone tells. One thing about a sea story, it can never be proved true or false, as those circumstances can never be put together again.

September 22 was our big day to transit the canal. A pilot and four line handlers came aboard at 5:00 A.M. We were to enter the first lock at 6:00 A.M. For fifty years I had heard of the canal, and now here I was going through it in my own boat. A thirty-two footer is put into the locks going up with a freighter. To a watcher from the shore, we must have looked like the freighter's shore boat, but it was one of the thrills of my life.

Everything must work like clockwork and I have never been here before, I thought. Who can go through with a thing like this and do it right the first time? It was about the closest to panic I have ever been. Here we are now and the canal is so narrow. It is impossible to turn around and the first lock is right in front of us. What do I do now?

The pilot says, "Hold right here."

Hold? I think to myself. This boat won't hold anyplace. The freighter ahead of us is holding, but he knows what he's doing. That skipper has a mate; in fact, several mates. They have been through this canal a hundred times, maybe. How in the devil do they expect me, a damned sheepherder, to do this impossible thing?

"Go ahead full," says the pilot. What he means is put all twenty horses to work at the same time. Big deal. The propeller on the freighter in front of us is churning the water madly. Our propeller is churning, but I think we are going backward because that twenty-foot prop ahead of us is causing the water to go by us like the Yellowstone River at floodtime.

The pilot gives me a look of disgust, but the boat ahead is way on now and his prop is slowing, so we are speeding up. Finally, we start inching ahead. The freighter already has lines run up to the sides of the lock. The lines are hooked on the mules there, railroad-type engines that will pull the freighter forward.

The four line handlers are ready when the lines come down on us from what seems like every direction above. Actually, there are only four lines fashioned in something like a spider web. We are inside the lock and our line handlers tie our one-hundred-foot lines to the lines thrown down to us from the men some forty feet above. The men above pull our lines up and secure them. The big gates close behind us. Those gates weigh over fifty tons each and are about fifty feet wide and must be forty feet high. Water starts to flood into our lock at a rate of millions of gallons a minute. The water is extremely turbulent and our line handlers have to keep adjusting our lines as the boat rises so that it will stay in the center of the lock. If one line is let slack, we would start to turn and could be smashed against the side of the lock. The pilot gives more orders to the line handlers. "Tighten the port forward line faster. Keep that after starboard line tight." Finally, he gives us the good news that the last yacht through had got crosswise and broken its bowsprit.

In a short time we are up and can see out.

"Slacken all lines," our pilot orders. Our green line handlers look at him as though he were crazy. They had just got them good and tight.

"Slacken lines," he shouts. They do, and we are cast loose. The gate in front of the freighter opens and the freighter is pulled forward into the next lock. We go ahead full again into the next lock and start the whole process over. This time it goes more smoothly, and by the third lock we all begin to feel like old hands. Then we are out onto the canal and have no more locks for fifty miles when we will be lowered into the Atlantic.

Rosie and I had both pictured the canal as a big ditch, straight across the Isthmus of Panama. It isn't. It's crooked; it goes through a lake and it runs north and south instead of east and west. It has crocodiles in it and a waterfall. On the S turns, the big ships blow their horns to let one coming the other way know they are just around the corner.

Late in the evening we arrived at the Atlantic side. It was a repeat of the Pacific side, except we were lowered by three stages into the harbor at Cristobal. Going down, for some reason, the powers that be placed us in front of the freighter. It might run over us, but at least we did not have its prop wash to contend with. Also, there was no surge of canal water, just the surrounding countryside disappearing as we sank down.

The gate in front swung open and we scurried to cast off lines to get moving so that that big monster behind us would not run over us. As he left the boat, the pilot (I hoped to get him in the Rocky Mountains someday) told me they had not run over any sailboats lately.

So, then it was the waters of the Caribbean keeping us afloat—quite a thrill for a country boy to change oceans all at once like that. On the Caribbean side the tide is less than one foot, while on the Pacific side it is around eighteen feet. My poor old mind can't quite figure this.

The yacht club at Cristobal was great, with floating docks we could tie up to, hot showers, a restaurant, and a bar going full blast twenty-four hours a day. The canal pilots work night and day and have to rehash the night transits.

Going east is the wrong way for a sailboat to go around the world because of the wind patterns. But we planned to while away a couple of months in the San Blas Islands and Cartagena, Colombia, then return to the Canal Zone, leave the boat there, and fly back to the United States to marry off our youngest daughter. Of course, Mama could not miss that.

Thoughts on Sharks

The San Blas Islands were as we had heard: beautiful atolls with good people, excellent skin diving, tropical weather. In the extreme southwest Caribbean, they belong to Panama. The natives are pure-blooded Indians and proud of it. In fact, they are so proud of their heritage that it is their custom not to allow a white man to stay on an island at night. The women are boss in the family and control the family wealth, which is mainly gold worn in necklaces and rings: earrings, nose rings, ankle rings, and just plain rings.

Their boats are dugouts. A fisherman who spoke English stopped by our boat for a cup of coffee. He told us that when he took his catch home, he handed it over to his wife. She divided it—first to her parents, then to the children, and then to herself. When she had eaten her fill, he could have what was left. I don't think it worked out that way often, but it was the law of the tribe. He did not look as if he had missed many meals.

All the drinking water was hauled from the mainland, about a mile away, in dugout canoes by both men and women. The women who did this manual labor wore beautiful, brightly colored dresses and head scarves. Their blouses, called molas, were made by starting with three to eight layers of cloth of different colors. If they wanted to picture a brown dog on the blouse, they cut down to the brown material in the outline of a dog, then stitched around it. If they wanted a green tree, they cut to the green material. The blouses were most colorful and had become a prized item for tourists.

Young girls wore their hair long; when they were mature and ready to marry, they cut their hair short to inform the young men. The San Blas Indians do not like to have their pictures taken. They believe that a picture takes away a part of their soul.

The area abounds with sharks. The people have built shark fences along the water's edge to enclose areas where they can swim. The fences were made by driving poles into the sand about three inches apart. Wire was twisted tight around each pole, then strung to the next. If a shark can get his nose between any two objects, he can exert a tremendous pressure. They reminded me of pigs in the way they seemed to plow up the ocean bottom looking for shells with the animal inside. With their powerful jaws they break the shell for their meal.

I had a face-to-face confrontation with a shark in these waters. We were walking in water about waist-deep out to the end of the shelf to do some skin diving. Rosie was behind me, as she was walking slowly, avoiding holes, spines, rocks, etc. It had taken us about fifteen minutes to walk some four hundred yards when I met, face-to-face, a shark about ten feet long. I looked at him. He looked at me. I shouted, "Shark!" Both the shark and I made 180-degree turns and took off at high speed. This time Rosie made the four hundred yards in sixty seconds flat.

Later, out on the edge of that same shelf, the snorkeling was the most beautiful we had seen in the water world. There were tropical fish of all sizes and colors; coral in yellows, purples, and reds; and plants waving back and forth in the water like trees in a breeze. Some were twenty feet high and all colors. It was really a fantasy world.

The night before leaving we went ashore to eat at a thatched-hut restaurant. For dinner we had rice and fish. Rosie had the fish tail and I got the head. Who received the middle of the fish, I do not know. The table was made of coconut trees split in half with the flat side up. Since there was only a kerosene lamp for light, the roaches were out in force. During dinner a cockroach about two inches long came up through one crack and down another. Still, the natives tried so hard to please us, even bringing a bottle of ketchup, that we did our best by the meal. They were a delightful people and we were sorry to leave for Cartagena.

10

Land of Thieves

Cartagena has the reputation of having more thieves per square mile than any other city in the Western Hemisphere. A friend of ours rented a car without turn signals. When he put his arm out the window to indicate a turn, his wristwatch was stripped from his wrist. One of our motorcycles was stolen from inside the walled city. I even knew who stole it. Going to the police turned out to be useless. They wanted me to give them rum. I thought I was misunderstanding, so they brought out an interpreter.

"First," he said, "they want you to give them some rum, then maybe they look." The interpreter was grinning and laughing all during the interview. He seemed a decent sort, so I asked him what he did there. He seemed so happy with life.

"Oh, I'm a prisoner in this here jail."

Several days later two young Cartagenians came to our boat with the information they knew where my Honda was: in the walled city in front of a restaurant. They said they would take me there. I got the key to my cycle and climbed on behind one of the boys on his cycle and away we roared.

It was a really black night, so I was glad of help. This is great, I thought. These two husky young fellows speak Spanish and look as if they can take care of themselves, so I'll have plenty of help.

They pulled up right behind my cycle parked in front of a restaurant. The streets in the walled city are dingy and narrow, and the only light came dimly from the restaurant.

I was shocked when I stood up to get off the bike and both my informants went roaring away, leaving me there alone. Since in Cartagena life is not valued too highly, I felt fast action and not talk was the only way to get my bike back. Casually, I walked up to it, swung a leg over, put the key in at the same time, and gave the crank a kick. It fired. People ran out of the restaurant, one lady screaming madly. She grabbed the handlebar. I got rid of her with a sideswipe of my hand and ran the cycle forward at full speed. A young couple jumped in front of me to block the narrow street, but I kept going and hit them with the cycle going at a fair clip. They sprawled away. I blasted away without looking back.

My two "helpers" were waiting at the gate to the inner city and we roared away. I knew I was hotly pursued, but I thought if I could reach the sailboats, some of my sailor friends would jump in to lend a hand. After we had gone about a mile and reached an open stretch of road, I turned to look behind. No one was following at all. I must admit that when we arrived back at the boat I was still shaking.

We had a pleasant sail back to Cristobal where we left the boat to fly home for the wedding. The trip was hectic. We were impressed that our friends and relatives were all doing about the same things they had always done. Shore life seemed quite far removed from the "cruising world." Hectic, but a little dull.

We arrived back in Panama six weeks later and found the boat in good condition. Home had been a pleasant interlude, but the time had come for the serious business of crossing the Pacific. In early February 1972, we passed through the canal again, old hands now, heading west. We tied up at Balboa on the Pacific side and set out to get ready for the great adventure.

It seemed prudent to prepare for a long crossing—maybe as much as six months. We at last decided, however, to stock for a five-month cruise. Actual sailing time to the Marquesas Islands, four thousand nautical miles away, should be only about forty-five days, but several factors present themselves on a long ocean crossing and we scarcely knew what to expect even after we arrived there.

So, five months' provisions: a pickup load of canned goods, ten dozen eggs, ten heads of cabbage, twenty-five pounds of beans, twenty pounds of sugar, twenty pounds of rice and potatoes, thirty cans of peanuts, eleven cases of beer, two cases of Scotch, two cases of rum, and hundreds of miscellaneous items. We filled every plastic jug we could buy or beg with water. We took on fifty gallons of diesel oil. The boat sank four inches deeper into the water than before, and I had to haul her out again to raise the painted waterline so that the top two planks would not be eaten away by teredos, the termites of the ocean. They eat away the inside of wooden planks and leave only a shell. To prevent this it is necessary to paint the bottom up to the waterline with antifouling paint, which has several pounds of copper in it per gallon and is supposed to discourage the teredos. I tell you, a sailor's life is a rough one.

The night before we planned to leave, Rosie left the valve open in the head and when we came back from our "goodbye" party, the boat had two feet of water in it and half our provisions were wet. She said it was a subconscious desire to stay in port. You can imagine what I said.

We spent the next day drying everything out after spending the night pumping water back into the ocean.

11

Lost at Sea

On February 9, 1972, we got under way from what would be our last U.S. port for some long time. As we motored to the fuel dock, the propeller shaft pulled out of the coupling on this boat, too. I could not blame a mechanic for this one. I had installed it myself. This little mishap almost turned into a major one. The fast-rising tide pushed us toward two other boats tied to buoys. I dashed for the bow and threw out the hook, which took hold and brought us up just short of striking. Hanging head down into the bilge again, I saw what was wrong. A nut had come off the coupling, letting the shaft loose. I fixed that in ten minutes and this time battered the end of the bolt with a hammer so *that* would not happen again.

From Panama to the Galápagos our noon shots showed that we were making between 125 and 165 miles each day. We knew that was impossible—our boat just couldn't make that kind of time, so we decided the sextant must be in bad condition. I kicked myself for not checking it in Panama. It is a terrible feeling to be lost at sea. All day and most of the night we took shots that always put us way ahead of our dead reckoning. For a while we just drifted while trying to decide what to do. If the sextant was off that much, it seemed foolish to try to find the Marquesas thirty-three hundred miles away.

How those few days made me sweat. Our procedure was for me to take the shot and for Rosie to figure the location. As we talked it over, with Rosie almost in tears, I recalled aviators saying, "You have to trust your instruments." One reason we knew we were off course was that if we were where the sextant said we were, we should have been able to see the Galápagos the day before when we would have been only twenty-five miles away. Now we were south of those islands and drifting farther south all the time. When we reread the sailing directions, they said that sometimes a thirty-knot current ran south along the South American coast, but we should have been too far offshore for that. At last, I decided there was just one thing to do: Assume the sextant was giving a correct position, set a course, and stay on it for two days. If at the end of that time we were not in the Galápagos, we would turn and go straight east until we found the Ecuadorian coast, for which we had no charts, and trust we could grope around to find a harbor. We were so concerned that we didn't really pay any attention to the fact that sometime between noon on February 15 and noon on February 16 we crossed the equator for the first time.

On February 21, while taking a 9:00 A.M. shot of the sun, I saw a strange-looking cloud on the horizon. Our two days would be up at the noon shot. I was afraid to tell Rosie it might be an island because, if I was wrong, she would feel all the worse.

After she plotted the position line, she said, "According to that we should be only twenty miles from San Cristóbal Island."

As casually as possible, I said, "I guess I'll go up the ratlines and take a gander." I was almost afraid to look myself, but there it was. You can bet I shouted loud and clear, "Land ahoy!" At seven-thirty that evening we set the hook in Wreck Bay, San Cristóbal. Rosie wrote in the log in capital letters: "TRUST YOUR INSTRUMENTS!"

I wrote in my diary, "I'm a damn fool." Ten times.

When we were approaching the reef to enter Wreck Bay, a name that doesn't inspire courage, the engine would not start. Approaching a reef with no engine and a dogleg turn in the entrance is enough to make you wish you were back on the farm. We made it, but the first order of business was to get the engine fixed.

I took the starter to a mechanic at the Ecuadorian navy base and he worked it over. He said it had rusted; I suppose from water in the bilge at Panama. He would not take anything for his labor, so I returned to my boat and took over a bottle of Scotch. It was well received. He said that if I needed anything else to be sure and come to him.

In many isolated ports, I found it hard to pay for small favors or jobs. The Scotch, which had cost two dollars in Panama, was worth twenty dollars in materials or labor. Later, the naval commander in Wreck Bay arranged to fill my five-gallon cans with diesel oil for another bottle. Of the two cases of Scotch I brought, I did not drink one drop, and it lasted to Australia. When I used it to pay a small debt, I made a good, solid friend and many times received gifts I could never repay in kind.

The navy base in Wreck Bay made orange wine. It seemed like a strange occupation for a navy base, but the wine was good. It took one year to process a batch and then they bottled it in any old bottle without a label, corked it, and placed it on the shelf in the PX. It sold for one dollar a bottle.

After three or four days we went ashore to buy all the vegetables we could find. This amounted to a gunnysack of oranges, very cheap; one papaya, delicious; two kilos of onions, very strong; and one dozen eggs, about half very old. We also got several pounds of raw peanuts, which were very good when roasted in a little vegetable oil.

We left that port in pretty good shape—with the motor running and stocked up—and went out through the narrow reef opening to Barrington Island. It was a barren rocky little island with no people, but interesting wildlife. Two other yachts were in there that we had known in Panama. The little bay was turquoise blue with clear water and a sandy bottom, really very beautiful.

A large herd of sea lions lived there. The little pups were about a foot long and the big old bulls ten or more feet. They must have weighed a ton. The docile, good-looking cows were only concerned with their young. The old bulls and the young ones were always raising hell. They would bellow, bellow, screech, yawn, gurgle, and bare their fangs at one another and at the cows. When we went ashore we could walk among them. They seemed gentle as kittens, not at all afraid of us. Although they were cumbersome on the beach, they were graceful in the water, and how they could swim. Often they swam directly for the boat as if to ram it, but at the last instant they would dive.

The dinghy tied to our stern seemed to be of particular interest to them. Many times the bulls would swim to the dinghy, then try to jump in it. Since they landed on the edge, it would tip and dump them back into the water. We laughed at their surprised expressions as they slid back into the water when the dinghy tilted up. We decided they must have thought it was a rock and wanted to climb it for a sunbath. One old fellow tried at least fifty times. I thought that if he ever succeeded in getting in, he would break it into a hundred pieces with one flap of his tail.

After several days of watching their antics, we motored over to Academy Bay. Our friends were there along with two other sailboats and five fishing boats. We became acquainted with the skipper of a lobster boat, a fine German fellow with a large crew of Ecuadorians. He kept us supplied with lobster. He was also the one who advised us to have the stamp canceled on outgoing mail. Otherwise, the post office people took the stamps off, resold them, and threw the letters into a scrap heap. The postmistress also sold eggs.

One local bar had a little thing going to stimulate business. When you ordered a beer, you also received a raw turtle egg in the bottom of a water glass. It looked rubbery. You were supposed to put a little pepper on the egg and swallow it in one gulp. All this is supposed to make a man of you, but I decided at once that I did not care if I was a man or not. When I looked around it was plain that every Ecuadorian in the house was watching to see what the Yank was going to do.

I looked at Rosie and she said, "Why are you so pale?"

"It's so hot in here."

"Oh? I notice it's making you lose your suntan."

I heard a few snickers. "Why don't you drink yours, if you're so smart?"

"I'll drink mine if you drink yours," she said.

I was having trouble breathing, but decided that I couldn't let the good old U.S.A. down, so I downed the egg in one gulp with my eyes closed. Rosie drank hers and the room burst with applause. We didn't order any more beer, though.

On the west side of Florence Island two sisters, the Wittmers, had a small store near Black Beach. We had heard that one could usually buy fresh vegetables, eggs, and beer here. They had a little of all three and a pleasant, homey atmosphere to enjoy it in. Also anchored there were Jim Mayo and Bill Elliot on the *Cloetta*. We had been port-hopping with these two retired Englishmen since Panama. In fact, we had helped each other through the canal. I had given Bill a ride on my Honda into Cristobal, and within one block of the yacht club we had been arrested and taken to a Panamanian jail. The crime was that Bill was riding without a hard hat. We argued a bit, but we could see that only money would soothe the irked judge. The jail smelled terrible, so we paid five-dollar fines and were told to "*vamos.*" Now, off Black Beach, we made plans to meet in the Marquesas, now but thirty-three hundred miles away. But, this was the last time we would see Bill.

12

The Longest Passage

On March 14, 1972, at 6:00 A.M., we raised the anchor, secured it, and headed west—with the motor going 1,200 rpm's. All day we motored. The previous week the wind had blown constantly, but now when we wanted wind, it was flat calm. Since we had to use the motor anyway, we decided to go straight south, as the sailing directions and wind charts showed the trade winds blowing farther south of the equator. We could not afford to use all our diesel. So, we turned the motor off whenever the slightest puff of air arose. After six days we had gone only three hundred miles. At that rate, it would take over two months to reach the Marquesas. Then, quite suddenly, we caught up with the trade winds. From then on the wind never let up. It blew a steady twenty-five to thirty-five knots. The seas were rough, about twenty feet high, with steady breakers all around. It was good sailing once you got used to the constant roll of the boat. I had always thought the trades blew a gentle ten or twelve knots, but after thinking it over, I could see that it would take thirty knots to push those big old grain ships hauling wheat from Australia to England and elsewhere. Besides the wind and waves, we were getting a boost from the west-flowing Humboldt Current, one of the mightiest rivers of the sea.

On these longer stretches between ports Rosie was in a perpetual state of anguish. She could not seem to stop worrying, and I felt sorry for her. She did not want to turn back, but she continually wished we would arrive at our destination. My mind, on the other hand, seemed to go more or less out of gear. If everything was okay, which it usually was for days at a time, I had the feeling that we should touch nothing, do nothing that was not absolutely necessary. Don't make any ripples; speak in a low tone of voice; maybe even whisper. Don't wake up the devil! Sit back and enjoy it while you can.

But, if something broke or went wrong, there was nothing to do but jump into the middle of it and fix the trouble. Total concentration was required at that time. Fix the ill that was there before Murphy's Law took effect and two more things broke, bent, tore, or went haywire.

In the continual high seas our gaff rig gave us trouble. The extralong boom it required was constantly dipping dangerously into the water. Every day or two I would have a new idea about how to tie it, so I'd raise the mainsail and tie preventers in a new direction. Taking the sail down in a storm was the best method I knew to commit suicide at sea. When the sail was up and the boat was rolling from side to side, often with the toe rail underwater, the great weight of that gaff would overpower the pressure of the wind and over the thing would flop to the windward side. The shrouds and mast would shudder, and the sail would crack loudly. A large sea might drive the boat off course and we were in the middle of a Chinese jibe—the boom out one side and the gaff the other. The only good thing was that we were so far out to sea that no one was watching. How I grew to hate, distrust, cuss, and fear that gaff. It finally got so exasperating that I tied the mainsail down and sailed with the big jib and a staysail, or twin jibs forward of the mast. The winds were so strong, we still made over one hundred miles a day.

On March 31, according to our noon shot, we were halfway to the Marquesas. Rosie baked two loaves of saltwater bread. Delicious. We made 110 miles noon to noon, and at sundown we had three rums with water and lime to celebrate our wedding anniversary. I had to tell Rosie again how lucky she was and how much fun this was. She tended not to remember that, especially when a large wave had come overside into the cockpit and dumped several gallons of cold water down her neck. Women are so forgetful.

After eighteen days at sea, we had developed a routine that

seldom varied. When the sun came up, I was on watch. Shortly afterward, about 7:00 A.M., Rosie would wake and start breakfast, usually fruit juice, bacon and eggs, toast or hot cakes, and hot coffee. After she had cleaned up the galley, it was time to take our morning sun shot, usually at 8:30 or 9:00. After that was figured and charted, it was time for a coffee break. When she made the morning coffee, she always put what we didn't drink then into the steel Thermos so that the coffee break was no problem. We often had some little goodie such as half a candy bar or a piece of left-over cake. After that little enjoyment, Rosie usually took the watch and I inspected the ship thoroughly: checked turnbuckles and sails, and maybe scrubbed the deck. Our mainsail was taking such a beating that I often had to sew sails. As we rolled continually, the lashings on the two motorcycles and the two plastic barrels often were loose. By the time I was done, it was time to take the noon shot. This was our most important shot of the day, for combined with the advanced morning position, it gave us a good position. Then we could tell our distance noon to noon. We were always pleased when we made over one hundred miles.

True noon, when the sun is directly overhead, could be anywhere from twelve to one o'clock local time. I hated it when it was five minutes or so to one, for by then I was so hungry that I could hardly wait until Rosie had the position charted. I usually thought we had done better than the fix showed. Trust your instruments. Immediately after that I was screaming for something to eat.

Lunch was always in the cockpit, then Rosie did whatever it is women do in their spare time. Sometimes we had time to read. Around three o'clock it was time for tea and another goodie. Although I had not drunk five cups of tea in my life before then, on the boat teatime became an addiction. Afterward, I did other chores around the boat, or read a bit, and then it was time for happy hour: six o'clock. We had two drinks, never more, and perhaps a few peanuts to tide us over until dinner about seven o'clock.

For dinner, we usually had a can of beef perked up with raw onions and potatoes, a salad—usually of cabbage, which lasted the best of the green, vegetables—and something sweet for dessert. After that it was dark and I was sleepy. Rosemary, who claims to be a night person, would go on watch until one o'clock. Then she woke me up and sleepily told me what had gone on. I sleepily listened, then took over in the cockpit and she went below. How I envied her being able to sleep until morning.

We had a rule that I would not leave the cockpit unless I called her topside and she never left it anyway. So if the wind dictated a change of sail, I would change directions if it did not put us too much off course, to allow her to get five hours of unbroken sleep. She did the same for me.

At 6:00 A.M. we started the day over again.

On long passages, we used salt water to wash dishes and ourselves, but the salt water gave me boils, so I decided I preferred to be dirty. If it rained, we caught rain. This was a bonus. With two quarts of rainwater, we would have a luxurious bath.

On occasion two dorado would follow us, sometimes for days, staying on the shady side of the boat. They are a blue-green fish found in these latitudes all around the world. Each morning we would look to see if our friends were still there. I never did try to catch one of them, as they seemed like friends. We never did find anything they would eat.

We got the greatest pleasure from watching the antics of porpoises that sometimes came around. I think they are all ham actors. We would applaud their gymnastics and usually one or more would roll over on a side and look at us with one eye. They seemed to enjoy darting in front of the boat as close as possible. I have watched them for hours and have never seen one touch the boat. Rosie said that when the high seas and high winds got her down, depressed, a school of porpoises always seemed to be smiling and enjoying life so that it cheered her up.

Rosie had an accordion on board that had been given to her after we wrecked the first *Mustang*. We both enjoyed it, but it was so large that it was almost impossible for her to play it sitting down. Since her birthday was to occur while we were

67

on this passage, I had bought an instrument called a piano in Cristobal. It was a glorified harmonica about twenty inches long with twenty-seven piano keys. The player blew in one end. I hid it in the engine room, wrapped well with oilproof cloth, and could hardly wait for the great day to arrive. I presented it to her just at happy hour, on her fiftieth birthday, and I have never seen anyone so delighted with a twenty-dollar gift. After that I dug out my old wooden drum and we often had a good old-fashioned jam session in the middle of the ocean.

Our radio was never much good to us. We did manage to get WWV, the U.S. government station that broadcasts the precise time twenty-four hours a day out of Fort Collins, Colorado, and the British Broadcasting Corporation out of London to receive the correct time for navigating, but music and news were normally so full of static that it was not worth trying to listen to it. Even WWV was hard to get. For six years we would hear the ticktocks that marked the seconds coming through loud and clear, but when the man started giving the time, it sounded something like, "The time at the sound of the tone will be glubbity, glubity, glubity, glub." Then the ticks would begin again loud and clear. When we were able to pick up BBC, the British announcer said, "This is London," five ticks and a bong and you knew it was the hour straight up. Over five sixths of the world, we could pick up BBC and for one sixth it was a struggle to receive WWV. This was humiliating to our national pride.

The days wore on and the farther west we went the better time we made. We had several 125-mile days, which made up for the doldrums at the first of the trip. Besides, the wind and waves seemed to moderate a little. Or, maybe, we were just getting used to it.

13

Tragedy at Sea

The closer we got to the Marquesas, the more we worried about what we would do if our navigation was off and we sailed on past the islands. Or, we worried that we might be closer than we thought and come upon the island without warning at night. So, the thirty-second night out, we both sat up all night staring into the darkness for sign of the land that if we were where we thought we were was no more than twenty miles away. After thirty-two hundred miles that seemed like nothing.

At daybreak, we saw the outline of Hiva Oa dead ahead. What a thrill! Without changing course we sailed into the opening of the bay and anchored there. Lordy, what a lovely sight was that mountainous, lush, tropical island. What delectable smells came off the land: flowers, dirt, trees, bananas. After thirty-three days of pure air, our senses were particularly keen.

Rosie said, "I'll never trade pure sea air for that marvelous land smell."

She decided also she knew why sailors drink: "They are so damned glad to get ashore and out of the dangers of the sea."

So, this seemed the time for an anchor drink. Everything was just so peaceful—a rooster crowing, a cow mooing, a jackass braying, the surf rolling on the beach. It was better than music to our ears.

A fifty-foot French sailboat that had left the Galápagos the same day we had arrived also that day. We shouted to each other as we drifted by them to anchor. We were all happy and gay to be in port.

After a short dinghy ride to shore, we had a pleasant walk into the small village. It seemed great just to be on land. After we cleared the authorities, the first thing was to exchange some dollars for francs, since these islands belong to France. At the market we bought Danish frozen chickens, Danish bacon, New Zealand canned butter and fresh cheese, and crusty loaves of french bread. On the way back to the boat, we passed a small vegetable farm where we dickered with the owner for vegetables. No sooner had we made the purchase when Rosie ate a nice, green cucumber, skin and all.

Everyone ashore was most friendly. One of the merchants asked Rosie what kind of a trip we had had and she said it was just like being inside a cement mixer for thirty-three days.

He laughed and said, "I fly."

The next day I looked up to see the boat with our English friends, the *Cloetta,* coming into the anchorage. Since only Jim was on deck, I decided Bill must be sick below. I rowed over to give them a hand. When I went on board I couldn't see Bill, so I asked Jim where he was. Jim broke into tears.

As he was getting close to land, I rushed forward to throw out his anchor. Then, he told me the story.

"It was on April second. Bill went forward to take down a whisker pole. See, we had our twin jibs boomed out and the wind shifted. I sent Bill forward to take the poles down. When he released the pole, the pressure on it threw him overboard. It—it happened so fast."

"Was it night? Could you see him?" I asked. "Was he hurt?"

"No. No, it was daylight. No, he wasn't hurt. He waved to me as the boat went past him."

"My God! You mean you just lost him?" It didn't seem possible. "My God! That's terrible. I can't believe it. Did you throw him a life preserver?"

"Well, yes, but Bill was a good swimmer."

"Nobody is that good. I can't believe it."

"Well, it took a while to get the boat turned around. A half hour."

"A half hour! Good Lord. Didn't you start the motor?"

"No. No, the motor wouldn't start. I—I looked for him for almost two days. It was hopeless. I would have been here sooner but for that."

Bill was one of the best guys and the best Englishman we had ever met, jolly and good-natured, always a good word for everyone. Rosie cried off and on for days and I felt like I had been hit between the eyes. I couldn't get the picture of Bill waving out of my mind.

The next day another American boat came in, *The Tuffy*, with Red and Ruth Brooks aboard. Red and I worked on Jim's motor and got it started. The harbor master told him to go to the main island to report the loss. The *Cloetta* moved out of the harbor under power, but slowly, as if in mourning.

After Jim had gone, I did some serious thinking and decided we were not going another mile with that gaff rig. Two hundred yards from where we were anchored was a slab of concrete about fifty feet square. Going up the mast in a bos'n's chair, I took careful measurements. Then, I took the mainsail ashore, laid it on the concrete, and struck a line roughly from what would be the top of the mast diagonally down to one foot short of the stern, then forward along the boom to the mast. As the boom stuck four feet beyond the stern, I had determined to cut five feet from it. It took three days to resew the sail, taking the peak of the gaffsail and sewing it on as the head of a Marconi rig. I moved the clew to its new position, then ran a rope the full length of the leach, or after edge, of the sails. The gaff timber became a new whisker pole.

This was a big step for a greenhorn sailor to take, but my hatred of that gaff rig overpowered my better judgment. I didn't know if the boat would ever sail correctly again, and we were a long way from a source of major repairs, but right then I didn't care.

After the sails were remodeled, we decided to see some of the other islands in the group, so we went to Resolution Bay, a favorite of Captain Cook's. It was a rough anchorage, too rough to go ashore in the dinghy. But on the twenty miles from Hiva Oa the new sail plan worked well, although it didn't get much of a trial in that distance. Hops to other islands didn't prove much either.

On Nuka Hiva Island in Taiohae Bay was the largest village of the Marquesas. It was the ideal tropical island, green right down to the beach with beautiful Polynesian women and well-built, muscular, noble-appearing men. All were friendly, helpful, and courteous. It was easy to see why sailors off the old sailing ships deserted by the score, and why they would pull the nails out of their own ships to give the girls for favors extended. It was truly a paradise.

We got grapefruit so huge that one person could hardly eat a half for breakfast; so full of juice that I think each contained about a quart. Limes, bananas, breadfruit, papayas, and cabbage were plentiful, as well as a few other vegetables. We found almost no white potatoes, but a lot of yams. Breadfruit was used as a staple much as Americans use the potato, which it resembles in taste.

We liked everything there except the beef and their method of procuring it. Beef meant either beef or goat. Both ran in steep and densely overgrown hills. The natives used dogs to hunt. The dogs ran after the animal until it was exhausted. Then the dogs usually ran it over a cliff where a hunter knocked the animal in the head. We watched them several times, and it was miserable each time. The meat was cut in chunks any which way and was the toughest we had ever encountered. We tried it once and couldn't run it through a meat grinder. We decided we'd rather eat fish.

The two little stores on Nuka Hiva had canned corned beef, chicken, ham, and tins of sardines. It astounded me that these people ate so many canned sardines when fish abounded in the ocean.

We were fortunate to be there on May Day, a holiday. The French navy sent a ship into the harbor and there was dancing and music. Can these girls, young and old, shake it! Wow! Much of the native dancing is done to only a chant and the beat of drums. The dance is called the Tamara, a fast version of the hula, more or less. Very sexy!

The jail was interesting. Prisoners didn't seem a bit un-happy. They were allowed out in the day and kept in jail only during the night. They swam and came out to the boats bumming cigarettes.

Before we left port I decided to buy a gunnysack of grapefruit. The man could only get twelve in a gunnysack and for this he charged me fifty cents. On May 7, we left lovely Tai-ohae Bay as newfound friends waved good-bye. I decided that nothing helps the beauty of a village as much as women wearing sarongs.

We sailed over to Tai Oa, a perfect landlocked harbor. It was nerve-racking going in, however, for it was a lee shore and the waves were crashing on the cliffs. I couldn't see the opening until we were within fifty feet of it because the entrance makes a dogleg turn. Had there not been an opening there, we would have crashed against the cliffs, but once inside we were in a picture-book harbor with towering cliffs, waterfalls, and sandy beaches. We could not figure out why so few people lived there until the next morning. Bugs! Oh, boy! This nearly invisible bug has several names: "no seeums," "nau naus," and "flying teeth." How they bite! Worse than mosquitoes! The only relief the natives get is to hover over a fire made to smoke all the time by putting coconut husks on it. They build the little fires inside and outside their thatched huts and sit around the smoke pot with their head surrounded by dense smoke, scratching their ankles.

The only relief we could get was to go swimming in the bay, and even then we'd get a few bites about the face. Thankfully, after dark the bugs went to bed. We gave a lady there three old magazines and just before we left, her boy brought us a stalk of bananas. The people were certainly most gracious.

Our next objective was to be an atoll in the Tuamotu Archipelago—Rangiroa. From studying the charts, I decided to try to visually pick up the atoll of Ahe first. From that positive position, we should be able to set a definite course for Rangiroa. At first, I had thought we might sail clear around this treacherous group of reefs where many, many ships and yachts have been wrecked. Captain Cook declared they were too dangerous to navigate. They are so low they can only be seen for about six miles, and then only if they have palm trees on them. I could hear echoes from the people back home who said, "He'll never make it."

Rosie and I talked it over. It seemed a shame not to see them at all, but one never knows when a decision could be the wrong one. The weather was clear for lots of sextant shots, and we proceeded as planned.

The sailing directions said that in that area we would have a current carrying us westerly, but that we would begin to lose the southeast trades and pick up the northeast trades. We found this to be so and on the fifth day spotted Ahe, then changed course from 220 degrees to 228 degrees and the next morning saw Rangiroa.

According to the sailing directions, we should enter the lagoon with the tide, as the tide coming out can create as much as a nine-knot current. Since we could not make more than five knots, we would be in trouble trying to buck nine. After puzzling over the phase of the moon, the time of day, and the crystal ball (we had no tide book for the area), I decided high noon was the time to try our entrance. When we got in front of the entrance, we could see the water coming out of the passage like a river at floodtime. The watch said to wait two hours before attempting it again. Good. We would do that. We tacked back and forth offshore a mile or so and had a Dutch lunch with cheese and crackers and a few peanuts.

This atoll is on a reef that encircles a lagoon about fifteen miles across and several miles longer. There are two or three openings through the reef. The action of the continually heaving sea pushes a lot of water up and over the top of the coral, but once inside there is not so much wave action and the only way out for the water is through the few openings. This all adds to the current flowing out due to the tidal action. Of course, wind speed, wind direction, the phase of the moon, how deep the lagoon is inside, and the shape of the lagoon all affect the current. Criminy, I cannot get it all straightened out. I think, If I had anything to do with laying out this old world, I would have made it simple for poor wandering sailors. They're not too smart anyway, or they'd be home plowing the land.

It was time to go in. I started the engine, upped another sail, and went to the bow to watch for reefs as Rosie held the tiller. "Don't cut that starboard side too close. A shoal spot is shown there.

"Watch that eddy. It's turning us around." I looked back and Rosie looked a little pale.

The entrance was no more than one-half mile long but in an hour we were barely inside. We had passed the narrowest part, so I figured it would slacken. "Yes," I decided, "we're finally in." A native sailboat was tied to a rickety wooden wharf. I directed Rosie to go past there to anchor. I started taking down sails. As I lowered and tied the jib, Rosie shouted that we were going backward. I raised the jib again and we sailed farther in to get out of the current. We went slowly. I lowered the jib again. Right away we started backing out of the opening. Whatever made me want to go to sea, I wondered.

I pulled the jib back up. A native onshore motioned us to where we ought to go. We followed his directions and, "Yes, it seems we're out of the current and the motor will handle it."

I lowered all the sails and dropped the hook. While I was tying the sails down I could see the anchor dragging. "Oh, hell!" We were headed straight for a boat tied to the wharf. Rosie started the motor again. Although the anchor was dragging, we could not get enough forward motion to get the damned thing in. We were back into the current out of control because the *Mustang* wouldn't respond to the helm. Within feet of the other boat, the anchor grabbed at last. The current caused the boat to strain on the anchor line. I yelled to Rosie to give the motor all it had. She did. We gained a little and I got the anchor line around the winch. I winched it as tight as possible but it wouldn't break free. I kept working on it, wondering what the hell to do next. The sweat ran off me. I couldn't winch it tighter without breaking my anchor line, and I sure as heck didn't want to lose my anchor in this lagoon. Suddenly, it broke free. Thank God! I raised all sails and we started making headway. We went even further inside. I took down the sails and threw the anchor out. The bottom was all coral and the anchor wouldn't grab. We kept dragging. Finally, we dropped over a sandy patch, and at last, the anchor held.

"Lordy, I'm tired. Bring out the anchor drink." The anchor weighed thirty-five pounds and the chain fifty. It was hand over hand to raise it in tight situations like that. "Oh, you bet—the joys of a quiet lagoon in the South Seas."

With the anchor well hooked we could finally enjoy the beauty of the place—everyone's idea of a tropical island—a gentle breeze, clear water, and palm trees. We counted our francs and decided we could eat ashore. We found a small, native-type bar and smaller restaurant, had a couple of beers, fried fish, and potatoes. While we were eating, the cook told us the potatoes were imported from New Zealand via Tahiti. "When my boy told me you were coming ashore, I got out the potatoes because all Americans want them." The Polynesians ate mostly rice and yams. These people were most pleasant, straightforward, and honest. The more we saw of them, the better we liked them. The gendarmes were not interested in our papers. They said something like this:

"Did you have them looked at in the Marquesas? Are you going to have them looked at in Tahiti? Okay, no problem here."

Most of the businesses were run by Chinese. It seemed the true Polynesians would rather fish and gather coconuts. I don't blame them. These atoll islands are much different from the mountainous islands of the Marquesas. The highest point on this atoll was only about six feet above high tide. Not much grows except palm trees, so that if it rains there is nothing to hold the water.

Thus, drinking water is a problem.

3 AROUND THE WORLD

14

My South Sea "Romance"

On the morning of May 17, 1972, I lifted the anchor to take off for Tahiti. We left Rangiroa through a different pass to shorten the distance by several miles and navigated around some invisible reefs by compass and time. The color of the water tells much about the depth, but when the sea is kicking up, the colors don't show well. By one-thirty I figured we were clear and set a direct course for the fabled island of Tahiti. On the morning of our third day at sea, we saw the beautiful mountains of Tahiti and thought we were nearly there; yet, it was dusk before we dropped our anchor and backed into the quay alongside forty other yachts in Papeete—the sailor's dream home in the South Pacific. Miles before we arrived we smelled the lush tropical vegetation. Now we could hear music and smell steak cooking in cafés across the street. We watched beautiful girls, fat women, old men, and young fellows, all brightly dressed, whizzing by on bikes and motorbikes. Everyone, it seemed, rode bikes, but it was against the law to use a horn.

Rosie said, "Carbon monoxide never smelled so good." She sat back and took a deep breath. "No matter. It's wonderful after—how many weeks?—about fourteen weeks of primitive living."

Our stern lay about five feet from the concrete quay. If we wanted to go ashore, I pulled mightily on the stern line and we stepped onto the planking. With the pressure off, the boat glided back out, so it would not strike the cement. Everyone else had a stern gangplank. Tomorrow, I would make one to fit our boat. Lacking one, we were easily spotted as a newcomer, and I couldn't have that.

Tahiti is shaped somewhat like an hourglass. Papeete is on the northern half.The southern half was closed to motor traffic to keep it natural. Certainly, the island is the brightest, largest, greenest jewel in the South Pacific. As we traveled around on our motorbikes, we smelled the sweet aroma of flowers everywhere. It was impossible not to crush flower blossoms as we took a trip around the edge of the island. The tourist hotels and oiled roads somehow did not spoil the beauty of mountains on one side and sea on the other. From our boat the peaks seemed to be always cloud-covered.

On Sunday it seemed everyone went to church, many on motor scooters. Ladies, young and old, wore white dresses, gloves, hats, shoes. Sometimes two or three would ride on one motor with their long hair streaming behind. On this island we caught up again with the travels of Captain James Cook. He, too, found these people friendly and helpful.

Living seemed to be separated among the French, who run the government; the Chinese, who operate the businesses and control most of the wealth; and the Tahitians, who don't want to be troubled by much of anything. An American told us that Tahitians learn English without much trouble. He said they take one word a day. Having nothing else on their mind, they just repeat that word over and over until they learn it. Next day they learn a new one. The Chinese claim the Tahitians are lazy. The Tahitians claim the Chinese brought here two generations ago are ruthless.

A night out on the town meant a night at Quinn's, said to be the oldest bar in the South Seas. The oldest seaman I had met told me not to miss Quinn's. He said it was the best waterfront dive in all the world, and I think he had seen them all. The place lived up to its reputation with seamen from many countries of the world; women of all shapes, sizes, and ages; honky-tonk music; and a rough floor with tables all around. The only *servicio*, or restroom, was off in one corner. After going through a sort of S-curve entrance, I came into a lighted room with water running down all four walls into a gutter around the outer edge. In one corner was a woman doing what comes naturally. Not accustomed to such a situation, I hurriedly started to back out, but she hollered at me and told me to come on in. Flustered I turned to go back in, but fifty years of tradition was too strong and I turned around and left. Back at my table, I tried to talk some of the others in our party into going in, but they all refused after seeing how red in the face I was.

We spent several weeks in Papeete, but the time always comes when you have to leave. We left Tahiti on a bright, clear morning with the island of Mooréa plainly visible about fifteen miles away. We planned to bypass it, however, because if you go in there you have to return to Papeete before you can get final clearance papers. When we were almost around Mooréa, we encountered a small, violent storm that loosened our tiller from the rudder stock. I jury-rigged a pipe wrench on the stock of the rudder where it protrudes above the deck and we were able to tack into Cooks Bay on Mooréa. Going through a narrow opening in a reef in this manner is no fun, but we had no other choice. The bay is about two miles deep and I determined we would go back into it as far as the depth of water would allow, since fixing the tiller might take some time. I wanted the boat to be in as protected water as possible.

It was a small mishap that turned out well. Back off in that bay was one of the most ideal anchorages we ever encountered. Beautiful, lush mountains came down on three sides. Two miles away we could see the sea breaking on the reef, but in our bay the swell could not reach us. Palm trees and flowers grew everywhere. In the evening thousands of hibiscus blossoms floated past our boat, a blanket of color gently moving out to sea. The water was warm, and morning or night we dove in for a swim. I am surprised we ever left.

The tiller fixed, we were ready to leave for Huahiné. We were just outside the reef when I noticed the engine heating up, so back into the bay we went. It was easy to return to a place like that. The heat exchanger was plugged with mud, an hour's work to clean, but then we decided to wait for tomorrow.

We finally left at 9:00 A.M., June 20, with no problems. We attached the log I'd worked on in Cooks Bay. It was a small propellerlike device towed on a light rope astern that shows how many miles we've traveled in a given period, similar to a speedometer on a car, but not as accurate. At midnight, I decided we might be getting close, so I took all sails down and we drifted, depending on Rosie, since I don't hear well, to hear the surf breaking on any reefs if we got too close. Neither of us could sleep in a situation like that, so we just sat in the cockpit and strained to see or hear something. The barrier reef extended about a mile offshore and I worried that it might not be breaking so we might not hear it.

But at daybreak we saw the island about twenty miles away over a wind-whipped, choppy sea. We studied the chart, which said the "range is a post and a white house bearing one hundred degrees." Once we were in the lee of the island, the seas settled down, but it was a slow approach trying to find the opening in the reef breaking fifty yards to starboard. From where we were we couldn't see a break in the reef, but the sailing directions said there was one. Then, we began to see smooth water and when the house was bearing the proper degrees, we turned and headed in. Often one or both sides of these entrances were marked by a wreck. We were told, "Keep that grounded freighter to port and you will be okay." Some poor devil had wrecked his ship, but at least it told us where to go.

Once inside with the anchor down, but not holding too well, I swung the ship around and with the dinghy took a stout line ashore from the stern. Two young Americans on the beach took the line and fastened it around a coconut tree. I rowed back to the boat and hauled in on that stern line. This pulled the stern around so that the boat was perpendicular to the beach, facing the swells so it did not roll as much.

The two boys were Mike and Ron Brethour of Los Angeles,

in these parts with their parents. Can you imagine being a teen-age boy, sailing through the South Seas without a care in the world? On the beach with the boys were about a dozen sixteen- to twenty-year-old Polynesian girls swimming. No tops and little bottoms—pants, I mean.

The girls rolled in the sand, then dove into the sea to wash off. Then, they would run up and down the beach chasing one another. Those two boys sat to one side watching the activity. I told Rosie boys are not like they were thirty years ago. Rosie said, "What would you have done that's so great?"

I told her, "I would have been chasing those girls all over the island."

Rosie suggested that we get our movie camera and go ashore. So we put on our swimming suits and went in. Rosie struck up a conversation and asked if they would mind if she took their pictures. They laughed and giggled, but indicated they wouldn't mind. Rosie took a few feet of film, then told me to put my arm around one and make my friends at home jealous.

Try as I might, I could not put my arm around any of those pretty girls in broad daylight with my spouse eyeballing me through the lens of a movie camera. I finally handed one girl a seashell, which was about as close as I got. There were thousands of seashells on the beach, so I'm wondering what the girl thought I was up to. That was the extent of my South Sea romance.

As far back as the Marquesas, the ship had developed a pretty bad leak. Now, it was getting worse. All I could determine from the inside was that it was coming from high up in the stern. It leaked much more while we were at sea and very little if we were anchored in a quiet bay. Since both of our electric bilge pumps had long since given up, we had to pump about two hundred strokes each hour or the water would be sloshing up on the floor boards when we rolled.

Mike and Ron volunteered to dive down and examine the stern planks and transom to see if they could find a hole. After a couple of hours of serious looking, all they found were a few hairline cracks that might open up and let water in when the boat was working in a sea. We smeared some so-called water-proof cement on this, but it didn't work.

One of the island people watching swam out and told me that he was sure the boat could be hauled out on the island of Raiatéa, twenty-five miles west. We had planned on bypassing that island and sailing on to Bora-Bora, about fifty-five miles away, but I decided it would be prudent to go into Raiatéa, another island with a barrier reef and a dogleg entrance channel.

The leak had put Rosie in a bad mood. She said, "I never thought I would have to go around the world in a leaky boat."

Once again it was necessary to remind her that we were having fun. In a sardonic tone, she added, "Oh, yes, cruising is fun, fun, fun." I changed the subject as soon as possible.

15

That Man Ah-Tune

With a thirty-five-knot wind pushing us from the northeast, we were off at 7:00 A.M. June 26 for the village of Uturoa on the island of Raiatéa. It was a wild, fast ride downwind in rough seas across a thirty-mile channel to a narrow entrance through another barrier reef. I didn't like going through reef openings at any time, but I liked them even less when they were on a lee shore. There is no backing up in a sailing vessel if you make a mistake. Sailors claim no one loses two boats. We had already lost our quota—but did the man upstairs remember that?

We spotted a break between the reef and a small island and

turned toward it. If it wasn't the opening, we would be in real trouble with a strong wind blowing us right toward the reef. The closer we got, the tenser we became. Reefs would always mean terror for us. Fortunately, a boat came out and we gained confidence and headed in. It was the opening.

We anchored in seventy-five feet off the village of Uturoa. I had no sooner rowed ashore than I met an English-speaking Chinaman who directed me to the little shipyard.

"You might have trouble finding it," he said. "Jump into this car and I'll take you there. I can practice my English on the way."

Not only did he take me, talking English all the way, but also spoke to the boatyard owner to make arrangements to haul our boat out of the water at high tide—five o'clock the following morning.

The Chinaman's name was Ahtchoung Chong, pronounced like Ah-Tune. For the next three weeks, Ahtchoung worked at entertaining us. We had gone into Uturoa intending to stay three days to fix the leak, but it was over three weeks before we made ourselves sail on.

At five o'clock the next morning we were in front of the marine ways ready to be taken out of the water. However, the Polynesian owner could not get the ways sufficiently down the track to accommodate our six-foot three-inch draft. Finally, we turned the *Mustang* around. With seven men and Rosie standing on the end of the bowsprit, we lowered the bow to bring the stern up. It was inched up the bank so that the problem spot near the waterline cleared the water.

For four hours the *Mustang* stood on her nose while two carpenters caulked, pounded, and puttied. This was to cut our intake of water in half. Unfortunately, the next storm loosened up the caulking and that leak later was nearly fatal.

The coconut tree telegraph had informed Ahtchoung that we had been unable to haul out. When the carpenters were finished, Ahtchoung was there with a young son who was to guide us to an old wooden wharf where we could tie up, an infrequent luxury for a cruising boat.

There was danger involved, however, which Ahtchoung

warned us about. To get to town—about a half a mile—we would have to walk two hundred feet through a coconut grove where ripe coconuts were falling. A big, ripe coconut that weighs several pounds and falls thirty to fifty feet hits the ground (or you) with a loud *kerwrack*! Sometimes you could hear them coming by the *swish* they made as they fell through leaves and branches. The only trouble was that, like a bomb or grenade, if you hear it, it's too late to duck. Ahtchoung told us that coconuts did not kill too many people, only broke shoulders and heads. We took our chances, and although we took some big, fast, fancy steps sideways and backward a time or two, neither of us was hit.

Land crabs were thick under this grove of trees. They were about four inches in diameter, not counting their legs, and could move despite their sidewise mode of walking. The crabs drove the local dogs crazy. The dogs would chase them and growl and bark, but never did I see a dog come close before the crab disappeared down a hole.

Waiting onshore once for Rosie, I decided I would try to catch one of those pesky crabs. I took a good look around, since I didn't want anyone to see me. I did no better than the dogs, no matter how I dodged and plotted the paths the crabs would take. It is embarrassing to be outwitted by a dumb crab.

Otherwise, what a place to enjoy life—tied to a little wharf with the motorcycles off the boat; riding around on a tropical island only seven miles in diameter. The road did not go all the way around, but who cared?

Ahtchoung was the reason we stayed so long. He had been born on this small island to which his grandfather had been brought to work the cane fields. Before the grandfather died he had owned a small interisland freighter, in reality a sail fishing boat converted to haul freight. As a boy, Ahtchoung had to pump the leaky old scow out each morning at 4:00 A.M. With a two-inch pump, this took an hour. He said his back ached until noon. Then he would be off to a French school where English was his favorite subject. He could speak four languages.

After seven years of schooling, it was time for him to go work with his father and grandfather on the freighter. Most of the freight they picked up at neighboring islands came onto the wharfs or beach at Raiatéa to be sorted out and, often, transshipped to Tahiti. When they had a good run with lots of freight, they would come barreling through the opening in the reef with the decks awash. To top off a load his grandfather would buy handsawn lumber on the outer islands and load it on deck to be sold in Raiatéa or Tahiti. Huahiné, Bora-Bora, and Tahaa were the best producers of lumber in these islands, and still are.

Occasionally, they made a trip to Papeete, Tahiti. On one of these trips, he met Ema, the most beautiful girl on the islands, according to Ahtchoung. After having five lovely children, she was still a most beautiful woman—a dear sweet person, always smiling, working, or cooking. It was five years and three babies before they could afford to be married. That year they opened a small restaurant and bar, a half a block from the new concrete wharf, right in the middle of town.

Some years later he acquired a boat large enough to take out sport fishermen. That was his business when we were there, sport fishing and the little bar and restaurant. The whole family worked with smiles. We never heard one complain.

Across the street from his house someone had opened a theater. Ahtchoung helped his eldest son start a little sandwich booth in the front yard. "Now," he said, "that boy make more money than me." Each morning before the bar opened the whole family, including two grandmothers, pitched in to make sandwiches. Ahtchoung usually had something else to do about then.

Ahtchoung told us one day about his best Chinese friend. The friend and his wife had a beautiful daughter. One day a Frenchman showed up on the island and saw this beautiful girl. They fell madly in love and moved into her parents' home. For a time everyone was happy. Then the bill collectors began to arrive, trying to collect bills the Frenchman had run up, some from as far away as Tahiti. This did not set well with Papa, especially after he found out there was a wife in Paris. Things got pretty uncomfortable and Mr. Frenchman departed for parts unknown.

The beautiful daughter was soon to have a child. Papa knew of several couples who wanted babies, so, as is sometimes done, he made the decision to sell the baby. First, he approached his brother and his wife.

"No," said the brother. "I know that Frenchman and he no good man. I don't think we buy baby."

Then the Chinaman approached two other couples, but they too said, "Bad blood. That Frenchman, he no good."

So the baby was born, and as is the custom there, the mother went about her business and the grandmother took care of the child. He was a husky, dark-eyed, stout little fellow and very smart. When we were there the boy was four years old. Good looking? You bet, with his ancestry one-half French, one-fourth Polynesian, and one-fourth Chinese.

Ahtchoung would slap his knee and laugh at the joke pulled on those three couples. Now many people wanted to buy the boy, but Grandpa wouldn't sell. As far as Ahtchoung was concerned, it was the best joke of the century on that island.

One day Ahtchoung came to the boat and wanted to know if we were doing anything that evening. "No," we replied.

"Well, would you like to come and eat with Ema and I? Eat, no charge, at the restaurant as guests?"

They were having something special and wanted us to share it with them. "Sure. We would like to. Seven? Okay."

It was not the best meal we had ever eaten, but it was not the worst. The meal started with raw fish, common in the South Pacific. Then we had fried bananas, breadfruit, and some quite dark meat. Ema did not eat the meat, but Ahtchoung cleaned up two big helpings. I could not decide what it was. First, I thought it might be duck, then I figured it must be a deep-sea fish because the bones were small. But it did not taste like fish either. Rosie and I both ate our portions but declined seconds. When french bread is fresh, it is so good that everything with it tastes all right.

When we were through eating, Ahtchoung sat back in his chair and said, "Now, let's talk about what we ate."

Rosie said, "Yes, I've been wondering what it was."

"It was dog," he said. "Ema won't eat it, but I like it. Do you?"

Rosie said it was fine. I didn't want to hurt his feelings. Neither did I want some to take back to the boat. I said, "Yeah, it was great. Where did you get it?"

"Right over there," he said, pointing across the street to a Chinese meat market. "They have it all the time. The last American I fed some to got mad."

On the way home, Rosie said, "I'm not going to buy any more meat in that meat market." I really think, though, that they kept the dog meat for special customers.

We enjoyed walking along the road to our boat because of a vanilla drying factory on the way. Vanilla was brought from gatherers on all the islands and dried at this factory. The vanilla bean resembled a large string bean. The beans were placed on trays and carried from inside to outside as the sunshine changed, since they could only be in the sun at certain temperatures. When properly cured, the beans were put in five-gallon cans that were soldered shut and shipped to France. The whole area smelled delectably delicious.

Copra was the main cash-producing crop in all the islands. It is dried coconut and we saw it drying everywhere. If a man owned only one coconut tree, he produced some copra off it. Copra is made by splitting husk, shell, and meat of ripe coconuts with one hefty blow of a machete. Then the halves are left to dry. As they dry, the meat curls away from the shell. If it doesn't all come loose, it is pried away with a knife or sharp stick. The shrunken meat, saturated with oil, is loaded into gunnysacks to be processed for margarine or any one of about fifty products.

Ahtchoung talked us into staying for the biggest celebration of the year, called Fête, the French version of the Fourth of July. It started on July 14 with a big parade. Can you imagine a big parade in a village of seven or eight hundred people? A parade it was, though, and a good one. There were hats made out of nothing but flowers, and bicycles so completely covered with flowers that the bike could not be seen. There was thatch and sisal tied together to make the best-looking canoe you have ever seen; two flower-bedecked dogs that walked on their hind legs for a mile; and ladies carrying baskets of fruit on their head. I surely liked those people.

Every night there were dances, parties, and fun. The second day they had bicycle races, each with about ten contestants. They worked at it, too. The roads were all made of coral rock instead of gravel. With those bikes zipping along, a fine, white, powdery dust came up from the road. The dust became thick as contestants retraced their tracks several times to make the required mileage. A contestant from another island won.

Then there was a banana race. Judges weighed many stalks of bananas. To make them all weigh the same, a banana might be taken off one stalk and tied with string to another. Then a stalk of bananas was tied to each end of a three-inch-diameter pole about six feet long. The racers picked up the pole with the two stalks, placed it on their shoulders, and ran a block. If a banana fell off, a spectator would run out and stick it back in the stalk. The muscles in the legs of the contestants were rippling railroad irons. The winner of that contest was the shortest fellow entered.

The most beautiful event was the sailing outrigger canoe races in which dugouts from ten feet to thirty feet long were manned by crews ranging from several ten-year-old boys to as many as eight men. There was also a woman's race. In one, five women were aboard a sailboat with a good stiff breeze blowing. With the first hard gust of wind, over they went. No one paid any particular attention and they righted the canoe and continued the race. When they came across the finish line, two still had flowers behind their ears. They were all laughing and enjoying the race immensely. All told, there were half-a-dozen knockdowns (capsizes) among the various classes.

An amazing thing about handling these outriggers was that when they came to a buoy, instead of making a sharp turn, they just reversed the sail and sailed backward. Since the canoes were double-enders, it did not matter. The rudder was just a giant paddle.

It was choppy that day and the bailers were the busiest sailors on board. The next busiest were the fellows who ran back and forth on the outrigger supporting timbers. The way they moved the ballast was to run out on the outrigger. If the wind was such that the outrigger was lifting out of the water, one, two, or three persons would run out on the outrigger brace to hold it in the water.

They also had dancing contests. Young girls from all the villages entered alone or as a group. Each wore flowers in her long black hair, a scrap of a bra, and a colorful grass skirt. They usually danced to just the drumbeat. The South Sea dance is not the slow hula of Hawaii, but a rapid, rhythmic shimmy that is supremely sensual without being offensive. The hands and arms form graceful gestures that tell a story. The dancing is done to torchlight and the spectators chant and applaud for the "home team."

To me the last day of the festival was the best: the spear-throwing contest. A coconut was impaled on a pole about forty feet high. The thirty-some spear-throwers stood about seventy feet back from the base of the pole. They got twenty chances to throw a spear at the coconut. The winner was he who put his spear nearest the center of the nut. They threw in relays—five men in a group throwing five spears each. When all had thrown, they would start over until all had thrown twenty spears.

The men made their spears from small bamboo trees. Each spear was about five feet long and tipped with an iron point. The spears were not necessarily straight. In fact, some looked like a piece of rope lying on the ground, they were so crooked. It did not seem to bother the throwers. One man told me, "It doesn't matter if the spear is straight, as long as it is thrown straight."

The throwers wore headbands made of flowers and brightly colored sarongs around their waist. They were bare-chested, muscular, intense.

A man would pick up a spear, balance it in his hand with his throwing arm extended behind him and the other arm extended full length in front for balance. Gauging the wind and its effect on the spear in the air, the man hurled with all the power he could muster.

Soon the air was full of spears around that nut. Watching this throwing of a rather crude spear, I could easily imagine these were the warriors of old attacking an enemy village, arching their spears up over a barricade.

When the spears fell to the ground they landed the length of a city block from the throwers. When the contest was over there were six spears in the nut and five in the slender pole under it. The officials took the pole down to determine which spear was nearest the center. The winner was a fine-appearing fellow about thirty-five years old from the island of Tahaa. He won fifty dollars, the largest prize for any of the events.

Part of the celebration that evening was the "walking of the rocks." About fifteen grown men and women walked across fifteen feet of very hot rocks and boulders. The rocks had been thrown into a pit and a fire built on top of them that morning and kept going until sundown. The fire had then been put out in rites conducted by priests. Then, the participants walked slowly across the bed of rocks to the crescendoing beat of drums. The only light came from torches that reflected from the painted faces and strange headgear of the priests. The whole event had an eerie, pagan atmosphere.

I thought it might be a trick, and so after they left, I went over to the pit. The stones were too hot for me to keep my hand on for more than two seconds. I decided their feet must be unusually tough from going barefoot.

In two years of sailing, of seventy-six anchorages and hundreds of people we had met, this was the one island I did not want to leave. Ahtchoung and Ema cried as they presented us with a dozen going-away gifts. Rosie wept as she hugged both of them and I had a tear in my eye, too. But all things come to an end, and if we were to get around the world, we had to move on. We did, but even after six and a half years of circumnavigating the world, we remember that one little island most fondly.

16

To the Rescue

Neither of us had much to say as we sailed to Bora-Bora, a deep anchorage inside another reef. I was sure there were good people there, but we were too sad to find them. After a couple of days we pushed on to Rarotonga.

One day out and the northeast trades switched to southwest gales. Two days of trying to hold our own against stiff head winds made us forget our sorrow at leaving Raiatéa. It took us eight days to go 540 miles. Actually, we got right up to Rarotonga's entrance at dark on the seventh day, but since it had a fringing reef and a narrow passage, we thought it best to sail in a circle in front of the harbor all night rather than chance going in. When we did go in early the next morning, I was glad we had waited, particularly when I saw the old brigantine *Yankee* plainly visible high and dry on the reef in front of the town. It is a sad sight to see a boat out of water waiting for time and weather to disintegrate it.

By nine o'clock we had the bow anchor out and the stern tied to a concrete wharf. Several other sailboats were inside along with a 120-foot interisland motor freighter. Two Australian friends, Theo and his daughter, were there, as well as a Frenchman, a New Zealander, an Englishman, and a Swede. Rarotonga is a protectorate of New Zealand and uses New Zealand's money. The natives are darker than the Polynesians. Many work in the cannery that processes the juice of the many oranges grown there.

I had only been tied up an hour when I was asked if I would help carry a dinghy with a pretty girl in it. All the yachts' crews were going together to enter a local parade. We had arrived just in time for another celebration. I was never sure what we were celebrating, but we helped them do it anyway. We entered as a serious entry and were somewhat taken aback when we won the twenty-five-dollar prize for humor. The yachties donated the twenty-five dollars to the local children's charity. It gave us a great opportunity to have a party after the parade.

Still tired from the crossing from Bora-Bora, the parade, and celebration, we planned to sleep late the next morning. But at 6:00 A.M., we were awakened by the master of the interisland freighter. A sailboat had gone on the reef near the old *Yankee* and was being pounded to pieces.

"I'm gathering some sailors to go give the fellow a hand." He planned to go out to sea off where the sailboat was on the reef and see if she could be pulled off. I agreed to go and went aboard his ship with several others. He put us to work getting big, stout, two-inch lines out of his rope locker.

Rosie, in the meantime, had gone with some of the other women to where the yacht lay on its side on the reef. She said later they could walk out to it and hardly get their feet wet, for it had gone aground at high tide. It banged on the reef with the wave and swell action created by the incoming tide, which also kept pushing it farther up the beach even as a strong, onshore wind rose.

That freighter skipper, a New Zealander, knew what he was doing. He dropped anchor in ten fathoms about one quarter of a mile offshore directly out from the sailboat. We line handlers tied the two-inch lines together and paid them overboard. The skipper figured the wind would drift the rope ashore in the vicinity of the beached yacht. The wind did carry the line shoreward, but a current running parallel to the island carried the rope to the west.

A young New Zealander seaman on the freighter dived overboard, swam out to the end of the line, and pulled it toward the boat. He must have been a tremendously strong swimmer, as he pulled the line in the right direction for at least two city blocks. When he was maybe one hundred yards from the yacht, a rowboat came from shore and pulled the line the remainder of the way.

Rosie said the men on the beach had pushed the twenty-eight-foot grounded yacht around and were holding it with the bow toward the breakers. The rope was tied around the mast at the deck and signals made to the freighter's skipper, who lifted his anchor line off the bottom, and with the engines slow ahead, the propellers churning the water, we inched out to sea.

Rosie said that the small yacht started across the reef with an awful screeching and scratching. Everyone hollered "Stop." But the skipper and his mate ashore had walkie-talkies going and the mate said to keep going, so we never stopped. Rosie said that as the yacht slid over the coral, it was hard to believe it could hang together, but in about one hundred feet it dropped off the reef—and floated. There was a big yell of joy from the people ashore. Those seafaring people wept at the death of a boat as they would that of a friend. The skipper of the yacht crawled aboard and back to the tiller while the New Zealander gathered his gear. Almost immediately the skipper had the yacht following us in a straight line.

When our skipper felt we were far enough offshore, he stopped the engines and winched the little boat alongside. We put over fenders, and soon the yacht was tied fast to our port side as we headed for the harbor. Untying the knots in the hawser lines tightened by the strain was a bigger job than tying them, but by the time we gained the harbor, everything was shipshape again. They tied the freighter to the dock, then hand-lined the little sailboat to a berth in shallower water.

We learned that the owner of the sailboat was a young Swede, single-handing around the world. He had also approached the island in the evening and had elected to hold offshore until morning, but had fallen asleep around midnight and the boat had drifted onto the reef. He was heartsick, thinking his boat badly damaged. He was lucky. A New Zealand construction crew on the island brought a large mobile crane to the shore and within an hour had lifted the boat onto the quay.

Amazingly enough, there were only three cracks in the fiberglass boat hull about one foot below the waterline. With help from other sailors, he was repaired in a few days and ready for the next jump. The yachties had another excuse for a party, this time a steak fry.

Two nights later there was a dance festival with village teams of dancers competing. The dancing done to torchlight and drums often told a native Maori story or legend, and was most exciting to watch. Rosie asked a native what the dancers were saying, but the native just giggled and said it was naughty.

Many houses had graves in their front yards. We asked why they did this and were told with a look of amazement, "Then it is easy to tend the grave."

17

Pago Pago

A number of people had told us, "Don't go to Pago Pago." They said the local government (Pago Pago is the capital of American Samoa) doesn't like yachts. But we had often found that sailors know local waters but will often volunteer advice on the next island without the benefit of having been there themselves.

We left Rarotonga on August 7 for a hard, rough eight-hundred-mile passage. We did not see the sun to get a fix for four days; the sails tore every day and had to be mended, and the autopilot quit completely. I was forced to rig lines from the jib sail back to the tiller, crossing them at the cockpit. By that method we could steer the boat automatically, although it was terribly hard on the jib sails.

I, at least, could only make the method work by having the boat fall off and a shock cord pull the tiller over. Then, when it was pulled over sufficiently so that the boat turned to fill the sails again, we would go back on course. When it came into the wind the sails flapped violently until the cord took over and brought it back on course.This frequent flapping tore the sails and I spent every morning sewing. Still, it was preferable to spending every minute at the tiller.

The boat was leaking badly again and, as usual, the motor had packed up. I began to wonder seriously if this boat would get all the way around the world, and I think Rosie was thinking about airplane schedules in American Samoa.

On this crossing we saw our first white-tailed tropic bird. What a sight! We were especially amazed because we were three hundred miles from land. Our bird book told us that these beautiful birds never follow ships, but that they appear out of nowhere, circle the boat once, and go their way. We had several do this and always wished they would stay longer so that we could study them more. The bird is snow white with two tail feathers twelve to fifteen inches long flowing out behind. They were content with one short look at humans, but we would have liked a better view.

On the eighth day out the storm cleared up some, so we got a fix and found we were likely to arrive at night. That night when the lights of the island came into view, we heaved to until morning and I threw out a makeshift sea anchor to hold us back. There was the usual reef off the entrance, but perhaps we were getting used to them. Rosie read the sailing directions, and I studied the chart. Follow the reef until you come to a wrecked Chinese fishing boat and make a 90-degree turn to starboard. That should be the entrance. It was.

The island of Samoa is very high and easily identified as an extinct volcano with the harbor right in the middle of the old crater. Evidently when it was erupting the lava cut a valley out one side, building up the outer reef in the process. When everything was over, the sea moved into the crater and there was the harbor—well protected but deep. Going in without a motor, we sailed until I was afraid of going aground, only about one hundred feet from shore. I threw out the anchor and it seemed as if it never would hit bottom. First, the 125 feet of chain, then the three-quarter-inch nylon line started out the hauser hole, and the first thing I knew all 300 feet were over the side. The anchor did grab hold and we swung around. I think we hung almost directly over the anchor with a scope no more than two to one. The big boys back home say it should be seven to one. We had no sooner anchored than the harbor master came out and said we would have to move.

I told him, "If I move, you are going to have to move me. There is no wind in here, the engine won't work, and I have no strength to pull that anchor up today. It would take me five hours."

I was surprised. He went back to shore and returned with a shore launch about thirty feet long and two husky men. The men pulled up the anchor and the launch moved us about thirty feet and dropped the anchor again. I couldn't see why he moved us such a short distance, but he must have had a reason. He was most polite, also.

As we were due for a new bottom paint job, I went over to the ship repair facility to see about hauling out and also asked them if anyone could look at my engine. They also were very nice and said they would send a launch over that afternoon to tow us alongside their wharf.

To a Samoan, to be fat is a status symbol. The fatter you are, the more income you must have and the less work you must do. Many must have weighed 250 pounds or more—men and women. I took our sails to the sail loft in the shipyard to have the seams resewn and some patches put on. In the loft were three women workers weighing well over 200 pounds apiece. Having to go back several times, I became acquainted with them.

One day one asked, "Isn't your wife good cook?"

"Oh," I said, "yes, she's a pretty good cook. Why?" I could tell they did not think she was.

"Well, if she good cook, how come you so skinny?" I weigh about 165 and am five feet ten inches tall. I had to laugh. When

I returned to the boat, I told Rosie not to be surprised if those three ladies brought her a cookbook.

Rosie had been given a ticket for not having a Samoan license on her bike. The police said she could pay five dollars or go to court. She chose to go to court (a matter of principle, she said, because she was a visitor there and should not need a Samoan motor license). It took three trips to court for her to get acquitted. She said it was an interesting process. The three judges, all great, fat black men, wore long black robes and had a most dignified bearing. When court was over they filed out in a stately manner. All were barefoot.

Later, as we were going through town on the cycles with Rosie ahead of me, she went through a stop sign, right in front of the police station. A dozen whistles blew. She pulled over to the side and was getting a lecture from a cop when I pulled up beside them. I took the side of the cop and told him I always had to contend with this sort of thing. I told him that when we got back to the boat I would beat her. He let us go. Go we did—off to the Tonga group and then on to Fiji.

18

Hot Showers—and French Lighthouses

Since we found Fiji, we guessed that Rosie had finally figured out the complexities of crossing the international date line. Finding the island was one thing, getting into harbor was another. With two or three wrecks in sight, we sailed back and forth looking for the channel. Presently, a small tug came chugging out from behind the reef. It came close alongside and the sailors asked if we were in trouble. We hollered back that we were not in trouble, but would like to follow them into the harbor. They obligingly turned around and proceeded slowly so that we could keep them in sight.

We had heard a rumor back in the Marquesas that there were hot showers at the Royal Suva Yacht Club. So right after the anchor was down, I went in to ask permission to stay at the yacht club and inquired about the showers.

"You are welcome to use all our facilities."

"Even the showers?"

"Certainly."

I made a mad dash back to the boat to gather up towels and soap. Wonderful! Those hot showers even had hot water. Soft water, too. I lost half my tan right there. Then, feeling scrubbed and clean, we went to the restaurant for steak and rice. It was all we could eat for $1.50 each. Never have I liked the British so well. American is spoken here with a strong British accent, difficult to understand at times.

The town of Suva was an exotic meeting of East and West. British, New Zealanders, Hindus, Moslems, and Fijians— members of three distinct cultures—spoke their own language and wore their own clothes. The Hindu women were stately and colorful in long flowing saris, beads, bracelets, and a spot on their forehead or on the side of their nose. The Fijians were coal black. The women wore long dresses and carried themselves very erect. Their hair was frizzy and many wore it several inches long. The men wore the lavalava and were muscular and well built. There were also a number of Chinese, all of whom seemed to have restaurants or be fishermen. The Hindus were the shopkeepers. Since Suva was a duty-free port, there were hundreds of little shops, all run by Hindus. A Hindu priest told us that to be a priest, your father had to be a priest. The castes were still there. The large stores and mechanical shops were run by New Zealanders or British.

Fiji is the picture-book South Sea island. Away from town

there are fertile valleys, mountains covered with all shades of green vegetation, rippling streams, quiet lagoons, palm trees, and offshore reefs abounding with shells of every variety. They also have their share of tropical storms.

The public market in Suva was an interesting place with exotic smells, sneezy smells, fishy smells. Tobacco is sold off a big reel, like rope, about one-half inch in diameter. Here comes a fellow with a pipe. He wants two inches. He crumbles it up, stuffs it into a clay pipe, and goes away happy. No labels on the reel saying, "Injurious to health."

We left Suva on October 3, 1972. We had waited for a good weather report, as I was concerned about the mast, which was getting worse. Only fifteen hundred miles to go to Australia.

About three hundred miles out of Fiji another tropic bird circled us. The ocean was full of porpoises. A large passenger liner passed us at night. The next morning a Chinese fishing boat was about two miles off. The ocean was getting crowded.

With New Caledonia still two hundred miles away, the barometer began to drop. I did not mention this to Rosie, for the weather seemed pleasant enough. One more day and the barometer had dropped some more, and we were getting wind and rough seas. The wind switched and came directly on our nose. In twenty-four hours, we made sixteen miles on course. I started up the engine and we bucked and pitched toward New Caledonia. As we raised the island, the seas settled down some and I was relieved to see the lighthouse on the extreme southeastern point.

The French build good, big lighthouses and it is a delight to be able to see them when you are a few miles out to sea. They are often concrete and painted white. Lighthouses made out of steel angle iron are almost transparent, as they blend in with the surrounding country. Since points of land often look much alike, seeing the lighthouse helps to identify the point. Past the lighthouse, up the channel, Canal de La Havannah, and off to starboard was an anchorage. Inside, it was smooth, deserted, peaceful. The storm had faded off somewhere to plague the next fellow. No one but a seaman will ever know what a great feeling it is to be in shelter. Big waves were not slapping us around; we could quit striving to move ahead.

Rosie made some tea. We took a swim in the warm water and settled back for a peaceful evening.

19

Another Tall Sea Story

We left the next morning for the harbor of Nouméa. At the entrance, a New Zealand woman in an outboard directed us to the yacht club. She was Lee Reilly, who later became a friend. Many luxurious yachts were tied up at the Cercle Nautique Yacht Club. The French here seemed to be wealthy.

While our boat was tied to the fuel dock waiting to be assigned a berth, I met a New Zealander. I asked him where the bank was and where we could find a good restaurant. He told of a restaurant about a block away, but said all the banks were closed.

"Oh," I said, "Rosie won't like that. She likes to eat ashore the first night in."

"How much do you need?" he asked.

"Oh, enough for a couple of steaks and a few beers," I laughed.

He reached into his pocket and handed me the equivalent of fifty dollars, saying, "Pay me back tomorrow when the bank opens." I had known him fifteen minutes, but that's a New Zealander for you.

Our best friends here were three New Zealanders: Ian Singleton, who had loaned me the fifty dollars; Lee Reilly; and Ian's buddy Don Mosley. Ian and Don could down six pints of beer in six minutes with no trouble. They were first-class sailors who delivered sailboats for a living and crewed on race boats for fun and play. Each had crossed the Tasman Sea many times.

The story I liked best was their last exploit at work. They were to deliver a thirty-two-foot fiber-glass sailboat from Auckland to Nouméa, over one thousand miles. Two hundred miles off the coast of New Zealand, the water tanks cracked and all the water drained into the bilge. The first they knew of it was when one went to get a drink and no water came out of the tap. Pay for boat delivery is usually by the mile. They don't get anything for going back. After they sounded the tank and found it as dry as the day it was built, one said, "This is a bloody bad situation."

"Shocking," replied the other. "How much beer do we have on board?"

They had two full cases left—forty-eight bottles. They figured they should be able to do the eight hundred remaining miles in seven days. That meant they had over three bottles each a day. Fair enough. On they went. They had a good breeze and did it in six days flat.

"We drank the last two bottles coming through the opening right out here."

One day a pretty New Caledonian lady and a small boy were standing on the dock looking at our boat. She started talking to me in rapid French. When she saw I did not understand, she sent her boy back to the parking lot and he returned with his father. The father introduced himself, the son, and his wife.

"My wife would like to have your U.S. flag."

I told them I was very sorry but it was the only one we had and I could not give it up. I explained that we were required to fly our flag in foreign ports. The lady was crushed.

Her husband said, "We love America and Americans and she wanted it for a souvenir."

We had found so many people who did not like Americans and here was a friend and we could not do her a little favor. Rosie asked them aboard and that turned out to be a boatful, since they had seven children. They were Mr. and Mrs. Marc Rossi and their five beautiful daughters, Marthe, Annick,

Bianca, Tina, Marinella, and sons Marc and Karl. The father said they appreciated America because, during World War Two, America had sent men to protect them and the men had been gentlemen through and through. Mr. Rossi wanted me to ask our president to send a big warship for their young people to see.

To have more time and quiet to visit with their parents, we introduced the five girls to four American boys in the yacht next to ours. From that meeting the oldest girl and Bob White of Costa Mesa, California, went on to fall in love and are now happily married. They live in New Caledonia. Just call me Cupid!

Besides playing Cupid, we toured the large island that is New Caledonia. The island is different from others we had visited in the South Pacific because it is dry. The brush in the hills was the short, stunted, hardy brush that survives with little moisture. It reminded me of Wyoming. We did not mind getting out of the rain belt for a while as we toured the island on our cycles.

On one eighty-mile Honda trip to the north of the island, a rear tire blew on Rosie's cycle. A New Caledonian came along with a jeep and hauled the motor back to the boat, thirty miles past his own home. I knew he wasn't rich, but he would not accept pay for it. In fact, the next day he brought us a large sack of vegetables and a carved wood temple. I finally talked him into taking a bottle of Scotch.

The next day I went out to buy a new tube and looked all day with no success. None of the tire shops or cycle shops could supply me. I decided it was the language barrier and the Spanish word *tubo* was not getting through. So, having an old tube on the boat, I started out with that. The first merchant I talked to produced a tube at once, saying, "Oh, *chambre à aire.*" Well, of course, any fool should know that a tube is a chamber for air. I suppose a balloon is the same thing.

All business, work, etc. in Nouméa came to a halt at 12:30 when everyone went for lunch. Lunch was a full meal with wine and the whole bit and lasted until 3:30 or 4:00 P.M. Only reluctantly did the stores open up then.

The day had come when we had to leave this fun place, Nouméa, New Caledonia. The hurricane season was due to start within the month. Having gotten this far with no major setbacks, it was no time to loiter around. We hoped to find an anchorage in Australia as far from the sea as we could go in the boat. Preferably up some deep creek or a river. Then, if we could squeeze in among some trees or mangroves for more protection it would be ideal. We would stay put for five months at least. There was no reason for us to gamble on weather if we did not have to.

In other words, study the sailors two Bibles, *Bowditch* and the *Sailing Directions*, and follow their advice.

Sadly waving good-bye, we departed on October 25 for Australia. Rosie said she counted fifteen people on the wharf who had come to see us off.

The channel out was twenty miles of winding between reefs, but they were buoyed or marked by wrecks. Two wrecked freighters appeared to be at anchor. They must have run up on those reefs while going full ahead as they were high and dry but upright as though floating. Grim reminders to keep our eyes open.

A few days out of New Caledonia, we began to pick up Aussie stations on the radio. It was pleasant to hear English again. We were excited at approaching Australia because we felt they would be our friends. We have fought side by side, speak the same language, and most of our forefathers came from the same country. We looked forward to being at home away from home.

We decided to go into Gladstone, the home of Theo and Muraika, and we set a course to go just south of the Great Barrier Reef. We took many sights the last two days and were surprised one morning to find we were twenty miles too far south. We set a course to compensate and the next noon found we were too far north and just off a reef. We hurriedly took some more shots and determined that this was definitely so. I climbed the mast, and sure enough, off to starboard not a quarter of a mile was a breaking reef. With a southeast wind and a set to the north, going south would be slow business.

Studying the chart, I saw an opening through this fifteen-mile-long reef just west of us. Turning southwest we headed for it. It was a little hairy, but we got through. I hate reefs.

We headed for Lady Mosgrave Island. Inside its large barrier reef we could see smooth water, but we could not see an opening even though the chart showed one. Presently an outboard motorboat came alongside. Its passengers shouted "hello!" I waved and asked if they knew where the opening was to the lagoon.

"Just follow us."

As they were camped on the small island, they knew the opening well and we followed them in. It was the island called Lady Mosgrave.

With the anchor out and our boat swinging with the current, we invited them aboard for a drink. There were George Osborne and his wife from Waihemo, Murringo, sheep farmers on holiday.

Lady Mosgrave had a busy anchorage. Two fishing boats came in. The smaller came to us and gave us a large fish for supper. I invited the fisherman aboard to help us eat it. We tied his boat astern so that it drifted out behind. He was Alex Reynold, fishing out of Bundaberg, Queensland. We had a great evening exchanging sea experiences and learning something of Australia. Alex told us the way the fishermen anchor in this little bay. They drop their anchor close to a coral head, then circle it once with a lot of chain out. The chain wraps around the coral head and all is secure. In the morning, they reverse their circle to unwrap the chain, then lift the anchor, and they are off.

He stayed on the boat until it was too late for him to go anywhere else to anchor. In the total darkness, he could not see the coral heads all over the bay. He decided to stay tied to our stern all night. About three in the morning a terrible thunder, lightning, and wind storm arose. If our line broke, or our anchor dragged, we would both end up on the reef. All three of us sat up uneasily watching the storm and trying to determine that we were holding. The lightning was spectacular as it lit up the black ocean and the white breaking reef. The wind howled, but the water inside the lagoon was not extraordinarily rough.

20

Meeting Hostility with Reason

At daybreak, the storm settled down. Alex told us he did not think our twenty horsepower engine could buck the current coming through the opening, so he gave us a tow out. We have never met a commercial fisherman we did not like, no matter what nationality.

Since Lady Mosgrave Island was about fifty miles off the Australian mainland, we could not make Gladstone in daylight. We planned to anchor in Pancake Creek that night. When we arrived off the creek, we could not find the entrance and, instead, went on toward Gladstone. Since the area for miles around was charted at forty feet, we decided we would just move until dark, throw out the hook, and ride out the night wherever we were. This we did. In the morning it looked as if we were anchored in the middle of the ocean—land was still twenty miles away.

With Alex's directions fresh in mind, going into Gladstone was easy. We followed the channel markers, then got behind Facing Island. "You'll go mostly westerly here," he had said. "There will be a small island off to starboard and Auckland Creek will be to port. There will be some sailboats there. Turn up that creek and if there is an old metal boat tied between two pilings, tie alongside and the customs will be out to inspect you."

We waited three hours for customs, and when they did not show up, we rowed ashore and Rosemary went to the post office. After a month or two, mail was always a big event, and I could not hold her back. I went to customs, two blocks away.

They were a bit mad because I had come ashore and madder still when I told them my wife was at the post office. Right off they had me in a car with a customs man, headed for the post office to "fetch Rosemary." They hauled us down to the boat and said, "Don't leave again until you are cleared in."

Customs, immigration, and health were out to our boat in fifteen minutes. They admitted they had not seen us come in, nor spotted our Q flag. They said the tugboat men were on strike and no one was supposed to come into port. I do not know how long we would have waited had we not gone ashore. They decided not to be mad, I guess.

The minute they left I went ashore again to the bank with our letter of credit to buy Aussie money. We wanted to eat ashore that night to celebrate a little. I had steak and chips with veges (pronounced vejees). The steak was one-quarter inch thick, the chips were shoestring potatoes, and the veges were carrots or peas. They usually do not serve beer in a restaurant, but serve food in the bars.

We decided to ride our Hondas to Brisbane, camping on the way, to look for some needed boat gear. The fear that we might lose the anchor at Rangiroa made me realize the necessity for a spare. The anchor chain was rusty, and we needed turnbuckles, stainless-steel wire, and, perhaps, a new sail. Name it and we could use it. The sea is hard on equipment.

With both cycles heavily loaded with camping gear, sleeping bags, a change of clothes, cameras, tire pump, ax, and water bag, we were off. We looked forward to getting away from that pesky boat for a while. Total square footage on deck was less than two hundred feet, like a room ten by twenty. We had enjoyed it, but with Australia in front of us we wanted a little of its available elbow room. The country is only slightly smaller than the United States but has only fourteen million people.

The four-hundred-mile trip to Brisbane was a wonderful ride. We camped along Bruce Highway. By riding off the highway less than a mile, we could be by a small stream. With a canvas lean-to up, our air mattresses under the sleeping bags, a campfire going, coffee boiling, and a steak ready to broil, could you beat it?

Building a campfire was a pleasure. The wood was a bit oily and even if there had been a rain shower, the fire would take off at once. Coffee was ready in fifteen minutes when hung over the fire in an old can. After the hot fire had burned away, the coals were red and glowing for a couple of steaks on a rack three inches above. I was fearful about getting Rosie back to the boat.

"This is the way I like to sail around the world," she said.

It was early summer there and the countryside was a picture. As we rode we got the warm land breeze and a glimpse of the sea occasionally through forests here or pineapple farms there or an apple orchard in the valley. The sugar cane fields were brilliant green and every so often there was a dairy farm with fat cows chewing their cud. It was a change from the ocean—a welcome change.

While the land was pleasant, the people were not. While we were shopping in a store in Maryborough, the owner saw our cycles with Montana licenses and asked, "How come?"

I told him we were from the United States visiting Australia on our sailboat in Gladstone. He turned to his wife and said, "Yanks always did have more money than sense." Nice fellow.

After our week's vacation north, we were, as after any vacation, glad to get home. There was a new boat flying the American flag tied up in the creek. It was out of Seattle, our listed home port. We had not seen a Seattle boat since leaving Panama, so meeting John and Joan Casanova on the trimaran *Tortuga* was like meeting your next-door neighbor.

We had dinner together several times, told sea stories, and talked about the United States. We were not the only ones getting the "Yank" treatment, and we talked it over and tried to decide what the big complaint was, but did not find an answer. The Casanovas were not worried about the hurricane season and had a commitment to get to Spain, so they left after a week.

It may not be as big a surprise to you as to me, but women are different from men. I knew, of course, about the difference in body construction, and that women were better looking than men. I also knew women were more even tempered— "always bad," I told Rosie. She didn't think that was as funny as I did. The biggest difference is the nesting instinct. I had been pretending not to hear certain utterances and mumblings coming from Rosemary, but about a week after our trip to Brisbane, while we were enjoying a morning coffee, she laid her cards on the coffee table, so to speak. I remember it distinctly. It was over the third cup.

"I'm going home for Christmas and to see the kids," she said.

I knew she had been thinking of this, but at that moment I had no defense ready, so I said, "You mean this Christmas?"

"Yes, this Christmas!" She banged her coffee cup on the cockpit table.

The upshot was that I, as an easygoing sort of male, said, "Yes, dear."

I was trying to figure out what a ticket to Billings, Montana, would cost. It was easy to visualize our savings account taking a beating. Almost that same day, she received a letter from her brother, a Billings businessman. He was having a bookkeeper problem. He would pay her fare home if she would straighten out his books. About the next day a letter came from my best friend in Billings, Bob Martin, saying they were going south and if we came home for Christmas, the key to his house was ours.

Being naturally bighearted, I told Rosie to go ahead and buy herself a ticket.

"I'm not going without you!" she said emphatically. Oh, lordy, double trouble.

"Theo told me yesterday that he would watch the boat," Rosie said. It dawned on me then that she had been working on this deal for probably six months. She must have had some code worked out in her letters. I really did not want to leave the boat that long in a foreign country, but being captain didn't seem to help much.

On December 19 we left Gladstone by train on the one-thousand-mile trip to Sydney to catch a plane for the United States. Twenty-three hours after takeoff we were greeting friends and relatives in Billings. It had taken that many months to get to Australia. Twenty-eight days and twenty-nine parties later, we boarded a plane and headed back down under. It took me two months to recuperate. That plane traveling is not for me. It is just too fast. We did not see anything; did not talk to anyone interesting; and were offered a crummy movie for three dollars. The hostesses were pretty and the food fair.

I was expecting a hassle with Australian customs over boat parts. The only thing they were stiff-necked about was a windup razor I had taken back to the States for repair. It was still in the box from the factory and the customs wanted to charge $10 customs duty. That was $14 American money and it had only cost $19.95. I finally convinced them I had taken it home for repairs. They were a hard-nosed bunch of bloody blokes—to put it in Aussie English.

Shortly after we returned to Australia, I ordered a new aluminum mast. During our last thousand miles of sailing, that old mast had got so bad it would bend about 15 degrees even under reefed sails. It was a miracle it got us to Australia and I was darned relieved to be getting a new one. The Mexicans had done their best for two hundred dollars in a small village. On close examination I found a few nails driven into that mast to hold down a scarf, the place where two pieces of wood come together. They were only small nails, but they let water or moisture enter to do damage. The old carpenter who built it had said he would not use nails, but I felt no malice toward him. With what he had to work with, he had done a good job. I still have a soft spot for him. Our new forty-four-foot-tall mast, made out of quarter-inch aluminum and teardrop shaped, was laid on the dock for four hundred dollars Aussie, about six hundred American. It would not rot, anyway.

Theo was going to Rockhampton, so he took our fittings to have them galvanized. They did such a good job that I later sent our anchor chain to have it hot galvanized. Our charts indicated that until we got to Singapore we would be in a backward area, so it seemed sensible to get as much as possible done in Australia.

We had decided to leave about the middle of April. About the first of that month we took another cycle trip, meandering 1,000 miles inland at a rate of about 150 miles a day. We continued to be surprised at the animosity the Aussies showed toward the United States. When we met a stranger it was nothing for him to start running down the United States with the third sentence. At first we ignored them, then we questioned them.

I had always been a flag-waver. The Aussies only made me wave it higher. After a while I quit turning the other cheek. About six of us were sitting at a small table in a pub one night: us, a couple from New Zealand, and an Aussie couple. The Aussie kept needling us about the United States. It finally got to me and I stood up, "I've taken all of this I can. Let's step outside and settle this."

I'd had my knees under that small table and when I stood up I just dumped the table and our drinks and everything into the guy's lap. By the time he'd got himself untangled and kind of backed off everything had calmed down. Several more arguments and fights later we had sorted out our friends and enemies in Gladstone and were treated with more respect. I later decided the Aussies just like a fight and a fighter. When we prepared to leave, we had about ten going-away parties that lasted far into the night. When we left port, I had difficulty seeing the buoys and we had on board cakes, food, vegetables, and addresses of many friends.

We planned to go through the Great Barrier Reef just north of Lizard Island. We waited there three days for the weather to improve. The anchorage was poor and rolly, the days gray and overcast. We could not go ashore through the surf breaking on the beach and throwing spray into the air; we would never have made it in our lightweight dinghy. So, we marked time. It had been so long since we had been on the open ocean that Rosie was reluctant to go.

On the fourth day the barometer rose a bit, and I decided we would take off. It proved to be a mistake. As we approached One-Mile Opening, named by Captain Cook, we saw tremendous breakers on the outside of the reef. The thunder of the breaks was like the steady rumble of a freight train. Fifty miles out the next evening, Rosie heard on the radio that we were on the edge of a hurricane. Our course lay directly across the big waves that continually washed over the boat.

21

An Elegant Stop at Port Moresby

One by one we tore up three jib sails. The last one ripped in half and the top half flew up the mast, flapping wildly. I climbed the ratlines trying to get it down. Rosie, in tears, kept pleading with me to forget it and come down, and I admit the motion of the boat was so violent that I decided it was no time for heroics and let it fly. In the next couple of days I tried a couple of other ways to bring it down, but could not.

The fourth night out we crept into Port Moresby in New Guinea at 3:00 A.M. by following the lead lights. The entrance is shaped like a dogleg; in fact, two doglegs, one over 100 degrees. We had faith in the British lead lights and were so damned sick of that Coral Sea, so beaten up and dead tired, that we decided to chance it in the dark. I learned later that we had gone so close to the barrier reefs that had I seen it in daylight, I would have been scared to death. Next day the sun came out and the storm was over.

The torn sail flying from the mast was embarrassing, but it gained us an immediate friend, Reggie Lincoln and his wife. They rowed out to our boat at daybreak and offered to help get it down.

"You must have been out in that terrible storm," Reggie said.

I admitted we had, but did not admit that, according to Rosie, it was because I was impatient to get away from Lizard Island.

The Lincolns were a New Zealand couple on a trip who had been living for a few years in New Guinea. As it turned out, I could straighten the mess out myself when we were in port, but it showed how these New Zealanders think. They were the first to step forward. They also told us a large freighter had gone aground in the storm somewhere around Mackay. It had been anchored and a fluke had broken off the anchor, so the freighter dragged ashore. The high wind and seas put him high and dry.

At this point we seriously considered taking the shortest route home: east a bit more around the southeast tip of New Guinea, up to the Philippines, and then north to Japan to catch the Japan Current for a ride downwind into Seattle. Rosie said she did not think the boat would hold together going on around the world. It meant we would be home in less than a year. I guess we really never seriously considered it, although we discussed it. Then Rosie said, "Oh, let's go on." She has a knack of occasionally saying the right thing. Of course, we were in port at the time and Port Moresby was certainly one of the more pleasant stops we made. Besides the items previously mentioned, often a dirty old fisherman or a deckhand on a freighter stopped by with a small gift of some sort—flowers, fish, or a seashell.

Outside of Port Moresby they raised a small, solid pineapple that was so sweet and juicy I thought it must be candy. The interisland freighters often came in with a load of them. Someone unloading would throw us one or two.

One day the police launch tied up across the wharf to unload about twenty prisoners. They all had musical instruments and were as happy as though going to a convention. I asked one of the guards what they had done.

"Oh," he said, "they caused trouble."

Three weeks later I saw we had better pull stakes or we would never leave. A sailor cannot stand having it too good or he bogs down and gets landitis.

The New Zealanders and the Aussies in the yacht club had a Fourth of July party for the Americans, and on the sixth we left this well-sheltered port for points west. It was hard to do. But, loaded down with enough supplies to make Singapore, we took off thinking our next major stop would be Dilli, Timor.

The day before we left, there were reports the Dutch sailboat *Rik*, with our friends Claus and Wilma Honig, had been wrecked on a reef in the Torres Strait. They had left Port Moresby a few days before. Apparently they had sent an SOS out on their ham radio, which was picked up in Darwin and forwarded to Port Moresby. We kept our eyes open but saw nothing.

The entrance to the Great Northwest Passage of the Torres Straits was very difficult to find from a small boat without radar or a high deck. It was marked to the north by Bramble Cay, an island about four feet high without palm trees. The cay was supposed to have a forty-foot-tall structural steel tower with a light on it. But as I pointed out before, since structural steel is not a solid object, a person can look right through it and not see it.

Rosie spent some time worrying about that. If we missed the entrance and went too far west before turning south, we would be near a large reef area that was poorly charted. So, the plan was to get within twelve miles at night, since there was a twelve-mile light. The third night out, however, when we should have seen the light, we saw nothing. As soon as the sun was up, we started taking shots. That seemed confusing, for it showed us very close to Bramble cay. I was doing something else when I happened to look somewhat out to starboard and there it was, quite close. It was only a miracle we saw it at all, for we were already past. It seemed strange that such an important navigational point could not have been painted white. The Aussies maintained it and Rosie was all for writing them a letter.

At daylight we saw that our position was about as good as it could be. We saw people on the island and figured that if we were in a bad spot, someone would come and inform us. Local people are usually good about telling you if you are anchored wrong. Often they had led us to a good anchorage.

We decided to stay there for a day and think things over, so I took the dinghy and went ashore. The chart said there was a mission there. That meant a church with a school. We took candy ashore for the children. I asked the headmaster if it was all right to give it to them and he said, "I'll take it and give it to them at a more appropriate time." I hope the kids finally got it.

It was an interesting little island with about sixty people including children. They raised a few pigs, chickens, and turtles, but most of their subsistence came from the sea. Besides the conventional method of fishing, they had built coral corrals out in the shallow spots. When the tide came in the corrals filled with water and fish. When the tide went out they walked out to the corrals and picked out the fish stranded there. The turtles were raised in concrete pens about six by six feet set at the high-water mark where the sea automatically came in twice a day.

Arthur Stevens was one of the turtle growers and later in the day he came to our boat for coffee. I've never met a man with more common sense. He had had only three years of school, but could read and write. He was well built, stocky, with gray curly hair and coal-black skin. He had a sense of humor that kept us chuckling.

"Raising these turtles is a government project," he said. "We get them when they come from the hatchery and they are about an inch long. We each receive a hundred at a time. They are put into pens about five feet square and as they grow we put them into larger pens. We raise them until they are about eight inches across, then the government takes them back to plant or sell. We receive money for each one we are able to deliver.

"Before I started raising these, I used to fish about three days a week and live good. Now, I have to fish seven days a week to feed those turtles. We live good, but no better. I was happy before. I'm happy now, only I'd rather work three days a week. I guess the government is happy, too."

Pointing to an island we had passed, he said, "That's Darnly Island. The men from this island go over there to get their wives. We have done that for years." He laughed. "Good-looking girls on Darnly."

Arthur told us everyone on his island was named Stevens. Rosie asked, "How come?"

"Used to be, no one have two names," he replied. "Only one. But when the government said we could vote, they said we had to have two names. A white man used to come to this island. We liked him, so we all took the name of Stevens."

He asked us how we liked traveling. Rosie said, "If you go with Keith, I'll stay and feed your turtles."

Arthur laughed. "Feeding turtles is hard work." Then, he said, "I've been to Port Moresby and Brisbane—when I was drafted during world war. Oh, yes, I've been to Caution."

"Where?" I asked.

"Caution," he said. He pointed west. "You know?"

I didn't, so I went and got a chart. About twenty to seventy-five miles west of Stevens Island was a large uncharted and unexplored area full of reefs, rocks, strong currents, riptides, and shoal water—everything to give a sailor nightmares. On our chart it covered an area of nine hundred to one thousand square miles. Marked in big letters across the chart in that area was the word CAUTION. Arthur had been there several times and returned. He was proud of it. We did not blame him.

That evening we bought several nice shells from Arthur and found a larger bailer shell on the reef. A bailer shell is from one inch to two feet long, shaped something like a bucket, so the natives around Australia use them to bail out boats. I asked a lady if I could take it and she said, "Why, certainly."

We waved farewell the next morning and sailed for Coconut Island. It looked interesting; so off with the dinghy. We stayed two days. After receiving permission from the chief to walk around the island, we did so for nearly twelve hours. We had bought 160 shells and some of them weighed a pound. I hired a small boy to help carry. He demanded and got ten cents.

22

Worn Out with Kindness

We had a good trip—everything worked. Nothing went wrong, and five and one-half days from our interim stop at Thursday Island we dropped anchor in front of the village of Aduat on the island of Selaru in the south part of the Banda Sea. The anchor line had no tension in it. I could clearly see bottom and we were just drifting around with a slack anchor line.

The islands were lush and green. Several native sailboats were tied up to the wooden wharf and every house had a thatched roof. There were no guns shot at us, and in a short time the boat was surrounded with dugout canoes of every size and description—leaky ones, dry ones, short ones, long ones, outriggers and nonoutriggers. None were painted except for decoration. On most of them the ax marks were clearly visible.

The people in them were obviously friendly, for they brought bananas, fish, and coconuts out to us. Each canoe was to the waterline with occupants; all with black flashing eyes, gleaming white teeth, and big beaming smiles. During the first hour, twenty-five canoes must have gathered around us. We did not like this as they bumped, bumped, bumped against our hull.

Each bump knocks a bit of protecting bottom paint off, giving those damned teredos an open door to get to our planking and eat their fill.

The smiles and loud talking of the natives made it difficult to tell them to please not knock against the boat. I used sign language, at which they laughed even as they gradually got the idea. I am sure they could not understand why, never having seen a can of bottom paint. At least seventy-five people were there, so we did not dare invite anyone aboard, since they all would have followed. All of them on board at once, especially if they gathered on one side, might well have sunk our boat.

Soon a young fellow arrived and spoke to us in halting English, "It is necessary I see your passports." I invited him aboard and offered him a cup of coffee. He put six heaping spoons of sugar and half a small can of canned milk into it. He was most polite. "I thank you. Is necessary I take passports to shore. You get them from policeman."

We really hated to let loose of our passports, but there seemed no alternative. Legally, I do not think that, according to International Law, we would have had to do that, but what was "legal" in this out-of-the-way place? A few countries had taken them and kept them until we left, but usually they just stamped them and told us how long we could stay in the country.

The young man stayed aboard for more than an hour. We were welcome to stay as long as we wished, he said, and to come ashore. He was only eighteen, a schoolteacher, and the only person on the island who could speak English. Although it was difficult to understand, his English was better than our Indonesian, which was zero.

We asked him if he would please tell the people in canoes not to bump against our boat. We explained about the paint and how there were little animals in the water that eat wood. He nodded and told the canoe folk about the problem. It did no good, however, as the canoes were always coming and going.

He drank several cups of coffee and I could see Rosie eyeing our sugar supply. He said he would come back the next day and invited us to come into the village the next day about one o'clock to visit the police. We said we would.

All the next morning I traded for shells. Since we had no Indonesian money, it had to be trade. I began to feel like Captain Cook's sailors who pulled nails from his ship to trade for the favors of the Polynesian girls. Every short piece of rope went, all of the loose bolts and nuts I had been saving for emergencies, spare shackles, pulleys, old tools, old clothes, matches.

Rosie protested. "This boat is going to fall apart like *The Wonderful One-Hoss Shay*—it will collapse all at once."

But I was like a dope addict selling his children. These people had shells we had never seen before. They would trade twenty dollars' worth of shells for a used six-cent one-quarter-inch eyebolt. And, oh boy, for a well-used shirt or pair of pants, I could have had a dugout canoe if I could have carried it. It shows that everything is relative. I really wanted one of those dugouts to take back to the United States, but I couldn't figure out a place to put it. With two motorcycles, a couple of five-gallon plastic cans, a thirty-gallon plastic drum for extra diesel, and our own dinghy, there was just no room. I did trade for two hand-carved canoe paddles of the native wood, a deep red brick in color. The shape was strange: The lower end was pointed.

As we rowed ashore in the afternoon, we saw people running down to the beach. The way they were congregating, we thought perhaps someone was hurt. There was also a policeman in a bright uniform. I changed direction so as not to land in the middle of the crowd, but as I headed up the beach, the people did too. When Rosemary stepped ashore, about three hundred persons gave a big shout and clapped and whistled. It was embarrassing. The policeman in his fine uniform had to clear a way for us from the beach.

The whole crowd followed us inland, crowding close. We, of course, could not understand a word of what anyone was saying until the young schoolteacher arrived. Both he and the policeman had on shoes, in honor of the occasion, I supposed.

We figured out that we were being given a grand tour of the village—all three streets. I didn't see a vehicle or motor on the island, not even a bicycle. The crowd stuck close to us, laughing, crowding in to tell us something, good-natured and jostling among themselves.

We wound up at the village center, the largest and most prominent building in town. Inside we were led to the only two chairs. When we sat down, everyone clapped again. It was something new to be a dignitary. The policeman stood in front of us and gave a speech. Then another official gave a speech. Everyone clapped. We clapped. Then different groups of girls danced. The people watched us. We watched the dancers. At the end of each dance we would stand and clap. The audience would laugh and shout and clap. It was easy to tell when the "majorettes" danced. Then the older grads did a couple of numbers and finally some very young girls did the cutest dance a person could ask for. They all danced to drums and one tinkly little instrument with two strings. It sounded half oriental, half South Sea Island native. The little girls mimicked something and the crowd cheered. It was a very good show that outranked Vegas—no booze, no dirty jokes, just fifty beautiful girls.

After the two-hour show we were escorted to the police station, a thatched-roof hut with a crude wooden desk made out of hand-hewn lumber, a rickety chair, and no bars on the window. The policeman did have a stamp. With much ceremony he stamped our passports and handed them back to us.

There was no restaurant, but there was a small store that had a few cans of corned beef, dried milk, tomato sauce, and peaches. There was rice by the hundred-pound bag. We did not consider our boat too well stocked, but I figured we had a lot more food than that store did. We didn't buy anything.

So many people crowding around and talking made Rosie nervous. "Let's go back to the boat. These people are wearing me out with kindness."

The minute I started rowing out, about ten dugouts followed. They pointed and talked among themselves, then usually laughed. I think it was because "that funny white man sits with his back forward and cannot see where he is going." Native craft are rowed facing forward instead of backward.

Back on board Rosie decided we would stay below for a while. Being a celebrity had its disadvantages. I also thought that we would eat below instead of in the cockpit as was our custom, for at previous meals they had gathered around and watched each mouthful from plate to mouth. I know they weren't hungry, only curious, but it was disconcerting. Even down below, at any time we could look up and see four pairs of eyes at every porthole. I don't know how they did it.

The next morning they were bump, bump, bumping against the boat before daylight. I spent the day trading for more shells. Since I was getting low on trading stock, the market on shells dropped considerably that day. It was soon apparent that I had paid 1,000 percent too much to start with.

The schoolteacher came aboard for several hours. He asked me to take the motorcycles ashore. I had prior experience with this. If you took one child for a ride, you had to take five hundred, so I declined. There was not one motor on the whole island, nor radios, nor electricity, nor any other modern convenience. Forty-foot boats came in from other islands, loaded with people or freight, but always under sail. Some of the sails had holes big enough to put your head through.

The next day, two of the larger boats loaded so many people we thought they would sink. They were going to a neighboring island for a celebration and contests. The dancing we had seen was part of it, no doubt. They sailed by waving good-bye, and we hollered, "Good Luck!" I thought then we might have some relief from the "eyes" and constant bump, bump on the boat, but no such luck.

Two days later there was not a nut or bolt left to trade and we had been invited to the celebration, but we both felt so tired of the constant surveillance and voices calling from morning until dark, "Meester, Meester," trying to get our attention for another shell.

It was a kick, though, to watch the kids in some of the leaky dugouts. If there was one kid alone, he bailed continuously. If there were two of them, they took turns. There were many double outriggers and the young boys walked on them as relaxed as if on a sidewalk. Usually the outrigger, single or double, was held to the dugout by a crooked piece of timber shaped like a bow and lashed with vines.

The village was clean and the schoolteacher told us girls got two years of schooling and boys five, if they wanted it. We thought these people were very poor, but after seeing more of Indonesia, we decided they were rich in the sense that they were healthy, not crowded, and had plenty to eat. No one begged from us there, but in all the rest of those islands, begging was a way of life.

------------------------- 23 -------------------------

"Oh, No, Not Again!"

After several short stops along the way, we were near the west end of Lombok Island. Our chart showed a couple of six-fathom patches, so we decided to go in and anchor again. We were more or less directly under the highest peak on the island—at which I was gawking—when we struck bottom with a loud thud. Looking overside, I saw we were on jagged coral. If we laid over here, that coral would punch a hole in the planking.

Rosie scrambled up from below and wailed, "Oh, no, not again! This can't happen!"

"Quick, the dinghy," I shouted at her.

We rushed forward and I untied the dinghy as fast as I could. Weak Rosie, with the strength of two men, picked up the stern and I the bow and we threw it overboard. I usually put the dinghy overboard with a halyard.

I yelled at her, "Start the engine! Find out what the tide situation is!"

I put the anchor into the dinghy and rowed out to deep water. It was slow going, for the weight of the chain held me back. I had to go back to the boat and put all the chain into the dinghy. The three hundred feet of rope was not so heavy, so I pulled it out to the end of the line and dropped the anchor.

As I rowed back, Rosie was calling, "Hurry! Hurry! It's less than an hour to high tide."

I took a couple of wraps around the muscle-power anchor winch and we started trying to winch the ship out. One hundred feet of three-eighths-inch chain and three hundred feet of three-quarter-inch nylon rope started to come back aboard—stretching as tight as the proverbial fiddle string. I dared not break the winch or we wouldn't stand a chance. When it was as tight as I thought was safe, I sent Rosie back to gun the engine. Nothing happened. We tried some more muscle on the winch. The anchor was straight to sea at 90 degrees to the hull and the hull was parallel to the swells coming into shore. I hoped we would at least turn the boat so that the bow would be turned toward the swell.

We hauled in on the line and gunned the engine forward and then in reverse. No movement. The anchor line had stretched so tight that the three-quarter-inch line was only five-eighths inch. We tried to tilt the boat toward the sea by standing on the outer edge. I swung the boom out and climbed to the end of it. If the boat would heel over 10 or 20 degrees, it would draw less water. Still, it would not budge. I tightened the anchor line a few more inches, even though I was afraid the winch might pull out of the ship, taking part of the deck with it. I recalled seeing a boat where that had happened. A sailor had tried to pull himself off a reef in the Tuamotu Archipelago and the winch had torn a two-foot-square piece of deck out. When the winch flew off, it broke the sailor's arm and knocked him into the sea.

I had to chance it. We had to get out of this predicament. Rosie and I both heaved hard on the winch handle. The anchor line quivered. It was then only one-half inch in diameter.

How much more of this will it stand before it breaks? I thought. I did not like the answer. I told Rosie to stay clear of the winch in case it should tear out. I wondered how far it would catapult through the air and if it would take the starboard lifeline with it.

I cursed myself for being so damned stupid and took a quick glance at the shore for any sign of habitation. None. I winched. Rosie ran the engine full ahead and full astern. Nothing moved. But, so far, the anchor was holding. If it dragged, we would be in bad trouble. At least the swells could not push us further up on the coral. I recalled the *Yankee* in Rarotonga. I remembered the first *Mustang*. Oh, damn!

And I was mad at Rosie. She must have figured the tide wrong. I told her so in no uncertain terms. She, in tears, went below to check the tide book again. Even the tide book did not tell the tide in this exact spot, for it only listed the Flores Sea in general. Damn the tide book! Damn the sea!

Rosie was always threatening to fly home when we were in a big storm. If this boat broke up here, I would have to fly with her. Then I was thinking, if we get off, I may fly home with her anyway. The sea is cruel. It's Murphy's Law! If anything can go wrong it will do so on the sea. I am sick of the sea. I just may go home from the next port and plow.

The trouble is, we don't have a home. This damned boat is our home. Now here it is—sick, crippled, lame. Damn the boat! Damn the sea! If this boat breaks up, we can walk ashore from here when the tide goes out. I'm going to walk ashore and not stop walking. I'm going to walk right straight inland away from the sea. I'm going to walk until I can't see the sea, hear the sea, smell the sea.

If Rosie is right, time is running out on us. Look at those miserable fish swimming by—they don't even care that we are in trouble. Why doesn't some boat come along to help us? A good strong pull might slide us into one or two inches more water. That's all it would take to float us. Hell, no! No boat will come along now. If we were trying to work up a narrow channel we'd have ten boats, all wanting to be in the same place we wanted to be. Now no one wants to be here where we are.

From where I was standing, I had the mast lined up with a bare rock on shore. All at once, I thought the rock moved. No, I must have moved to change the line of sight. It had been forty-five minutes since we'd struck.

"Keith, Keith," Rosie screamed, "I think it bumped!"

We both shouted as we felt another bump. For sure that rock had moved. Another bump. The sea was moving us a bit. I strained harder on the winch and kept all the tension on the line that I dared. We bumped harder. Surely we weren't moving toward shore. Bump, bump—two in a row. Gun the damn engine, heave on the miserable winch handle.

Two minutes later we were afloat. I pulled the winch line in by hand to get us away from that damn piece of real estate. The anchor came over the side and, using the motor, we headed directly out to sea. I hugged Rosie. She was a great girl. She was never wrong. If she figured the tide, I could count on it. Yessiree sir!

"You bet, honey. I never doubted you for a minute. I just wanted to keep your mind occupied. Give you something to do, you know."

We heaved to for a moment to take the dinghy back aboard and tie it down. I asked Rosie if she wanted to go back in to anchor for the night.

"Don't you dare turn this boat toward that miserable place!" she said. "Thirty nights on watch is better than one hour on a reef." We voted to sail all night and to forget anchoring for a while. I proposed a happy hour with two stiff rums to soothe our jangled nerves. We set a course for the north coast of Bali and relaxed. It was a beautiful, beautiful night.

24

No Mail at the Post Office

The only real harbor on Bali is at Benoa, about eight or ten miles south of Denpassar, the capital. Both are on the protected south side of the island. But, we decided that since Benoa was fifty or more miles out of our way, we would go into a harbor on the north side, Bueleng, for Singaradja. Our sailing directions said Bueleng was protected some by reefs and to take care going through them. Oh, brother!

At daybreak, after our night at sea, we saw Bali about fifteen miles distant. The mountains rose out of the sea to an awe-inspiring height, so green they looked artificial. We were lucky the sun was behind us so we could see the reefs. By ten o'clock we were firmly at anchor, by ten-fifteen four officials boarded us, and by ten-thirty we were cleared to go ashore—but we couldn't take the motorcycles ashore. We would have to cross the island, the policeman told us, to talk to higher officials in Denpassar to try to get the permits for the cycles.

The next day we went to the local bank listed as an agent on our letter of credit, but were told we would have to go to the main bank in Denpassar. When we returned to the boat, a policeman was waiting on the little wharf.

"The harbor master thinks you should move a bit to be in a better holding anchorage," he said.

"Okay," I said. "Where should I move to?"

Benny, as he introduced himself, said, "I'll come out and help you move."

After we moved the boat only about a hundred feet, Rosie

made coffee and Benny sat down to drink with us. I think he really just wanted to visit with Americans. He was a fine example of manhood: tall, dark, husky, and well-mannered. He told us his Dutch father had been stationed in Djakarta on Java when he married an Indonesian girl. Benny's father, killed in World War Two by the Japanese, had talked to him in English as well as Dutch. Since there are many Chinese on Bali, he had also learned that. He spoke English, Dutch, Indonesian, and Chinese.

When we told him we were going to Denpassar the following day, he said, "Good, I meet you on dock and make sure you get seat on bus."

The next morning we learned what this meant. At the marketplace from which each bus left was a mob trying to get on board, good-naturedly pushing and shoving. Benny's police uniform cleared a way for us and we sat. Our bus was one of the better ones, not over twenty years old. A sign said, "Limit 27 Passengers." The Balinese interpretation was thirty-seven standing passengers, thirty-seven sitting. They are a small race and always sat three in a seat for two. I am five ten and stood a head taller than most of them. They also didn't seem to mind a lot of body contact, where most Americans want elbow room. Between short stops on the thirty-two-mile journey to Denpassar, people stood on the bumper, hung out the door, and shouted and laughed, having a good time.

That was quite a ride! The road went one and a half miles straight up, then one and a half miles back down. The driver kept the throttle to the floorboards all the way—around narrow mountain curves, through villages where the many exotic temples went by so fast we hardly got a look. At the summit, the driver jumped out of the bus, ran to an idol at the side of the road, left some token of gratitude, bowed three times, and ran back to the bus. He slammed the door and with brakes screeching and horn blowing, we started the descent, taking our half out of the middle of the road. Rosie closed her eyes. I thought I might as well see what we were going to hit. No one else paid attention, including the driver. He could not keep his eyes off a pretty girl who stood next to him. I could not take mine off the road.

Donkeys, water buffalo, goats, babies, pigs scattered as we flew by. If the driver did take a quick look, he pressed the horn, never the brakes. I wondered if we should take a plane back but thought that, perhaps, aircraft could not climb that fast, only drivers. I thought back to the stop at the temple. I never did figure out if the driver was offering thanks to the gods for getting us up there or asking help to get us down. I felt like giving a few tokens myself when we got to Denpassar safely.

We went for mail—there was none—then to immigration where, for good-size fees, we got our passports stamped and got permission to put our cycles ashore. I never did make it clear to the officials why we brought the cycles to Bali. By the time we left that office, I couldn't remember myself.

Denpassar, which I believe means great marketplace, is certainly that with hundreds of shops, street vendors, peddlers on foot, peddlers on donkeys, and peddlers carrying wares on their heads. I had to drag Rosie away. We never did find out Bali's population, but the island is crowded. That public market was a mass of people. To walk between the stalls we had to turn sideways and force our way through the aisle. To us it was very tiring and sort of nerve-racking. After a bit, we just wanted to get out and take a deep breath.

We had another harrowing ride back on the bus. It was a real pleasure, later, to make the trip on the cycles. The island is so beautiful, it is beyond description. Rice is raised everywhere, but they are not allowed to export any. This seemed a good idea, as they did not go hungry. In its different stages of growth, the rice shoots were different shades of green. The paddies were terraced over the top down to sea level. At the top they got rain, while lower down water was carried from high volcanic lakes and streams to each paddy through ditches with waterfalls in between. Where rice was not growing, flowers were.

After getting the cycles to run, our first short trip was from

Bueleng to the post office in Singaradja. On the boat before leaving, I typed my address: KEITH JONES, YACHT MUSTANG, POST RESTANTE, SINGARADJA, BALI. At the post office I handed this to the lady.

She smiled.

I said, "Hello."

She said, "Hello."

I presented my name card and inquired, *"Poste Restante?"*

She said, "Hello, yes."

I said, *"Correo."* My Spanish always pops up at times like this.

She said, "Ha, ha, hello."

Reaching over to an untidy pile of mail, she fished a letter from the bottom and handed it to me. I was jubilant. "This will cheer Rosie up."

Then I looked at the letter. It was addressed to Mr. Robinson. I gave it back to her and showed her the name tag. I said, "No, me! Me no Mr. Robinson. Me, Keith Jones." She laughed, "Oh, ho, ho."

I said to the lady, "Me no Manly; me, Jones." She smiled and took the letter and said, "Yes, yes, yes." She went to a dark corner and started to fish around in a pile of mail for a letter she must have remembered. The pile was covered with dust, so she called for someone of lower caste to dust it with a feather duster. He was chewing something; I believe it was betel nut. The pile was, at last, dusted off. She hunted around in it gleefully, came up with a letter, and ran back to the cubbyhole where I stooped to look through the bars at the proceedings. She smiled broadly and triumphantly handed me a letter. Ah, ho, ah, ho, what happiness to show this European the last letter in the office. She was so happy, I hated to let her down, but, sadly, I handed back to her the letter addressed to Mr. Yjourgenson and went outside to Rosie. No mail. I never went near that post office again. Rosie tried a couple of times, but finally gave up. Later, in Singapore, we received some mail forwarded from Denpassar.

Everything else about Bali was beautiful. The land was gorgeous, and the girls pretty, well built, and long-haired.

They walked down the road with a large load of pans, bananas, or whatever, on their head, bare-breasted, erect, their sarongs flapping in the wind. Often they had one hand for the load and one for the sarong. They thought nothing of stripping down and bathing in a stream of water. Playing in a cool, soft stream of mountain water seemed their greatest delight. They would wear bathing suits in a swimming pool, but fifteen feet away, at the pool overflow, they would take a nude bath with suds all over them. You can imagine how this affected me when I was swimming. Twice, I almost drowned.

After ten wonderful days in Bali, we prepared to leave. Rosie fought the public market for supplies. I got water carried down to the dinghy in five-gallon plastic jugs. Diesel oil was another problem. Benny again helped. We walked to what I thought was a service station, but was a truck repair shop. Benny and the owner talked for a half-hour and at last decided I needed a fifty-gallon barrel. I bought that at ninety cents a gallon and we walked to the delivery establishment. Benny did some more dickering, and it was finally decided that they would deliver it to the wharf for one dollar.

The next morning, at exactly ten o'clock, an ox pulling a two-wheeled wood cart came around the corner of the warehouse. In the cart were two men and a fifty-gallon drum. The men unhooked the ox and backed the cart by hand to the wharf. I rolled the drum out to the end of the wharf, upended it, and siphoned the contents into two five-gallon jerry cans, which I ferried out to the *Mustang* in my dinghy, emptied into my fuel tanks, and returned for another load. It took about an hour while the two men and the ox waited.

When I was through, I indicated it to the men. They rubbed their thumb and forefingers together, saying "Teep. Teep." They were getting pretty obnoxious when our good friend Benny arrived. He had made the original deal and he soon told the men to make tracks. I would not have minded giving those men a tip, but if an American does, he is considered a fool. The poor devils only receive about fifty cents a day. Benny, a sergeant in the police, received seventy-five dollars a month.

On September 22, 1973, we left for Djakarta. We decided to

take the eastern side of Madura, although the western side was the shortest and showed a large port at Surabaja. But the chart also showed lots of shallow water, reefs, rocks, and wrecks. With our recent experience fresh in my mind, I decided the longest route might be the shortest.

At sunrise the next morning, Madura was about ten miles away. We had a good wind and a northerly current, so we hustled up the channel between Madura and Sapudi and by ten o'clock were setting a course straight west—toward home. We seemed to spend a lot of time going north or south. The north coast of Madura was pleasant. Since there were no off-shore obstructions, we were in close and could watch the land, until we had to go out to sea to avoid being in a dangerous area at dark.

In this area we met some of the most beautiful sailboats in the world: big cargo sailboats of native construction with two masts, three foresails, and two topsails. They fly them all. They have no engines and are loaded down, so the deck is barely out of water. One we passed in the moonlight about a block off our starboard. We were heading straight west and it was going east. Under a full moon, it glided along, stately and majestic, without noise, without lights. It was so lovely, Rosie and I sat spellbound.

People had warned us of pirates all along the way. There were supposed to be pirates off Nicaragua, off Colombia, in the South Americas, off New Guinea, the Tanimbars, and, especially, Indonesia. Two days out of Djakarta we had our first pirate scare. We were going downwind when, five miles ahead, I saw one of these beautiful two-masted schooners coming toward us. All its sails were up, as usual. As I looked through the binoculars, it was easy to imagine myself back in the days of sail with a privateer bearing down on us to board, plunder, and scuttle. As we were going downwind and he was working upwind, it was, by the law of the sea, our responsibility to keep clear of him.

When we were about a mile apart, it seemed to me we were on a collision course. I made an intentional jibe to starboard to keep out of his way. He tacked to port, which again put us on a collision course. What was this? Rosie said, "Maybe he was just going to tack and did not see that we had jibed over."

"Yeah, that's about it."

We were still the burdened boat, so I hauled in the main and jibed again to port. Two minutes later he tacked again. Now, I am not one to run from a fight, but through the binoculars I could see between ten and twelve men on that boat, all out and pulling on sheets, and bringing that ship around just when it ought to be brought around.

"Those guys are sailors," Rosie said.

"Yes," I said, "and there are a dozen of them and two of us. Start the motor." For a change, it started.

Now we were less than one-half mile apart. We jibed again. Immediately, he tacked, so he again headed straight toward us.

"Get the gun," I shouted at Rosie.

She went below, brought the gun up, and handed it to me without any shells.

"Holy smoke," I asked, "where are the damn shells?"

She brought up the shells. I was so nervous by then I could hardly load the damned thing. We had carried it all that time and I had never fired it. Will it fire or blow up? I wondered.

That ship was getting so close that I was wondering if they planned to ram us. I counted twelve men on deck. Rosie decided to scare them, so she went below, put on one hat, and stuck her head up from the forward hatch. Then she ran through the cabin, put on another hat, and showed her head in the cockpit. Back through the cabin and and, with a sou'wester hat on, she showed her head and shoulders through the forward hatch again; back through the cabin and she came into the cockpit with no hat on. Maybe they thought we had six men below. Maybe they thought our men were loading the cannons.

Well, that boat was so pretty and we were so close that we could see it in detail. "Get the camera, Rosie," I said. She did and when she stood up to get a clear view and they saw the camera, that crew, almost to a man, started combing their hair, waving, adjusting caps, and so on. We waved back and broke into roars of laughter at ourselves. Those sailors had been just as curious about us as we had been about them. There weren't many yachts in this part of the world.

Our approach to Djakarta was at night. The entrance was supposed to be buoyed, but the one light we could distinguish did not have the same sequence the chart indicated. Finally, using the lead line in the bow to measure the bottom, I found thirty feet and we threw out the hook to wait until morning.

When light came, we found we were right in the middle of about three hundred fishing strakes. These could be five miles from land if the bottom was not too deep. They are really a fish trap, but in this part of the world they were called fishing strakes. They looked like a house with the frame up but no siding, and usually were made of bamboo, tied together with hemp or vines. I never did see what was under the water, but I knew it would be bad for a boat like ours. We had come in the previous night playing footsie with this bunch in the dark. They are difficult to see even in the daytime if they do not have a structure above water. These must have been around for a long time, as our chart, which was over twenty years old, called attention to them. When we entered, however, I had not realized we were so close to them.

25

Freighters, Freighters Everywhere

We spent a short stay in Djakarta and continued on to the South China Sea. We set a compass course to go through the Bangka Strait, which we knew would take at least a day and a half. It seemed that every freighter in the area had planned to quit the China Sea that day. Maybe there was always that much traffic in the strait, but I did not want to go back and find out. At times that night, four freighters were chugging up astern of us while five were in view headed south. The rules of the road were out the window, for it was impossible to figure who was going to do what.

It was spooky, to say the least, with a twenty-knot breeze blowing, choppy seas, and everyone wanting to be in the middle of the channel. We, of course, should have moved way over to the outside, since we drew less water than the freighters. But we had never been here before, and the charts showed rocks and shoal water to starboard and port. We, too, wanted to be in the middle with lots of water under the keel. Everyone liked the middle. No one liked it over near the land—especially in the dark.

Every freighter looked to me as if it were bent on running us down. The first thing that showed at night on these ships were their range lights: two white lights, one on the bow and the other usually about halfway back and much higher. If the two white lights were one under the other, he was, for sure, trying to run over us. This was not true, of course, but when you are thirty-two feet long and all the others are from three hundred to one thousand feet long, you get the feeling you're just too insignificant to bother about.

And, there was another hazard: The little interisland sailing freighters carried no running lights, no range lights, nothing. They didn't light up their ships until they saw someone coming toward them at night. They carried a five-gallon can or something similar filled with palm fronds, coconut husks, dried banana leaves, and anything that would burn readily. When they sighted a ship approaching too closely, they took the cover off the can, touched a match to it, and lighted the tinder. It flared up to make a quick, bright light.

We were on a collision course with one and did not see him until, all at once, that fire appeared directly in front of us. The flames showed the boat up well, with the sails silhouetted in front. They also scared me half to death. I was staring out in total darkness, watching some freighter lights in the distance, when a big fire flared up right in front of us. Rosie claimed I jumped three feet straight up, but I claimed I only gave a slight nervous twitch and went on with my business. We avoided a collision and the fire went out the minute they were past us. I suppose they clapped a metal lid on it and snuffed it out.

Our own running lights were at best only six feet above the water—and that was one light in the bow. The others were lower. In that channel we showed every light we could: a spreader light, a cockpit light, cabin lights, and, of course, our running lights. Sometimes we placed a kerosene lantern in the rigging. I knew what a mouse feels like when an elephant walks by.

We finally passed the straits and entered the South China Sea. It was full of fish and we saw flying fish all the time. One hit Rosie in the chest one day. That meant he had to have been over five feet above the water. I wondered if a flying fish had to hold his breath while flying.

When we saw we would make the approach to Singapore at night, we anchored just off a small island called Pandana, which, according to the chart, was just north of the equator. The first time we had crossed was heading south at the Galápagos. There it had been dry, but the area around Singapore must have had 100 percent humidity. Our clothes were damp, the bedding wet, and my straight hair got curly.

Rosemary complained, "The flour is caked, the sugar is syrup, the salt won't shake, and the crackers are soggy."

The slightest bit of effort would make the sweat run into our eyes and sting.

26

You Can't Win
Them All

Singapore Harbor is only a harbor by virtue of being surrounded by so many islands that it is protected from the action
of the sea. "Singapore" is the name of both a country and a
city. I was told its total area was less than five hundred square
miles. I think that was about one fifth the area of the county
we lived in in Montana.

Singapore makes up for its area in the fast pace of its harbor
and on the island. One hundred fifty big freighters must have
been at anchor. Fifteen or twenty freighters were moving
around at any given time. It took us by surprise, as we had
pictured it as a little oriental harbor where we would go in
among the sampans and tie up.

There were a lot of sampans, but they were rafted up in
front of the wharves and every few hours moved about and
changed places. It did not look as if we could stay there very
long. Our Q flag was flying, but no authorities paid us any
attention, so I finally hailed a taxi boat and we went into the
customs office on the wharf. When they found out what we
were there for they were quite nasty and told us to get back on
the boat as soon as possible, leave the harbor, and anchor in
the roadstead among the freighters. This looked like an impossible place for us, but the official said that if we did not go at
once, we would be placed in jail. We went!

We had no more than anchored out among the freighters
when the customs launch pulled alongside. Three men climbed
aboard and cleared us into Singapore. Sometime later we be-

came friendly with two young Americans in Singapore from Bangkok. They had anchored out in the roadstead and had been told they had to go in and anchor in the spot we were told to leave.

Usually the authorities would help a small boat like ours find a place to tie up or, at least, point us in the right direction. These people refused to give us a clue to where we might go. We stayed where we were all night and then took a water taxi ashore. Rosie got on the phone and called two boatyards and three yacht clubs listed in the phone book. We planned to spend some time in Singapore to get some work done on the boat where it was still leaking. One boatyard told us they didn't usually bother with yachts, but they would do the work for twenty-five hundred dollars. The other said we could stay for twenty-five dollars a night. Two of the yacht clubs said they had absolutely no room. The third said they would take us, but we had to join the club. They gave us sketchy directions on how to get there.

We decided on the third club. We could not stay where we were. We were five miles from the shore. Our boat was like a cockleshell compared to all the large freighters running around, turning around, being pushed around by tugs, or standing by awaiting water or fuel barges. We had not known there were that many boats in the whole Pacific, much less this one harbor. I read there were 171 ships coming or going every day. Nor were we wrong in our appraisal of the danger: In the three months we stayed in Singapore, there were collisions every day and one boat was sunk while at anchor.

Hauling the anchor up from fifty-five feet was no easy task. While I was doing that, a Japanese bulk-ore carrier drifted to within ten feet of us as three tugs were turning him around to start him out to sea. The ship was about nine hundred feet long. The pilot on board was tooting signals on the ship's horn. The tugs were tooting back. Rosie was screaming that they were going to wipe us out. I was cussing the whole Japanese nation, especially the merchant navy. Actually, we had found them to be good seamen. Our near-collision was just one of those things bound to happen in any crowded harbor.

But it was a bit heart-stopping to watch that big ship bearing down on us.

Actually, it was interesting to watch the activity. There were ships from every nation, including ships flying the flags of countries that do not have a seacoast, such as Switzerland, Austria, and Bolivia. There were a half-dozen Russian ships. They were always the dirtiest; Swedish and Danish the cleanest. The countries with the most flags flying were Panama and Liberia, which had no taxes on ships registered in their countries. I was sorry the American flag was hardest to find. Having been gone for over three years, we would cheer to see an American flag flying. The few American seamen we did meet told us the American merchant navy was almost a thing of the past.

At last we started up the coast toward the yacht club. Rosie had verbal directions given by the club manager. Our harbor chart showed shoal water the whole distance and the manager had said that a boat of our draft should be at the last mile into the channel an hour before high tide. I was nervous about being too late and having to enter on a falling tide, so we managed to be early. The boat took to the ground a few times, and looking astern, we could see where we were causing muddy water. We didn't strike hard enough to stop completely, however, so we were off the club dock an hour before high tide. The members came out and kept waving us directions until we slid into an anchorage in the muddy water.

Once again we felt that fine feeling of contentment when the hook is down, there is land between you and the sea, and civilization is close. That is one of life's greater pleasures after playing footsie with strange reefs and islands for a few days. We went ashore to the club. Like most foreign yacht clubs, it was a product of the former governing country; in this case, Great Britain. Now the Chinese and Malaysians ran it. They tolerated Europeans because they needed the money. The Chinese and Malays rarely took their boats out of the harbor. Owning a boat was more of a status thing with the wealthy.

There were six American boats at the club. All of the Americans had bought their boats in that area: at Hong Kong, Thailand, or Singapore. Two were deep-sea divers working for oil exploration companies in Indonesia. Indonesia would not let them live there for more than three months, we were told, so the Americans maintained a home in Singapore. In that case, on a sailboat. One diver had a young wife, two children, and a big dog living on a forty-six-foot boat.

I told the club officers we would appreciate the privileges of the club for about three months.

"Certainly. All that is necessary is to join."

That was not too bad, really, as it was one hundred dollars to join and about twenty-five a month. For this we got cold showers and use of the restaurant, bar, and swimming pool. We could also keep the motorcycles under a nearby shed.

Singapore has almost five million people, mostly Chinese. It rained every day, a hot, tropical downpour that stopped a motorcycle rider instantly. We could only try to get under a large tree or overhang.

Prices were high. I had planned on doing a lot of work on the boat, but they wanted twelve hundred dollars for three men working two days to put on a new toe rail. Beef was about four dollars a pound, but eating in an ordinary café was reasonable—if you were content to eat noodles, rice, and skinny chicken.

One area in the older section was called Thieves Market. The island teemed with thieves of every type. Many people claimed that if something you valued was stolen, you would find it three days later in Thieves Market. Vendors there even specialized in certain items. If you had lost hand tools, you just went to about twenty dark, crowded holes in the wall and looked for the tools. If you found them, all you had to do was to buy them back. If you claimed them as yours, you would have been laughed out of town. Why should you complain? You only had to pay a price for them.

We badly needed foul-weather gear—those stiff, waxy, yellow, uncomfortable rain suits. They were not to be found in this busy seaport. One day, wandering in Thieves Market, we found two very good suits, almost the right size, and about half price. They had the name of a ship out of London stamped on them. I jawed the Chinese owner down to about one half his asking price. Then, I pointed to the name of the ship. He turned around, picked up some stenciling material, and stenciled out the name. Grinning broadly, he handed them to me, took my final offer, and away we went. It's every man for himself in this cruel world.

We made friends with an American named Brown. He was superintendent on a drilling rig off Indonesia owned by Reading and Bates. He had to keep an apartment in Singapore where he only spent two days of each month. He also had a Choy Lee forty-four-foot sailboat at the yacht club. He offered us full use of his apartment, which had a maid in attendance every day, and his little foreign sports car. He gave us the keys to his apartment and the car when he left for Djakarta.

Oh, the pure pleasure of hot, steaming baths! It was a beautiful apartment and we did spend a night or two there just to see how the other half lived. The car was another matter. We took it around town several times, but we were used to a motorcycle and felt a little unsafe in the car. In the first place, getting into it reminded me of Rosie squirming into a girdle. And once in the car, the driver was sort of lying down; it made me sleepy.

Sleepy or not we decided to drive the car up the Malay Peninsula. To do this we had to talk the Singapore immigration authorities out of our passports. They almost did not give them to us. Why would anyone who came in a yacht want to leave in a car? Surely, anyone who wanted to do that was smuggling something. No! We just wanted to go up the road a couple of hundred miles, we told them, to see the interior of Malaysia. After a big conference in which a higher man on the ladder had to be consulted, we were given our passports, but for only forty-eight hours. Bureaucrats are bureaucrats the world around.

We had a wonderful time. For fifty miles, we drove through rubber trees: forest after forest of evenly spaced trees. Each had a river-shaped runway cut into the trunk. Creeks ran into the river and the river emptied into small clay cups that held about one pint of the latex. On small rubber plantations, the latex was laid out and dried into thick blankets about three feet square that were loaded onto stake trucks and hauled into buying sheds. The buyers were all the large rubber companies whose names we see on our tires in the United States. The latex coming out of trees was almost pure white. This was a great surprise to me. I had thought all rubber was black. I guess that is why white sidewall tires cost more: The rubber must first be colored black and then, if you want white, they have to bleach it out again.

I finally settled down to do some much-needed repairs on the boat, such as trying to find and caulk a leak somewhere under the footrail. I also painted the boat a bright orange. We'd had so many close calls with freighters that I'd decided not to travel another foot in a blue-and-white boat, the color of the ocean when there are a few white caps. The name of the paint was rescue orange. I thought that appropriate.

I also bought five gallons of kerosene for our stove and, as a consequence, I had to work on the stove every other day for five thousand miles. I decided it must have been diesel. I cussed that Chinaman who sold it to me until that stuff was finally out of our supply tank.

Christmas came and went. For that celebration, we had beefsteak, which the women bought and had the cook prepare. Rosie tried to tell him that steak was even more of an American dish than sauerkraut and wienies.

27

Cecil

An Englishman named Cecil came into the club harbor from Malaysia. We invited him aboard for coffee, but he stayed until dinner, so we invited him to dinner. He spent the whole time telling us what a lousy country America was. According to him, we had only entered the two world wars for monetary gain. Our military men were overpaid, thereby creating unfair competition with the English military. He said that if we had done so and so before the war, it would never have occurred, etc., etc., etc.

When he left, Rosie said, "Never ask that man aboard this boat again. He wants to start a fight and his manners are atrocious."

I told her he was just blowing off and not to pay any attention.

The next day he wanted us to come on his boat for tea. I finally talked Rosie into going. It was a disaster. Cecil began to tell us how much better his boat was than ours. "See, whereas you only have ribs every twenty inches, mine are every eight." He had several other little things to point out, such as how much better English charts were than American charts.

Rosie said, "Let's get out of here before I get mad."

A couple of days later Cecil left the club with a charter, a paying passenger, on board. He ran onto a reef within a half-mile of the entrance to the club anchorage. I took our hand-operated bilge pumps and was the first one out to help him. I pumped steadily for several hours, as he had knocked two holes in the planking in spite of the eight-inch ribs. When the tide came back in, he righted and floated off the reef. But he got a line snarled in his propeller, and we almost drifted onto another reef before a little Malay boy dived down and disentangled the line.

Cecil kept hollering over the stern to the boy, "Hurry, hurry, please hurry!"

The rope was finally removed and we motored back into the harbor towing the dinghies of the four other sailors and myself who had gone to help him.

That night he invited us all to dinner to express his appreciation.

Rosie said sweetly to him, "Too bad you didn't have an American chart. The shoal water is shown in green to alert you. We could lend you one."

I kicked her under the table. No use having an argument at

his dinner. He only glared at her. We kept the peace, but that was not the last time we were to see Cecil, even though it was time for us to prepare for sea again.

Our route from Singapore would be north through the Straits of Malacca to Port Klang, Malaysia, then to an island off the most northern point of Sumatra, and across the dreaded Bay of Bengal to Ceylon.

Every part of the world has its stretch of water that everyone fears a bit. In Singapore, it was the Bay of Bengal. This bay, 950 miles across, has given sailors good reason to respect it. February was the only month no hurricanes had been reported there.

Rosie said, "We cross in February!"

Since the sailing directions said frequent violent storms often lasted for days in certain months, I agreed February was the month to cross in a small boat like ours.

Brown, the fellow who had lent us his car and apartment, came over to our boat on our last day in port. He brought Rosie a bottle of champagne.

"This is for you to drink when you have dropped your anchor in a safe place in Ceylon."

Chinese New Year was January 20. We watched the parade and ate dinner with our New Zealand friends. We left the club on January 21, which would give us ten days to get to the northern tip of Sumatra. Singapore authorities charged us $158 to clear the port. It was strictly a bandit fee, as they charged us as if we were a freighter. We therefore left Singapore on a sour note. The New Zealanders, Harry Young and his wife, accompanied us to the reef outside the club in their motorboat and waved good-bye.

The Malacca channel proved another narrow, shallow channel with freighters everywhere. We met a U.S. aircraft carrier at midnight in this narrow channel. Watching him bear down on us, I would have sworn there was not room for us both in that ocean, but we passed with a half mile between us.

We were outside the entrance of Port Klang on a rising tide, so we decided to go in to get a bath and a good meal. Cecil, the Englishman, lived there, but I thought there wasn't much chance of running into him in a city of fifty thousand.

Chugging around in the various fingers of the harbor, I finally found the little yacht club and anchored out front. Next day, I rowed ashore, cleared with customs, and asked at the club if we could use the facilities.

The manager said, "Certainly. The club is yours. Take all the baths you want. The restaurant opens at five P.M."

We spent the day looking the town over. When we returned, a young English airline pilot and his wife stopped by our boat and invited us into the club that evening to have a drink. We accepted and thought how wonderful it was when local people made a friendly gesture.

As we reached the top of the steps to the little restaurant, Rosie said, "Wouldn't you know it. There's Obby."

Obby, for obnoxious, was the nickname we'd given Cecil between ourselves. We nodded as we passed his table to join our friends. He called over for us to join him for a drink. I made some excuse and declined. I knew Rosie and he would get into a big argument if he started in again about the United States.

He asked a couple more times, and finally the pilot and I went to the bar to accept his invitation. Rosie sat at the table and I thought this would keep my little wife from arguing with him. I had hardly taken a sip when this character started in again on Americans. I listened to a few insults, and then he said, "The trouble with you Americans is—"

All at once I had had enough of that guy. I felt my face getting hot and I was overwhelmed with murderous rage. I grabbed his necktie and gave it a good twist.

"You son of a bitch," I said. "I think I'll kill you."

I decided I'd either choke him or drag him out to the veranda and drown the bastard. He kept backing off and trying to scream, but my grip sort of throttled his voice. The pilot, who was well over six feet, Rosie, who is five feet, and the club manager, who was five feet tall and five feet wide, were grabbing me and trying to pull me off. I was so mad, though, that I hardly noticed them and pulled the whole bunch toward the water. Dimly I heard Rosie shouting, "Keith, Keith, for Lord's sake, let go! Let go! You'll end up in jail!"

Weight finally overcame anger and I was forced to let go.

Obby was blue in the face and not breathing too well, as I had been gripping his tie all the time.

When it was all over, I felt a little foolish and went into the restroom to wash my sweaty face and hands and comb my hair. The manager followed. I fully expected him to ask us to leave. I said, "I apologize for causing a ruckus in your club."

"It's all right," he said. "I heard what Cecil said and I don't blame you a bit."

When I went back to the bar, the pilot and Obby were standing at the bar and the pilot said, "Keith, come over and have a drink. I'm buying."

Not wanting Obby to think I was afraid of him, I went over. The pilot said, "Keith, why don't you shake hands with Cecil?"

I said, "I wouldn't shake hands with that SOB if he was the last man in Malaysia."

The pilot said, "Oh."

He invited Rosie and me to dinner elsewhere and while we were at dinner, he told me, "I'm glad you tackled Cecil. He needed it. I damned near took a poke at him myself this morning."

I had heard that in Malaysia, if one European kills another, the police wouldn't do much about it. I am still sorry I did not get a chance to test the theory. We had liked the Englishmen we'd met, but that guy was just too much. I had formed several opinions about countries we had been to, but I would not discuss them in front of people who lived there.

28

The Tame Bay of Bengal

A couple of days later we were back out in that damn Malacca channel again. We cut right across to Sumatra so we could go up the coastline, more dangerous, but also more interesting. We had a pretty good blow. Rosie swatted a big fly with her hand. She said she thought it was seasick.

Right in that channel, at about longitude 100 degrees east, there was no compass variation. We had not had that circumstance since we had been between Cristobal and Cartagena, Colombia. This means we did not have to subtract or add a certain number of degrees to our compass reading to maintain the correct course. Often our true course would be, say, 180 degrees, but to get to wherever we were going we had to steer a course of, perhaps, 197 degrees. The variation is pointed out on most charts on the compass rose. It comes about because the compass always points to magnetic north, which is not in the same place as true north.

Because of bad weather, we did not sail into the harbor at Pula We until the seventh of February. It is a lovely harbor, landlocked and with a good holding bottom. We anchored close to shore, so I did not have to row the dinghy a mile every time we went ashore. The Sumatran authorities came out at once to clear us in. They were pleasant and did not ask for our Indonesian sailing permit—which was lucky because we did not have one. I had figured that if they demanded one, we would just go on to Ceylon.

I met a young Indonesian who could speak English, sort of a gun-packing character on a motorcycle. He said he carried the gun because he hated Communists and shot them on sight. I don't know how he judged this. He insisted on taking me to meet the chief of the island. The chief was a pleasant sort of fellow who had spent seven years going to school in New York. He sort of held court for me in a big council room of at least five thousand square feet with benches in it for council members. He said forty men governed the island.

Five servants waited on the chief, the gun-toter, and me. The chief was interested in our trip around the world and said the things Americans did never failed to amaze him. His general attitude, however, was pro-American. They had just declared the harbor a free port and hoped to attract some American industry. I decided there must be a lot of unemployment, for at any given time we could look ashore and see up to two hundred persons on the little wharf just looking at the water or at us.

Our gun-toting friend took us to a Chinese restaurant one evening. I had invited him to eat with us and he showed us the best place in town to eat. When I paid the bill, our Indonesian friend noticed how much it was. He patted his gun and started cussing the Chinaman. The Chinaman finally shrugged his shoulders and gave me back six hundred rupees.

The next day the gun-toter took me on his motorcycle to his place of business, where he exported rattan. He was very proud of his operation.

While in Sumatra, we took the dinghy and went diving on the reefs. Or, rather, we went snorkeling, for we both enjoyed just looking at the coral, tropical fish, and underwater fauna. I had a spear gun along, but never used it, since we usually looked for shells.

When we had a bad stretch of water to cross, I always wanted to get at it and Rosie always wanted to wait one more day. I finally got her out of this harbor on February 9, 1974. She informed me that if we got into a hurricane she was going to fly home from Colombo, Ceylon. She was so definite about it, I asked if she already had the ticket.

Rosie always got scared in any kind of storm. When I came on watch one night at 1:00 A.M., she was still shaking. I did not feel too sorry for her, though. Even when she was scared, when she went to bed she went right to sleep. When I was scared, I could not sleep. I was better in one thing. I could sleep in a wet bunk. If we had forgotten to close the forward hatch and a wave came in, soaking down the bunks, I didn't mind. I just lay in one position for five minutes and the bed warmed up and I went to sleep. I dared not move, however, or it would feel cold and clammy.

Women worry about the oddest things. At least Rosie did. She came on deck one day after figuring the noon shot and said, accusingly, "It's two and a quarter miles deep here." She looked at me as if it were my fault.

Once more I explained, "It's necessary for you to swim in anything over five feet because you are only five feet, so there you are. Why worry?"

I had to keep explaining little things like that to her.

The whole crossing of the bay was rough, but it never got any rougher. At noon on February 17, we dropped the hook in the harbor of Galle (pronounced Gaul), Sri Lanka. Protected from all but a southerly wind, it certainly looked good. I had just thrown the anchor overboard and was waiting for the boat to drift around so that I could put the engine in reverse and dig in the anchor, when I heard a gun go off in the cockpit, or so I thought. I looked around and there was Rosie with the bottle of champagne. She had popped the cork. It had flown over the side and she was trying to catch the bubbly in a couple of glasses. With no cork there was nothing to do but to drink to a safe crossing of the Bay of Bengal.

We said a toast to Ralph Brown, our benefactor.

29

Adjith de Silva

A motor launch pulled alongside and we were told that where we were anchored always had a bad swell and we could move to the inner harbor where the freighters tied up. Later, the chief of police moved us to the police wharf where he and his buddies could keep an eye on the boat. He said the people would take anything loose.

The chief, Mr. Senonayarke, was a big man, a widower with four lovely daughters, very feminine in their chiffon saris. We were invited to take a bath in his home over the police station. The four daughters were in constant attendance to help Rosie bathe, but ignored me. When I teased them about that, they blushed and laughed.

The chief had worked for the British while Ceylon belonged to Great Britain and he thought it was a mistake for Ceylon to be independent. He said it had gone almost entirely Communist since becoming independent and the economy had gone steadily downhill.

We had gone into Galle intending to rest for a day or two, but stayed over a week and hauled the boat out to work on it a bit and paint the bottom with copper paint. The marine ways was owned by the government as were many other industries. Young engineers at the fishery and the marine yard had us to dinner and tried in every way to be helpful. We, in turn, had them on our boat for dinner.

Ceylon, of course, is noted for its tea. We were given about ten pounds by various people and we eventually used every bit of it. The city of Galle had a lot of poor people and the usual military men around carrying guns. Of course, on the waterfront, we tended to see the shady side of a country. The well-to-do do not hang around that area.

The numerous oxcarts and oxen interested me. As they say, you can take the boy off the farm, but . . . The carts often had a cover shaped like the old covered wagons, although these were made from thatch, with the bows made from a bataan tree. We were told that if correctly made the covers were waterproof. The Buddhist monks were everywhere with bright orange habits wrapped around their bodies. They shaved their heads and all carried an umbrella. We were surprised that so many were so young. An engineer friend told us that many young fellows entered the monasteries to gain an education. After four or five years, they dropped out with the equivalent of a college degree.

From Galle, I wrote to my brother Lyle:

There are practically no imports here, so you can imagine the black-market activity. Rosie had to pay one dollar for one roll of toilet paper the other day. The poor people just back up to the water trough and wash off with their left hand. Then they, the Muslims, don't use forks or chopsticks, but dive right into any food, rice, or stew and eat only with the right hand. We were invited to one house for dinner, but they gave us silverware. The host asked, "Will you be offended if we eat in the traditional manner?" I, of course, said, "No." All their food is hot, pepper hot. Even in a restaurant, a hamburger steak is full of pepper, salads full of pepper, cabbage full of pepper, carrots full of pepper. I'm full of pepper. Regards, your brother, Keith.
    P.S. He's full of baloney, too—Rosie.

One morning I arranged for the boat boy to buy diesel oil and get it to the boat by a two-wheeled cart pushed and pulled by two men. When the forty gallons were delivered, I insisted some be poured into a glass jug so I could see it. It contained at least a pint of water and over a handful of dirt. I had explained specifically about dirt and water, and how it would give me much trouble and could even cause a wreck if we were going into a harbor or were near land. So, I told the boat boy I would not pay him or the delivery boy. I told them I would call the police and the God of Muslims would descend on them.

Everyone and everything disappeared. When they returned about three hours later, they all had a seashell for me and a bouquet of flowers for Rosie. I felt ashamed of myself and invited them aboard for a drink of rum. My only excuse is that dirty diesel oil will stop a motor, usually right when you need it most.

February 27 and 28, we went up the west coast of Ceylon to the capital at Colombo. Two hours after tying up and taking our Hondas off, we met Adjith de Silva. We were in the tiny yacht club where the rattle of huge raindrops on the tin roof drowned out most of what, with my hearing loss, I can hear, when he came up and introduced himself. So began a wonderful friendship.

"I have a lot of free time," he said. "If I can help you in any way, let me know."

One day Adjith said, "Can you two Americans leave your boat for a few days?"

Before I could answer, Rosie said, "Yes, where are we going?"

Adjith laughed and said, "Neetha and I have not been back into the center of the island for several years. If you will come with us, we will take about a five-day trip and see the other side of the island. In the interior there are wild elephants, water buffalo, tigers, and whatnot."

Rosie and I both said, "We can be ready in fifteen minutes."

Two days later we started around the island in Adjith's four-wheel-drive jeep. He was off the road as much as on it, up one creek and down another to view something he had known as a boy. At night we stayed in rest houses run by the government; not fancy, but clean and comfortable. The price was three dollars for bed and breakfast with a bath thrown in.

Now I have never laid claim to being anything but a country boy. On this whole trip so far, my eyes had been as big as saucers. They got bigger here, if possible, more like plates. Adjith took us into a large game preserve. The trails were narrow and dusty, and occasionally we were brushed by the sharp thorn of some tree, but that trip was a high spot of our journey. The third day out, Adjith slammed on the brakes. Motioning for us to be quiet, he pointed to the left. There, not a hundred yards away, were four full-grown elephants and one calf. The old bull was a monster, at least twelve feet high. The calf, about three feet high, stayed close to mama.

We had the 16-mm camera ready and got some pictures. A year later, when we finally got to see them (at almost every stop we mailed shells and film home, where the film was processed), they were good. One of the beasts had pulled up a big clump of tall grass, lifted one forefoot as daintily as a ballet dancer and, with his trunk holding the grass, beat the clump against his foot to knock off the dirt before stuffing the whole thing into his mouth. The herd crossed the road in front of us and disappeared into the jungle.

Less than a half-mile down the road, Adjith again slammed on the brakes. He jumped out of the jeep and said, "Come."

We walked back up the trail and he pointed at the dirt. A very small bug was pushing a round ball about ten times its size down the trail. The green beetle was called a dung beetle. The ball it pushed it had made from green water buffalo dung. Inside the ball was an egg put there by the beetle. He moved it to what he considered a safe place. Two weeks later, after the egg hatched, the young beetle would live off the dung for about ten days until it was able to go out into the world. The wonders of nature.

After that we saw water buffalo, peacocks, a hundred species of birds, wild pigs, and monkeys. I hope someday to take Adjith and Neetha to Yellowstone Park. From the game preserve we went up over a range of mountains on a road Adjith said had been built by the United States. It was blacktopped and, although it had only been finished about two years before, was in a state of disrepair. This seemed typical of our foreign aid. The United States would build a wharf, road, airfield, or hospital and the natives would use the dickens out of it, but never maintain it. Yet in Ceylon, half the male population sat on the streets all day doing nothing.

The next night we stayed in a government guesthouse on

the summit of a mountain range overlooking a fantastic valley. The summit was at an altitude of five thousand feet and we could see for a hundred miles, it seemed. The jungle foliage, the flowers, and the green, green valley sent up a faint mist that gave the whole view a fairy-tale look.

The following day we went to the city of Kandy where we saw working elephants bathing in the river or plodding slowly home at night with no taillights. Adjith said that if a car hits one, bystanders throw rocks and bananas at the auto's passengers. Kandy is the old capital of the island where the kings of old built forts and palaces as well as a complicated, but efficient, irrigation system.

A few days after we returned to the boat we began the usual hassle with the authorities and the stocking up that preceded leave-taking. Canned food was scarce, film was ten dollars a roll, and there was no canned meat except sardines. There were few potatoes, onions, or cabbages, our mainstays, in the vegetable line; and sugar, rice, and bread were rationed. We left quite poorly stocked. Several of our friends offered their month's ration of those items, but we declined. We felt they should not go without just because we had sailed into port. Adjith took us to someone he knew and we did get three loaves of bread at a bakery.

Many told us that in the Maldives, five hundred miles to the southwest, we would be able to buy anything we needed, so we were not much worried about our supplies, for we thought we could stock up there. The Maldives form another small, independent country comprised of hundreds of atoll-type islands. So, we left Colombo with deep regret at leaving our friends there, mostly Adjith and Neetha.

30

The Arabian Sea

Since there was little wind, we motored most of the way, and so had an easy five-day trip to Male (pronounced Maul). From our anchorage we could see a breakwater and a not-too-prosperous-appearing town. Some of the native craft behind the breakwater had masts as high as ours, so when a boat somewhat larger than ours passed us and entered, I decided that if it could do it, so could we. The harbor was very small and jammed with native craft. The first thing the immigration office gave us was a sheet of paper stating that "no dogs, cats, liquor, or pork" was allowed ashore. We were also told that fresh provisions were scarce. That was shocking news, since we had a twenty-three-hundred-mile passage ahead of us across the Arabian Sea and Gulf of Aden.

We purchased two cans of corned beef, a bottle of olive oil, six cans of sardines, six bottles of beer (for which I had to sign my passport number), ten pounds of wormy rice, five loads of bread, and twenty-eight gallons of diesel. We also got a couple of squash, which I dislike, and a few onions. There were no other vegetables, as there was very little water, hardly enough for drinking.

The diesel oil people insisted on delivering the oil to the boat. I would have preferred to make three trips in my dinghy with two five-gallon cans, but no, they insisted it would be delivered to the boat the next morning. At 10:00 A.M., five men rolled an oil drum into the harbor and swam it out to the boat. Asking me for lines, they put two around the barrel in a rolling hitch and rolled it up the side of our boat, onto the deck, and stood it upright. I could see they all intended to leave then. I asked them what they wanted me to do with the empty barrel.

"Just throw it into the water." After I had siphoned the oil out, I threw the empty barrel into the water and one man swam out from shore and pushed it onto the beach.

That evening we sat down to analyze our situation. The islands were beautiful and interesting, but we couldn't stay there even one extra day using up our permanent rations. We were down to where this crossing would use every bit of our reserve stores even if things went well. We were heading for the most easterly point of Africa, which the sailing directions described: "Cape Guardaful, a bold, two-thousand-foot headland, desolate and dry, sometimes called the 'Horn of Africa' because of violent storms and contrary currents."

Fourteen and a half days out of Male, we were off Cape Guardaful. Plainly, anyone who had the misfortune to run aground there would be finished. The cape was the most barren piece of real estate I had ever seen. From the boat, two miles off, we could see drifts of sand on the rocks that reminded me of drifts of snow in Montana. In relief we turned away on a four-hundred-mile downwind race.

I told Rosie, "We are beginning to see the North Star again. Not seeing that star made me a little uneasy. It's nice to lie back and keep track of your course by glancing at the North Star."

Nineteen and a half days after pulling up anchor at Male, we entered the harbor of Bera Bera. It had been a fantastic trip— the kind you think you are going to have when you start sailing and seldom do: gentle seas, balmy nights, clear hot days, and lots of fresh fish.

Bera Bera was a village of mud huts, goats, and black people. The Russian navy was there in force, with seven large ships of war and two submarines. When we entered the port, the crews would not even wave; they just stared at us as though we were some kind of secret weapon. The Somalian authorities, however, were pleasant, although they told us not to take pictures. A young Somalian in the bank wanted to be friendly. He could speak good English, which he had learned in six months with the Bank of England in London.

The banker, Hassan Mohamud Siad, took us out to view the ocean from a beach near town. The beach was black sand and the entire area was barren. The wind felt like a hot draft from an oven, and still he thought it was one of the most beautiful places on earth.

On Easter he had us to his boardinghouse for dinner. Of course, he was a Muslim and did not know it was Easter. For dinner we had boiled goat meat and mutton stew. The fat from the goat was all on top, about one-half inch thick. We ate it all to be polite, but that grease about finished me. Knowing Europeans had different customs they gave us two large kitchen spoons. Everyone else used their fingers and mopped up the last of the juice with pan-baked bread.

We bought goat cheese and bread, so we had no problem getting on to Djibouti, two hundred miles farther downwind. We entered Djibouti at night, having found that the French had dependable navigation lights.

31

Oooh, La La

After the better part of twenty-three days at sea, Djibouti was a small oasis like a little piece of heaven. It had a nice yacht club, cold beer, hot showers, plenty of fresh vegetables and meat, and lots of crusty loaves of french bread. First evening there we had steak and french fries.

The next day we got a bonus. A sleek, graceful American destroyer came into port. It had hardly put the gangplank down when I pulled alongside on my motorcycle carrying our autopilot, which had given out again between Bera Bera and Djibouti. The ship was the U.S.S. *Mullinnis DD944*. I talked to an officer at the gangplank for two minutes. He summoned a rating to take me to Chief Warrant Officer Vern Eubanks. The next day the autopilot was repaired and they asked if there was anything else they could do for us. American efficiency can't be beat. I said we were short some charts to get us up through the Red Sea. In two hours they gave us spares or made photocopies of the ones we needed. They also invited us to a movie and dinner and told Rosie she could pick the movie. They left shortly afterward to help a French ship in trouble in the Gulf of Aden.

Djibouti is the home of the French Foreign Legion. The enlisted men in the legion all seemed to be Germans, big husky fellows. A Frenchman told me most of them cannot go home as they have committed a crime there. He said they are fiercely loyal, not so much to France as to the legion, in which they take great pride.

A young French high school teacher took us into the desert in his four-wheel-drive. Back fifty miles, the land became total, absolute desert—not one thing growing, not one blade of grass. He told us a person not familiar with the mountains in the far distance needed a compass. That particular stretch was not sandy, just hard-baked dirt. When we came to the far side of the fifty-mile stretch we saw a family of baboons, which scurried off into high rocks. The Frenchman said they lived on insects and brush and must know of a small water hole. We were looking for a small desert tree supposed to grow only in that area. Our friend wanted to send it to a friend who raised exotic plants. We found several, about six inches high, up on the side of a hill. They certainly didn't look like much, just a scraggly gray green.

We also took several motorcycle trips out of town, but never went over forty miles. We saw many camels running around loose. We assumed they all belonged to someone and had been turned loose to feed on the small tree called a camel tree. If it was a short tree, the camel would be down on his knees nibbling at the leaves. The camels ran loose, but goats were always herded by a child or woman. Even if there were only five goats, someone was herding them. We were told that goat milk is put into a kind of knapsack made of leather. A woman packs it around all day on her back and by evening it has formed a kind of curd, the mainstay of the nomads' diet. Since it is a pretty complete food, the nomads rarely suffer from malnutrition.

We did not see one commercial fisherman in Africa, which was hard to understand as the oceans seemed full of fish. We had sailed through a number of schools with thousands of good-size fish.

Several French couples were very friendly to us, particularly Danny and Evangeline Moreau. Almost every evening we went to someone's home for dinner or had some of them aboard. They liked to practice their English and Rosie worked hard at learning French. I can only learn that which is absolutely necessary, such as bolts, pipes, oil, ice, food, drink, good morning, and good night. Danny, who was in the French air force, and Evangeline, his wife, brought home again that it is the people who make a place fun and interesting.

One evening Rosie and I were riding around town on our motorcycles and decided to stop someplace for a beer. French sidewalk cafés were all over town. We happened to be riding down a secondary street and saw a rather nice-looking café with many customers and four or five young women. Usually there were not many women around in these countries. We stopped and the lady who owned the café came scurrying over, all smiles. She wiped the table at least twice, demanded and got instant attention from the waiter, and changed chairs to give us two better ones. About my second bottle of cold beer, it dawned on my shy wife that the fellows were coming in, having a drink, and disappearing upstairs. Soon they would come back down, have another drink, and go on down the street. But all the time we were there, the staff gave us every attention. We laughed about that visit for several days.

A couple of days later, I decided it was time to get ready to leave for Massawa, Ethiopia, 350 miles away up the Red Sea. We had been hauling provisions all day, so late in the day we decided to take a shower at the yacht club. The shower room had two stalls in it. On one the door would not close completely and the other had no door at all. As this was the rest-room where people were constantly wandering around, we usually went to shower together. Rosie got the shower with the door and I got the doorless stall.

That day, I was standing in the nice hot shower, naked and soapy, when I heard someone talking to me. I turned and there stood the most beautiful, shapely, gorgeous, sexy young Frenchwoman I had ever seen. She had on only the bottom part of a bikini and she was untying that, talking to me ninety miles an hour in French at the same time. Now, my French has never been the best and, besides, I am a little deaf, and on top of that I was goggle-eyed and confused. I think I must have been a bit embarrassed, although the situation was not of my making. I must have been squeezing the bar of soap awfully hard, as it flew out of my clenched hand and slid across the floor to stop beside the woman.

She didn't pick it up and hand it to me, so I stepped out of the shower to retrieve it, and she stepped into my shower. I thought that over for a second or two and decided that was going too far. I yelled "No!" and stepped back into the shower with her, so we both stood under the water. I expected Rosie to do something any minute, but she hadn't reacted by the time the girl finished and left. The whole thing left me some-what shaken.

Rosie said later she just figured, "He's a big boy. I guess he can take care of himself."

That evening at dinner, Rosie had a stern look and told me we had to leave this port tomorrow at sunrise. Sure as shoot-ing, the next morning, with tears in my eyes and a last fond look toward the shower rooms, I pulled up the anchor and we left. As I have told my friends, Rosemary is sometimes very strange.

32

Dust on the Sea

We had not been looking forward to this Red Sea trip, since everything we had heard about it was bad. We made good time, however, and the next morning we were well inside the Red Sea. By evening we were off the town of Assab, Ethiopia. Although a favorable wind was blowing hard, visibility was less than five miles due to blowing sand and dust. It was hard to resist the thought of a pleasant night behind a breakwater, so we went in. I anchored twice before I was satisfied that we were okay. I had just sat down to an anchor drink when a launch pulled alongside. Speaking kindly, but firmly, the men in the launch told us we could not stay where we were since it was the turning basin for freighters. We had to tie up to the wharf. It did not look good to me, as big swells were heaving up and down at the wharf. They made it clear, however, that I could either do as they said or go back to sea. With darkness coming fast, I said, "I will do as the port captain desires."

Maneuvering in a crowded harbor can be difficult with just two people, but the men in the launch went in ahead and gave every assistance as we approached the wharf. It was as I feared. All night long the boat banged against the wharf and we were up dozens of times. Before morning I had ten lines going ashore at various places and every conceivable thing that could be used for a fender hanging over the side to keep the boat from being broken in pieces. I could not chance going out through those reefs in the dark, but at daybreak I started untying lines.

About twenty-five miles out of Assab, according to the chart, was an anchorage in three fathoms behind a point of land called Bail Builel. I decided we would go into that anchorage and attempt to get some sleep. When we rounded the point, even with the motor going full ahead, we could barely creep forward. We were behind a hill at least three hundred feet high and yet the wind felt like fifty knots right on our nose. It took us two hours to make the mile to get out of the rough seas. When I found the three-fathom bottom with the lead line, we were less than a quarter of a mile offshore. I threw out the anchor and was surprised that it held. It was a mess though. Water from the tops of the whitecaps blew onto us as well as sand from the land. By nightfall one-eighth inch of mud covered our decks. I let out almost two hundred feet of line, tied rags at the chocks to prevent chafing, and went below, glad to get out of the wind and dust. The wind screamed in the rigging and the anchor line moaned with the strain of the boat tugging and swinging back and forth on the anchor. I checked it twice and the anchor was holding well. Rosie fixed a hot stew and we went to bed and slept soundly from 6:00 P.M. to 6:00 A.M. I'd intended to get up and check the anchor, but I was so damned tired, I couldn't wake up enough to do it.

That was such a miserable stretch of our trip that I cannot think of anything good to say about it.

May 8, 1974. Massawa. I thought we would get into Massawa before dark, but the contrary winds came up and we did not come into the harbor until 11:00 P.M. There was only one breakwater light working, the red one. When we were inside, we turned to starboard where the chart said three fathoms. We went slowly past some small Ethiopian navy boats who immediately began to whistle and yell at us and turned a powerful spotlight on us. I quickly made a 180-degree turn and tried to leave that little bay. It was a pitch-black night. I went into the main part of the harbor about one-half mile and found a vacant place in six fathoms and dropped the anchor. I don't like anchoring in six fathoms. In about ten minutes, a navy gunboat came alongside with two fellows on deck with Bren guns pointed straight at us. The driver of the boat must have been roaring along at thirty knots straight toward us. Within about ten feet he put the engines into full reverse and stopped inches from smashing into us. All the time the big ten-inch searchlight was lighting us up and blinding us. An officer came out on their bow and asked why we had come into their bay. "You're not supposed to go in there. That's a navy base."

"I didn't know that," I replied. "We are from America and were just looking for a place to anchor."

He had me sign a paper with the *Mustang*'s name and my name and they left. Early the next morning they came roaring up again. The same young officer came forward and asked how we were.

"Okay," I said. "No problems."

"I'm glad to hear that," he shouted back. "If you need any help just call on the navy. We'll help you all we can."

He pointed out the harbor master's office and told us to go in there and sign.

"You are welcome to Ethiopia," he said. They roared off.

My advice is, don't go to Ethiopia. One reason is the filth and the flies.

Anywhere along the waterfront, men relieved themselves fore and aft, then backed up to the sea and washed themselves with the left hand. I guess only Americans would let that bother them. When we went ashore, there were piles everywhere until the tide came up and washed it away. The stench was everywhere, but especially near a wall or building.

Then, there were the flies. They woke us up in the morning and remained a nuisance all day. We had to brush continually to keep them out of the coffee or off the cheese.

While I was in town by myself looking for bolts, I walked through the prostitute district. Grimy-looking girls sat in doorways or looked out through open windows. They would spread their legs and motion for me to come inside for a good time. Later, Rosie and I had to walk through the area while looking for something. The girls just smiled at us then.

One night, as was our custom when water was plentiful, I took my usual sponge bath on deck. I took my shorts off and forgot and left them there. In the morning the shorts were there, but my money and expensive jacknife were gone. Rosie is a light sleeper, but had heard nothing.

On the tenth of May we decided we could stand no more of the filth, the stench, the flies, the thievery, and the whole bit. We left early in the morning and planned to pass a certain island before dark to firmly fix our position because we would have to pass close to a second island in the dark. Although we came within less than three miles of the first island, we could not see it because of poor visibility and finally turned and went straight east toward the island so that we could locate it before dark. Just before dark we finally located it and were able to set our course so that we wouldn't hit anything in the dark.

On the evening of the twelfth we were working our way through the reefs of Jidda, Saudi Arabia. We had crossed the Red Sea and the trip had not been too difficult. The only way we could be certain we were in front of the city was several wrecks on the reefs were identified on our chart. The reefs out in front of the harbor overlapped one another so that we had to make several 180-degree turns. The whole thing was hair-raising. It seemed a pity that so many skippers had run their ships onto these reefs, but that was what made it easier for us and others to follow the channel.

We met several Americans and a Turk, all of whom treated us royally during our stay in Jidda. Mike, the Englishman, was on a trawler and he introduced us to his good friend Selim Kenan, the Turk. Selim spoke perfect English and was planning a world cruise, so he was particularly interested in our travels. He was working with a mapping crew of Americans as a cartographer. The Saudi government had hired the American crew to map the country and not only paid them well, but provided them with American-type housing in a compound surrounded by a high wall. Gordon, one of the Americans, invited us every day for a hot bath and drinks, or dinner if we were free. Everyone had us to dinner, and it was just great to talk to Americans again. Someone said, "How did you get permission to come to Saudi Arabia? They don't like tourists."

I replied, "We didn't have permission. We just sailed in."

"Amazing."

The harbor master told Mike we were the first yacht in the harbor in at least ten years. They were very suspicious of us and the assistant harbor master asked, "Why did you come here?"

I replied, "Just to visit Saudi Arabia."

"But," he asked again, "why did you really come here?"

We were never allowed to take the motorcycles ashore. Even if we had been, Rosie could not have ridden one, for it is against the law for a woman to ride a cycle, drive a car, or hold a job.

Women were completely covered with a drape from their head and face down to the ground. They were almost always accompanied by a male, even if the male was only four years old. I never figured out how they saw through that drape, but I never saw one bump into anything.

Man was supreme and could take up to four wives. He never took his wife out in public but spent a great deal of time in the coffeehouses drinking a thick, strong coffee that about tore the top of my head off when I tried it. Along with the coffee most of them sucked on a water pipe. Every sidewalk café or restaurant had from five to a hundred water pipes to rent to patrons. A good Arab would go into these places and sit down at a table. If he was known, no word would be spoken. Coffee would be brought by a young boy or an old man. Next would come the water pipe. It usually stood about two feet high. The pipe had a new refill of tobacco, then the boy held a good live coal over it with tongs to light it.

Usually two or three Arabs sat at a table. They did not seem to talk much, but seemed to be pondering something. Mostly they sucked on the pipe, which gurgled as the smoke passed through it. Some of the pipes I saw in cafés must have been sucked on by ten thousand Arabs, the handles the smoker holds were so worn and polished.

Some time around noon the chant came again from the mosque. That was the signal for the faithful to close up shop, stop work, stop everything, and get ready to pray. If a merchant did not close up, a religious policeman came to the front door and beat on it with a big stick or billy club. Often a big fellow, he commanded instant attention. One of these policemen hit an American woman on her legs and told her she was wicked for showing them. Her husband was from Texas and not too small himself. In five minutes there was a riot and the policeman wound up second best.

One day a policeman reprimanded our Turkish friend, Selim, for not praying at noon. The policeman pushed the end of his stick into Selim's chest. Selim grabbed the stick and broke it over the policeman's head. When the policeman got back to his feet, Selim offered him the broken half of the club. He told him in Arabic to watch who he hit the next time. Selim was only about five feet seven, but he was a Turk. Nevertheless, the Muslim church and its religious policemen wielded a great deal of power in Saudi Arabia. Movies were not allowed and only recently had they allowed TV, strictly supervised by the church.

Selim was a Muslim by birth. He told us that when he went to see the city of Mecca some thirty miles away, the guards would not let him through the highway since only Muslims can visit Mecca. He brought out his ID card that showed he was, indeed, a Muslim. The gatekeeper reluctantly let him through, but said, "Turks are not good Muslims." Selim told us they weren't, either.

33

Red Sea Storm

After a pleasant two days, we left Jidda for Suez. Fourteen hours out we were hit by a helluva storm right on the nose. Fifty-knot gale winds pushed up short high waves. The *Mustang* pitched and plowed as we tried to keep going for several hours, but the bow rose almost vertically and came down with a crash with each wave as if it had been dropped on cement from twenty feet up. I hardly dared to heave to for fear we did not have enough sea room, since we were no more than thirty or forty miles from the reefs in front of Jidda with the wind blowing us directly toward them. I tacked to take us farther out to sea, but had no sooner done so than I realized the bowsprit was loose. With that I had to take down most of the sail, since the mainstay which was attached to the bowsprit was popping and crackling from the violent action of the boat.

Since I couldn't see what was happening, I had to go forward to determine the problem. When I looked away from the compass light, it was absolutely black, like looking into a hole in every direction. I put on the safety harness, shoved a flashlight into my pocket, and crawled forward. Every few minutes a wave washed over me, and I had to stop to hang on. It was slow going. I had left Rosie at the helm, shivering and scared. When I finally got forward, I saw the bobstay was broken. It holds the bowsprit in place, connected from the end of it to the boat about at the waterline.

I crawled onto the bowsprit, but it was flopping up and down with every wave, so loose I expected it to break at any moment. I couldn't fix it in these conditions. About then, the jib halyard must have parted, for the jib flew to leeward and over the side.

I crawled back to the cockpit and told Rosie I was going to start the engine. As usual when we needed it, it would not start—not a rumble. It was absolutely dead. I took over the helm, trying to decide what the next move should be. Rosie went below.

Immediately she yelled up, "Keith, Keith, it's leaking bad. There's at least a foot of water down here. Oh, dear, oh, dear, what shall we do?"

She had already started pumping. I looked down and could see water sloshing around as the boat rolled and pitched. That settled one thing: We had to head back to port and hope we could make it with no bowsprit, no headsail, no engine, and with a bad leak.

I jibed over and we started downwind. Since it was about 3:00 A.M., I figured we wouldn't be close to the reefs off Jidda until after daybreak. I thought about our inflatable raft and wondered if I should start to inflate it or spend my time pumping. Deciding, I set the tiller and went below. Now that we had headed downwind, a lot of the strain was off the mainstay and conditions eased somewhat.

Down below, I looked into the stern. The water was coming through the old leak we thought had been repaired in Raiatéa. Now it was worse in the heavy seas. At least, I thought, I think we can keep up with that.

I took over from Rosie, pumping steadily while she went up to take the tiller. In those conditions, the *Mustang* would not steer herself for five minutes. After about an hour of pumping, I thought I had gained on it a little. We spent the rest of the night taking turns at the tiller and pumping until our arms ached.

At daybreak, we were able to take stock. We'd gained on the water and could stop pumping long enough for Rosie to make coffee. Nothing is quite so bad in the daylight with a cup of hot coffee in hand. The jib I had thought gone for good was dragging over the side nearly under the boat, but we managed to get it back aboard. The one thing we didn't see was the entrance to Jidda, and several hours later I was beginning to worry that our reckoning was off when I spotted the wreck on the outer reef. At least I hoped it was the right wreck, for we had no sun for a shot. In another hour we were sure of our location and began the tricky entrance back into Jidda. Late in the day the wind eased so that it took us three hours from the outer reef to the harbor entrance, since I could not use more than the small staysail.

"It would be just our luck for the wind to quit altogether," said my crew who, nevertheless, was a lot more cheerful with land in sight.

Once inside the harbor I drifted right up to a stop at the customs dock. I was patting myself on the back a bit when the assistant came running out and asked, "Why are you back here?"

"We had much trouble," I replied, "no motor, no sails, and a big leak."

That seemed to satisfy him a bit. I knew from our experience here before that I didn't dare try to move on our own in that crowded harbor, so I went right down and started to work tearing into that damned diesel.

Three hours later the immigration official came down with our new permit to stay in the harbor until repairs were made. Ten minutes later I asked Rosie to try the engine, and it started right away. The fellow in the customs shack came and looked down at us from the wharf. I knew they were saying to each other that there never had been anything wrong with the motor. Rosie gave me heck for fixing it so fast.

With the engine going, it seemed best to get away from all those uniforms, so I asked permission to move back to our former berth. Another reason for moving was that the customs wharf was concrete. When the tide was down, we could sit in our cockpit and watch hundreds of rats scurrying around on the underside of the dock. Some were nearly a foot long.

When we reached our former berth, our Egyptian friends from Massawa were unloading potatoes. They waved to us to tie up alongside them, but since Mike the Englishman was still there, I coasted up to tie him where it would be easier for Rosie to climb ashore than over the much higher Egyptian boat.

Our American friends soon invited us to come in for hot baths and Selim came down and offered to take some time off from work to drive me around town to buy parts for repairs. The Egyptians came over and were surprised to find out we had been in the port before. The skipper found an interpreter and through him told us it was impossible, almost, for a sailboat to go up the middle of the Red Sea at this time of year.

The news discouraged me. I think we were about as low in spirits as we had been on the whole trip. The *Mustang* was no great thing beating against the wind, and our motor was pretty feeble. I hated to turn back and go clear around Africa, and in fact, that would have been nearly impossible in this southwest monsoon season. I doubted that we could stay in Saudi Arabia. Inflation was eating a big hole in our modest income. We talked about it for several days, but every avenue seemed difficult if not impossible. The poor old *Mustang* had taken a lot of beatings and it seemed that I could hardly repair it as fast as something happened. I, at least, really wanted to finish this trip around the world, not necessarily to prove anything to those who'd said, "He'll never make it," but to myself.

I went to the Egyptian skipper and, through the interpreter, asked how he planned to go up the Red Sea. He said he would go up on the Saudi side (a lee shore) and stay behind reefs all the way until nearly east of Safaga, Egypt, then cut directly across the Red Sea to Safaga. I asked the interpreter to ask him if he would mark my charts along that route and he said he would. We set a time and place for the following day. When we planned to come up the Red Sea, we had read the Suez would be open. A visit to the Egyptian embassy gave us the information, however, that it would be at least a year before the canal would be open to traffic such as us. That night I asked Selim if it was possible to haul our boat from Jidda to Beirut by truck. He said he would find out.

"I know they haul cars and freight on that road all the time," he said. "The main trouble is that you have to go through several countries. Going through any of these countries can mean days of red tape at the border."

That could be bad. The *Mustang* was built in such a way that I could not afford to let it completely dry out and shrink, or it might never swell up again.

34

With the Help of Allah

The following day the skipper, his mate, the Syrian interpreter, and I met in the Syrian's office and I started marking our three charts up the Red Sea. It became apparent rapidly to me that I could not follow this route. At several different times, we would have to go within feet of knife-edged, treacherous reefs. A couple of the openings the crazy Egyptian was going through were less than fifty feet wide. It was no place for a stranger, not this stranger, anyway. My chart had that entire route marked "unsurveyed."

I must have looked pretty sad when I saw the route because the interpreter and the skpper talked a bit and the Syrian said to me, "He says you can follow him when he goes up in about two weeks."

That sounded good to me until I realized that four knots was our top speed. I mentioned this and asked the Syrian to find out how fast the skpper traveled.

"Six knots," said the Egyptian. Then there was a lot of discussion in rapid Arabic between the Syrian and the skipper. Finally, the Syrian turned to me. "The Egyptian and five other Egyptian schooners were caught down here when the canal was closed. They have been here over six years. Now, they are going home through the Suez when it opens. They are going to Safaga to wait there."

He also said the Egyptian was the most experienced and was going to lead the other boats. Since one of them was disabled, the skipper would tow him all the way home. This would probably bring their speed down to four knots. We could follow and if we could not keep up, the skipper would tow us, too.

I had dealt with enough Arabs to think I had better get it in writing as to what he would charge. I told the Syrian to find out. They talked some more and I was told there would be no charge. The skipper said they would be glad to help and have another sailor along.

"Also, there is in Jidda right now an Egyptian trucker who can haul your boat from Safaga to Alexandria on the Med. If you want to make contact with him the arrangements can be made at once."

Things were coming a little too fast for this Montana boy, so I asked for two hours to think it over. Everyone agreed and the meeting was adjourned. I went back to the *Mustang* and Rosie and I talked it over. We decided that our present circumstances were bad. We were in a country that did not want us and facing a bad piece of water if we tried to leave. After about our tenth cup of hot coffee on that blistering day, I said, "To hell with it. Let's go." Rosie, who was ready to fly home yesterday, said, "Okay." I found the Syrian and told him to tell the skipper we'd like very much to go with him.

That evening the skipper and I went to town to meet the trucker in a coffeehouse. With everyone but myself puffing a water pipe, the deal was made. The trucker said that for eight hundred dollars American, he would lift the boat out, haul it from Safaga to Alexandria, and put it back in the water.

Everybody shook hands and the Arabs drank a couple more cups of coffee and had a new pipe full of tobacco, so the pipe gurgling started in earnest. I was drinking Coke, which I don't like, but which was better than their coffee.

During the two weeks of waiting, Rosie and I started calling the skipper Big Daddy. One by one the other boats he was to lead up the Red Sea came in and anchored off the wharf. No one had a radio, so I don't know how the arrangements were made. Big Daddy and some of the others took on a lot of cargo. Big Daddy loaded his holds and put barrels of something on deck along with two cars. Everyday the crew tried to give us something; diesel, water, fish, potatoes. We took some of the potatoes.

Meanwhile the Americans and Selim and ourselves were having a series of parties, dinners, teas, and trips out to the desert. One thing happened here that occurred no where else in the world: We were running short of money. Our letter of credit was good at a bank, but it took six hours for them to make out the proper papers and hand the money over. It was an all-day job. I mentioned this to Selim.

"Come with me if you have a checkbook," he said. I got the checkbook and went in Selim's car to the center of town to money-changer alley. Selim led me to one dirty, small five-by-five booth. "This man will cash your check."

I did not believe it, but I handed the man a check for two hundred dollars, and without a word, the fellow gave me two hundred dollars' worth of rupees—no driver's license, no passport, no nothing.

I told Selim, "Just wait until the American hippies get wind of this."

I don't know what the Arabs do to a bad-check artist, but to a thief found guilty—and there are no soft judges in Jidda—it is bad news in Saudi Arabia. The thief is led to the public market and his left hand cut off at the wrist with a heavy knife like an ax. The hand is picked up and thrown high into the air for all to see. The stump is cauterized and the thief let go. The humiliation is that forever after than man must wipe himself with the same hand he eats with. An Arab never eats with his left hand.

During the last three days before we were to leave, Big Daddy watched the skies with concern. We almost left a couple of days earlier, but the clouds did not look quite right. Then, one of the crew came to our boat early on June 10 and said we would leave in one hour.

Not knowing what lay ahead for us in this convoy, I was somewhat apprehensive, but it was still exciting to see the six sailboats string out for a mile. Our thirty-two-foot *Mustang* looked like little brother tagging along behind the big kids. Right from the beginning, even though Big Daddy was towing a boat, little brother had a hard time keeping up. We had all sails up and the engine going full ahead. The other boats had three-hundred-horsepower Caterpillar engines as well as being full gaff-rigged schooners. The flotilla had not gone ten miles before Big Daddy flew a signal and one of the other boats came around in a circle to pull alongside us. From his stern, he threw us a line and went ahead about one hundred feet. We were in tow.

It was soon apparent that we were among a bunch of expert sailors. I had been told that every one of these men had been on a sailboat from the time he was five years old. They had little formal education, but they knew boats and the Red Sea reefs and anchorages. From the second day out, I copied everything they did. If they put up their mains, I put up mine. If they put up two jibs, I put up two jibs. We kept our motor going full ahead, and Rosie prayed every day that our motor would not fail. Despite motor, sails, prayers, and willpower, we always seemed to fall slowly behind. After about the fifth day, after we had raised anchor and were strung out, Big Daddy would throw us a line and would tow us as well as the disabled schooner.

Big Daddy was a goer. We usually left anchorage before sunup, with the barest amount of light. I suppose that because they were up praying to Allah at 4:00 A.M., he figured they might as well get going. Rosie and I talked and laughed about it, but were a little afraid they might cut the line in the night and slip off without little brother. She has excellent hearing, and so at the first sound such as a motor starting or an anchor winch grinding, we were up and pressing the starter. We stuck to them like glue.

Every night we slipped behind a reef or island and anchored for the night. One day we made only twenty-eight miles. The wind was so strong from straight ahead that Big Daddy anchored at two o'clock in the afternoon. We never put out an anchor, as Big Daddy told us to tie to him at night. Since the anchorages were often one hundred feet deep, this was a great relief.

Big Daddy was up in the ratlines of his rigging all day, every day, scanning the water for reefs and the route through them. We think he must have made this miserable trip many times, for we would get out of one mess of reefs and he would seem to know just which way to turn to find the opening through the next barrier. As we marveled at his seamanship, he grew in our opinion. Every day the wind blew about forty knots, but the reefs stopped the seas so we could make headway. By the time we reached Safaga, I thought Big Daddy must be ten feet tall, although in reality he was about five feet eight. In my opinion, he was the best sailor I had ever met.

All the boats trailed a fishing line. If Big Daddy or his tow caught a fish, they always gave some to us. If we caught one, we gave them most of it. Each night they would ask us by sign language if we needed diesel or water.

One day the wind was especially strong as we went through a small stretch of unprotected water. The three-inch-diameter line from Big Daddy's boat to the disabled ship broke. The two made motions to us to cast off, which we did. With all the boats pitching and rolling, it took several tries to get a new towline to the disabled boat. When the job was done, they made a big circle and threw us a line.

I went over to their boat that evening because they wanted to show me the broken line. The mate picked up a piece of string and broke it with his hands to show me how easily the big line had parted. As usual when I was on their boat, they served tea while Big Daddy puffed on his water pipe. We communicated a little by sign language, but mostly just sat and pondered. If he had a problem he thought nothing of kicking off his sandals and stepping outside the wheelhouse to pray to Allah.

One day we didn't pull the anchor up. It was so windy that although we were anchored only fifty yards off a reef, the boats were bouncing and straining on the anchors. It was a very uncomfortable twenty-four hours. Another day we anchored early because we could not get to another anchorage before dark. Rosie and I took the dinghy off and went onto the reef to look for shells. There were thousands there, live ones. The crews on the other boats also went after shells, but they smashed the shell and ate the meat, sometimes raw.

Once we anchored only two hundred yards from the Saudi mainland. The shore for as many miles as we could see had a haze of dust and the land was a series of undulating plains or desert. These rises were always in the form of a bench, each rising abruptly a hundred feet for miles, then another steppe, until there were some bare, rocky, dry mountains. The chart said they were about three thousand feet high. I did not see a tree. One village on the side of a hill was nearly one continuous building with flat roofs of various heights, arched doors and windows, and walls and covered passageways between the apartments. Everything was white. I supposed clay or mud painted white.

The fourteenth day out of Jidda we had gone 450 miles, and there we crossed the Red Sea. Following the Egyptians, we wound up in a port called Huragha, thirty-six miles north of Safaga. Why they went there instead of Safaga, we never knew. We thought as we crossed the Red Sea that they were heading too far north, but, as I said, we were not going to let Big Daddy get away. However, we thought we were in Safaga, the entrances appearing almost the same.

We had been sitting in port two days, had gone through quite some hassle with authorities, and had been told we could not leave the boat, when an official came out and began asking all the same questions again.

Finally, Rosie asked, "Who are you?"

He acted rather puzzled, but pretty soon he said in his halting English, "I am the doctor for the port of Huragha.

Rosie and I looked at each other. "Where?"

He said it again, slower. It was one of life's embarrassing moments.

35

Ali Baba and the Thirty Million Thieves

Two young Arabs also came out to the boat that day. They brought their clumsy old scow to our stern, and talking some English, started making smart remarks. In a rude and unpleasant manner they asked me how many aboard, how long we would be in Huragha. As they talked, they kept climbing farther up on the boat. They were trying to look down inside the cabin at Rosie. In Huragha there were very few women. I motioned them to stay off the boat, but they ignored me and kept working up on the deck from their boat.

We always kept a switchblade knife in a small leather sheath. I called down to Rosie to hand it to me, as I did not want to leave my position directly in front of them. If I moved, they would be up on the boat in a flash. Rosie came out of the cabin and handed the knife to me. In one move, I clicked it and had the point one inch from the Adam's apple of the Arab closest to me.

I chuckled at the way they practically fell back into their boat crying, "No, No, No!" We never saw them again.

The next day we pulled out with Big Daddy for Safaga. While we were calling him Big Daddy, he probably was calling us the glue twins.

In Safaga we were immediately put under boat arrest. We had not known it, but it was an Egyptian navy base and we were suspect. The harbor master was a navy officer and very kind, but firm. I told him I had to go ashore for water and food. Within an hour he had a launch out to us with an open barrel and water, and a rather dirty bucket to transfer the water into our tanks. We asked the two fellows who brought it what we could do for them and they said they would like a bar of soap. We gave them two bars of hand soap with which they seemed very pleased. About two hours later they returned with potatoes, watermelon, squash, and some Egyptian bread. It is a flat like pancake, about one inch thick, and twelve inches in diameter. It's unleavened, I think, but does not taste too bad at all.

The second morning I looked ashore and saw a big semi-truck driving along the waterfront. I said to Rose, "There goes a truck that could haul our boat."

Two hours later Big Daddy came in a launch with two of his crew. They indicated I should pull up anchor and move to the wharf. Big Daddy himself helped me pull the anchor up from fifty feet and we motored alongside the wharf where there was a truck and crane. The crane could lift about two tons and we weighed ten tons.

First, the mast had to be lifted out. All the time I was taking the shrouds, stays, and boom off, I tried to tell them that crane would lift the mast, but not the boat. There was one big problem: I was speaking English and nobody understood a damned word I said. Big Daddy was right there helping me, though, so I felt fairly safe that he would, in the end, set them straight.

The semitruck stood close by, ready to take the boat. On the

truck were over a hundred bags of sand. I finally found out by
sign language they planned to use those sandbags to prop up
the boat. They would set the straight keel on the truck, then
pile bags of sand around it to hold it upright. It seemed to me
any schoolboy would know it would not work and I was getting really worried. The ones in charge seemed too confident,
and everyone was running around talking like crazy, and nobody was listening to me, nor, do I think, to one another.

At last someone showed up from the navy who could speak
English. I explained the situation to him and tried to get him to
talk to the man in charge, but it was plain they all thought the
plan would work. Then the English speaker and I went to Big
Daddy. He had sense enough to agree with us and said he
would talk to someone about it.

The day before I had told the harbor master that the first
thing I had to do was to get to a bank and buy some money.
There was only one small bank and not one right to pay on the
letter of credit, but we still had about five hundred dollars in
traveler's checks and I planned to cash those.

In the middle of the crane argument, the immigration man,
the customs man, and three policemen arrived to escort me to
the bank. I tried to explain that I could not leave just then, but
in two minutes I was in a jeep bound for the bank. The appointment had been made with the bankers, and by the will of
Allah, no one kept a banker waiting. Besides, they thought my
boat was in capable hands. I did not get back to the boat for
three hours. I was told then to get the suitcases and be ready
to leave shortly. I screamed bloody murder that it was necessary for me to be there when they loaded the boat. The police
screamed just as loudly that we could not stay on an Egyptian
navy base.

By the time I returned to the boat, they had built a rather
insecure cradle under it. I asked Rosie what had happened to
the sandbags. She told everything that had happened while I
was gone.

They had moved the lightweight crane over next to the
Mustang. "I was sitting in the cab of the truck," she said, "for
women just are not allowed on the base, but no one knew

quite what to do about me. I was hoping Big Daddy was going to supervise. The amazing thing was that there were thirty men running around trying to get the job done, all yelling at the tops of their voices. It was nerve-racking. I could not help comparing it with what would have been happening at an American navy base. There would have been two or three men and one officer in charge and that would be that.

"Anyway, two drivers went down and got slings under the boat and the crane moved over and tried to lift it. I could feel the hair rising on the back of my neck, for it was obvious that crane was too light. If they dropped our boat, what would we do? Nothing. After all, we were on this navy base illegally. For ten minutes I resisted the temptation to get out of the cab and run around yelling like the Arabs. When they began to lift the boat out of the water, I could stand it no longer and got out and went to Big Daddy, who also looked worried. The crane got our ship up a few feet, but began to lift up itself, and the boat sank back into the water.

"Big Daddy went over and told the operator something and they unhooked from the boat and moved the crane off, for which I was greatly relieved. I tried to tell Big Daddy that you did not think the sandbag idea would work but, of course, I could not get the idea across, so I wandered around until I found an officer who spoke a little English. I told him my husband did not think the sandbags would work. He looked at me as if I were crazy and said something like, "Yes, yes, very good." I didn't know if he agreed or disagreed.

"They spent another hour getting the slings in place, the crane, and the whole operation going again. Even the new crane seemed little enough to me and I was right, for it could barely get the *Mustang* out of the water. I closed my eyes and prayed as they started swinging the ship across the semitruck. Then, something happened and they stopped the crane with the boat in midair and could move no farther. The truck driver, who acted as if he had a lot of common sense, hurriedly got into the truck and with ten men yelling instructions at him, backed the truck in under the boat. As they lowered the boat, men started pushing sandbags up under the hull. Almost as fast as they pushed them, the bags slid away and by the time the *Mustang* was sitting on the truck, most of the bags had been pushed to the side or fallen off. If I had not been so worried, it would have been hilarious.

"So, I conferred with Big Daddy and he pointed to the cradle of a small boat out of the water nearby and I could see he was telling them that they had to build a cradle. But the idiot in charge continued for another half hour to try to make the sandbags work. Then, he finally sent for some carpenters and wood and the men started trying to build a cradle. The truckdriver scouted around and found a sort of frame for one from a much smaller boat and between the truckdriver and Big Daddy some intelligent progress was made. All this time the slings were still the only thing holding the boat upright and I dreaded to see what was going to happen when the crane finally released the boat.

"In an hour or so they had some kind of cradle built, and they started to release the slings, but no one had thought to put something under the keel so that the slings could be pulled from under, and they had to lift it again to do that. On top of all that it was a blistering hot day with a hot wind blowing off the desert. I could see Big Daddy thought it was a pretty weak outfit. He sent his mate to get some shrouds and he instructed the men to wrap them around the boat and under the truck, strengthening the whole arrangement."

After she told me this, I told her to get a suitcase ready because we had to leave. "You mean we can't follow the boat?" she said.

"Not as far as I can figure out," I replied.

I got a ladder for Rosie to go up and into the boat to pack a suitcase as I looked the boat over. It seemed damned insecure to me and I talked to one man who said they were going to put it back in the water the next day and built a better cradle. I did not know if that was a good idea or not, but I couldn't do anything more because a jeep arrived to take us away. From the boat, we were taken back to the bank. The banker had not, in all that time, got the proper papers signed. All this just to cash a few traveler's checks.

Then we were taken to the customs barracks. They told me a customs man would ride to Alexandria on the truck with the boat. I would pay his expenses. It is 1,200 kilometers from Safaga to Alexandria, so I could see this would be no small item. Then we were taken to the immigration offices to have our passports stamped with approval to travel on roads not normally open to tourists. From there, we went out of the buildings to the sentry-patrolled gates. There sat an old car—the taxi that was to take us across 125 miles of desert. I wondered if I would ever see my *Mustang* again.

I made another attempt to tell the officers I could not leave until my boat was properly loaded. No one paid the slightest attention, and our bags and ourselves were directed into the crummy old taxi. A young policeman climbed into the taxi carrying his gun. We left the gate as various officials waved and wiped their brows. The taxi driver was grinning all over the place. This ride I didn't want was costing us fifty-five dollars.

Next stop was at a Safaga-style filling station: seventeen barrels alongside the street. The attendant and his wife and six kids all lived in a tent by the barrels. The policeman told me in sign language that I had to pay the fare so that the driver could buy gas. I was really over the well-known barrel. I had not figured out the rate of exchange for sure, so all at once I was supposed to put out fifty-five dollars U.S. in Egyptian rupees. The policeman kept reaching into my billfold, presumably to extract the right amount. I soon put a stop to that. With Rosie figuring out about what she thought the exchange was, I gave him, I think, about fifty dollars U.S. You should have heard the screaming and jabbering then. All the bystanders got into the argument. I had found some time ago that if I was wrong, I would eventually have to pay, but if I overpaid, I never got any back. So I thought it better to underpay first.

Finally, we were paid up, gassed up, and ready to roll. We drove to another part of the village and picked up a boy of about twelve. He was to open doors and change flat tires; the driver only drove. Then we were stopped by a group of army men and took on three of them. So my fifty-dollar fare is carrying an extra boy, three army men, and a policeman. The car was crowded, so the boy was put into the trunk. I thought that boy would surely die in the trunk the way the sun was beating down on us.

In that 125 miles there was one small watering hole where two forlorn trees and a mud army post grew. Otherwise there was no grass, no cactus, only an occasional shriveled up bunch of brush and sand and rocks. At my insistence, the driver let the boy out at the watering hole. I fully expected him to be dead.

At dusk we reached Qena. By then we were hot, tired, dirty, and mad. The driver pulled into the train station, the policeman went in and came out with a note saying our train would leave for Cairo in four hours.

I was really mad at the Egyptians by then. In no uncertain terms, none of which he could understand, I told the policeman how mad I was. I said we were going to a hotel until morning. I said I wanted to travel down the Nile in daytime when I could see something. He understood the word *hotel* and understood what I mean when I put my head on my folded hands and closed my eyes as if I were asleep.

Finally, reluctantly, he took us to a hotel. I signed for a room at, at least, three times the usual rate, I am sure. It was a local hotel and pretty crummy. The policeman and the proprietor escorted us to the room. It and the bed were so dirty that Rosie sat down and started to laugh. I thought she might have hysterics. There was one-eighth-inch-thick dust everywhere—on top of everything, between the sheets, on the floor, everywhere. Even the cold shower was dirty. I called the proprietor and he and the policeman came in. When I held up the dirty bedding, they both sort of shrugged as if to say, "Well, what did you expect?"

There was no café worthy of the name, so with the policeman following we bought some cheese and bread in a little store and with some warm Coke had our dinner in our room. The policeman slept outside the door all night. I never did know if he was protecting us or watching us. Rosie shook clouds of dust out of the sheets out the window and we managed to sleep out the night.

In the morning the policeman escorted us to the train depot, reached his hand into my wallet, and bought two tickets to Cairo. Right up until then, I had thought he would accompany us there, also. He got us onto the train and watched until the train moved out. We were really glad to see the last of him, although he actually was a nice young fellow only doing his job. We shook hands and parted friends. He had evidently been instructed not to let us out of his sight until we were on the train.

The train trip down the banks of the Nile was a pleasure. It was a good train, crowded but sufficient, and we had good seats. It was full of all nationalities. As we sat back and watched the Nile slide by, we decided not to worry about the boat. It was in the hands of Allah. I thought we might never see it again. When I mentioned this later to Rosie, she told me she'd been thinking the same thing.

The Nile valley was like any large river valley: green and fertile, busy and highly populated. People, donkeys, goats, and camels were all over amid date trees, palm trees, and farm crops of every type. Irrigation pumps by the thousands were run by humans, donkey, and ox. Men walked up endless steps with a chain of buckets that they dumped into a ditch to irrigate a field a little higher in elevation. Every species of farm animal walked around a pole in the center, thrashing rice, wheat, and barley. It was interesting travel for us—no holding a tiller or watching the compass for hours. That train did not need one sail change. Nixon had just made a visit to Cairo and all the Egyptians would say, "Nixon, Sadat brothers." Yes we were old buddies—Nixon had just promised them something like $1 billion in foreign aid.

Our room in the Capsis Hotel in downtown Cairo was clean and the clerks courteous. A walk over to the Nile Hilton showed us we were on the wrong side of the tracks, but from the Hilton, Egypt was not visible, nor were the Egyptians. The menu in our hotel was in Arabic and the food was Arabic. We had no toilet paper, soap, or towels, but brought our own. Boys did all the cleaning and waiting on tables. Only one clerk spoke English and he was kind enough to give us a card saying where we lived in Cairo so that if we got lost, a taxi could return us to known territory.

On the Nile we were interested in watching the dhows, a truly native Arab boat. They went up and downstream with about equal speed. The constant northwest winds blew them up the river, even though the big sails were often full of holes and sometimes of several different pieces of colored material. The dhows worked from one side of the river or canal to the other to avoid strong currents at different places. When they came downstream, the sails were usually down with just the current carrying them along. Since there were numerous low bridges across the Nile, the dhows could lower the masts and lay them flat on the deck to pass under a bridge. I asked several people how much tonnage they carried in a year, but no one had any idea.

I got in contact with the Cairo office of the company hauling our boat. They told me they would call me at the hotel as soon as the boat arrived in Cairo. Communicating with them was a problem until they produced a tall, young Arab who spoke good English. I was told he was their public relations man. I think he had been hired just to deal with us. A pleasant young fellow, he insisted on calling me Mr. Nixon, so I called him Mr. Sadat.

"Mr. Sadat" came to our hotel on our third day there to tell me the boat was being held up about fifty miles north of town by officials and low telephone wires. He said they would need me and our proof of ownership to go farther. I was glad to hear the *Mustang* had not disappeared somewhere in the desert and went out to where it was. I was really pleased to see the old girl again. That truckdriver was one of the few craftsmen I saw in Egypt who knew what he was doing. He had hauled the *Mustang* 1,250 kilometers and not put a scratch on her.

It was three days before we arrived back in Cairo because of low wires, back roads, and police. Twice that combination led to my arrest. Foreigners could only travel over certain roads. As long as the *Mustang* remained on the main road, I was okay with her. But when we came to low wires, the driver would turn off on a back road where foreigners weren't supposed to go. As soon as someone saw me with the boat, I was arrested and hauled off to a little mud jail until "Mr. Sadat" could bail me out. The police treated me well: I was always served tea by the highest authority there and told how sorry they were to hold me. Five hours was a long time in a filthy jail, however, and I was glad to see "Mr. Sadat." Then came another set of wires, another back road, and sooner or later, another visit to a jail.

As we were only making about fifteen miles a day, it was eat or go hungry. I did hold off on the water as long as I could, but I finally had to drink it. I think seeing the conditions were what made me sick. We stopped at a little restaurant where I took a drink. Later, I went out to the back. The hole for the outhouse and the well were only about six feet apart. I got sick. It was about the only time on the whole trip that I became ill, but it took me a month to get over it. The outhouse was close enough to the restaurant itself that the flies didn't have far to fly.

As we neared the outskirts of the city, the Cairo authorities took over with their own set of objections: "It is not possible to take the boat through the city." For three days the truck with the *Mustang* sat in the shade of a pyramid, but pyramids don't give much shade. The boat was stripped mahogany planking, one-and-one-quarter-inch thick and had already been ten days in the hot, windy atmosphere of, maybe, the driest place on earth. I could almost feel the planks pulling away from one another while some two-bit bureaucrat threw his weight around. Never have I been so frustrated. I could not speak that language and knew of no one who could help. I felt I was at the mercy of Ali Baba and the forty thieves. Rosie had great faith in the American embassy, but came back thoroughly disillusioned. We looked at the Nile with hope, but our freeboard was too high to pass under some of the bridges even with the mast down.

At last, after three days of going in and out of offices, I got permission to go through. The trucking company owners claimed they had had permission, but that the wrong man had signed it. The truckdriver, who had become a friend, told us he doubted it.

The boat was in the center of town when the trucking company called me again. They wanted the money for the hauling and three hundred dollars more than the agreed price because it had been so much trouble. It was a typical Arab deal. I never made a deal with one, except Big Daddy, that they did not renege on.

The big hassle began. Four of them screamed at me. I screamed back. The English-speaking "public relations man" interpreted. It was so bad that when I returned to our hotel I would laugh as I told Rosie of the day's activities. It was not so funny, because they had me at their mercy and they and I knew it. They even threatened to unload the *Mustang* right in the middle of town. Two days later I agreed to pay one hundred above the agreed amount, eight hundred. They said they wanted the money right then, that very hour.

It was after banking hours, so I told them I would have to get my wife and go to the American Express office, where our letter of credit was good. I told the public relations interpreter, "Tell them I will meet them at the American Express office in an hour and will pay eight hundred now and the other hundred when the boat is delivered in Alexandria and the mast is set in." I thought I might be making a mistake, but I was anxious to get the *Mustang* back in water as soon as possible. "Tell them also I want a piece of paper in English stating the total price and how much I have paid, with the company stamp on it."

He rattled off something to his employers, then told me he would pick us up at the hotel. He came by in a taxi. On the way to the American Express office he stopped by his apartment and returned with a suitcase.

I drew the money, which he said had to be in American dollars or traveler's checks, and he gave me a receipt with the company stamp, seals, and his signature. We left the American Express office, walked a block, and had a beer to consummate the deal. After he left, Rosie asked, "Did you notice how he was shaking?"

"I suppose that much money made him nervous," I replied casually.

The next day we took the train to Alexandria where we went

to a hotel recommended by the public relations man. It was another local hotel in the middle of the city. The first thing the next morning I called the office of the trucking company. The man there told us to come to the office at once and gave directions in English as to how to get there. Since it was close by, we walked through narrow streets on which sidewalk merchants took up most of the sidewalks. We had to push our way through crowds of people. I was hanging onto my billfold and Rosie was clutching her purse because a customs man had told Rosie Alexandria had the best pickpockets in Africa.

When we entered the transport office we were taken at once to the head man who started right in shouting and yelling, in Arabic, obviously angry. I asked the interpreter what the problem was.

"He wants his money," he said.

I told him, "I will pay the balance when the *Mustang* is in the water as agreed in Cairo."

The head man blew up.

"He wants the eight hundred dollars right now," the interpreter explained.

Then I blew up and started shouting. Words flew back and forth faster than the interpreter could translate. It was just as well. I was telling the head man what I thought of him and Arabs in general and he was apparently telling me to get out. At last I got out the receipt and handed it to the interpreter who read it in Arabic. The head man calmed down a little. He took the piece of paper, looked at it, and turned it over. Right then I reached out to get it back, practically snatching it out of his hand.

Rosie told the interpreter we would call the American embassy. She knew it would be a waste of time but thought the Egyptians would not know that. Now, the head man got on the phone and started making calls. The phone system was not too good and he got frustrated and yelled into the unhearing phone a few times, then banged it down. Then he'd try it again. After a while he got through to someone and they yelled back and forth about fifteen minutes. Our friend, "Mr. Sadat," had disappeared, along with our eight hundred dollars. To our knowledge, he was never heard from again.

Rosie and I left the office with nothing settled. We caught a taxi and went to the American embassy. They were polite, but would do nothing. Next we went to the tourist police. We had been told it was a bureau set up to protect tourists so that they would spend their dollars in Egypt. It was hard to get our situation across to them. Tourists didn't arrive in Egypt in a thirty-two foot sailboat—they came by airplane. A sailboat sitting on a truck on the outskirts of Alexandria was just not a problem they could comprehend. I couldn't blame them. I could hardly comprehend the business myself. We went back to the trucking office and told them we had contacted the tourist police. "Maybe they will shut this place down," I said. They were not scared, but were, as always, doing a lot of talking among themselves.

At last the interpreter came into the room and said, "If you will give him the receipt for eight hundred dollars, they will start to put the boat in the water. He wants to make a copy of it. He needs it to be able to prosecute the thief."

"I will go with them while they make the copy," I said. I did.

The next morning they called me and had me come over again. I was told the boat would be on such and such a dock at noon.

We were down on the dock at 10:00 A.M. and the boat came around the corner at 2:00 P.M. I don't know of anything that has ever made me feel any better than seeing the *Mustang* coming slowly up that street. It was now only one-quarter mile from the Mediterranean and I felt that somehow I would battle it on into the ocean.

36

It's Great to Be Back in the Water!

Three days later, the *Mustang* still was not in the water. Two attempts had been made with cranes too small for the job. Most of the time at least twenty-five Arabs were around yelling at the tops of their voices, giving advice. Two laborers were trying to do what twenty-five chiefs were telling them. The fourth day they brought in a floating crane designed to lift one hundred tons. It was built on a barge and the only way the crane could turn either to left or right was to maneuver the whole barge. They tried to do this with lines run ashore to the wharf. When they let out a port or starboard line, the barge would move slowly to right or left.

They had placed cables under the boat and when they finally got the crane into position, they thought they were going to lift the boat without spreaders, poles to hold the slings apart so the cables won't crush the boat. I kept trying to stop them—by gesturing that they needed spreaders—but no one paid any attention. As they started to lift the boat, the toe rails crumbled and I could hear other boards cracking and breaking. Having no ladder, I scrambled up the bobstay onto deck and grabbed the boss of the crane crew by the shirt and threatened to throw him to the ground fifteen feet below if he did not stop the crane.

He didn't understand English, but he did understand one mad American. I told the one "chief" who spoke English that I would personally kill the next man who gave orders to tighten up on the slings. I could not believe that any group of grown

191

men could be so damned stupid. This monkey business had gone on long enough.

One man from the trucking office said he would try to find some spreaders. About an hour later, he returned to say that there were none in Alexandria—this in a port unloading thousands of tons of freight a day off freighters. Once more I threatened to kill any man who did more damage to the boat. Then, I left to look for spreaders.

Rosie told me later that she had been very upset when she heard the wood cracking on the *Mustang* and had begun to cry. One of the transport company men had said, "Don't worry, little lady, we Egyptians can do anything."

I was looking for something hard to explain in a country where I could not speak a word of the language. I could not even hire a taxi. But Allah was with me. I headed for some shops that looked like machine shops, and walked through to the carpenter shop. Standing in one corner of that shop were fourteen-foot four-by-fours.

I got two laborers to help carry them to the *Mustang*. Then I climbed up, got into my tool box aboard the boat, and, taking a saw and hammer, made suitable spreaders in about a half hour. I checked the hull below the waterline for damage and told Rosie to get into the boat as soon as she was able and start pumping. With the spreaders in place I directed the crane operator to start lifting the boat. I was nervous as hell as the crane swung the boat over the cement wharf, but the operator got the job done and lowered the ship into the water. They set the mast in with all the rigging tied in knots. The truckdriver, his helper, and I literally threw the anchors, chains, motorcycles, dinghy, and one hundred other pieces of loose gear that had been removed onto the deck of the boat.

Then I went to pay the trucking representative the other one hundred dollars and was told I had to pay all the extra labor that had been "helping" me. I was too tired to argue and paid some twenty useless helpers. Ever since Cairo, I had been sick to my stomach, probably from the water, and I was sick in the head from fighting with Arabs. The shrouds were loose, the stays likewise, and everything was a total mess, but the engine ran and we motored off.

Rosie said, "Where are we going? It's nearly dark."

"I don't know where, but we are going!" I said.

I saw a vacant spot with one boat anchored across the harbor a couple of miles behind the breakwater. "Let's go over there and drop the hook for the night." Hurriedly I tied the anchor, chain, and lines together and threaded them through the hawser hole while Rosie steered for the spot. We anchored.

Twenty minutes later two Egyptian gunboats pulled alongside, one on each side of us. Both had Bren-toting seamen pointing their guns at us.

"What are you doing here?" a young ensign said.

"We just got our boat into the water and we are anchored."

"I'm sorry, but I shall have to place you under arrest. This is a forbidden zone."

It was almost too much. I was sick and tired and no spy. All I wanted was a few hours of peace. "Couldn't we stay the night?" I asked. "I'll leave first thing in the morning."

"Pull up your anchor," he said adamantly. "We are going to take you over to our wharf. You are under arrest."

I looked at Rosie and we both started to laugh. We laughed until we had to sit down we were so weak. I had had so many guns pointed at me in the last month I had almost become nonchalant about it, but not quite. A BB gun looks big when a nervous kid is holding it.

I finally went forward and hauled in the anchor line and they led us over to the navy wharf and tied us up with a stout line. Our ensign said he would call the "Admiral" to find out what to do with us. Typically, they offered tea. Rosie said, "No thanks, but do you have any ice water?" In about ten minutes they returned with two big glasses of ice water. Honest-to-goodness ice. That glass of ice water after the day we'd had was better than ten Tom Collinses.

I had been going on willpower for the last four or five days. I'd had it. I told Rosie I did not care what happened, I was going to bed. "The Egyptians can sink us, blow us up, or haul us off to jail, I don't care." I went below, crawled into my bunk, and passed out. While I was asleep, Rosemary pumped about ten minutes out of every hour. She was below pumping when the ensign returned and said we could move over to the commercial wharf.

She said, "Can't we please stay here the rest of the night? My husband is sick and dead tired."

"I'll find out," he said and left. He really was a nice young man. He was gone about two hours. When he returned it was getting close to midnight. "I'm sorry, but I cannot get permission. You will have to move."

Rosemary was thinking how ridiculous that was: First, he insisted we come and now he was insisting we leave. She said, "If we move you will have to move us. My husband is sick and I don't know where the wharf is, and besides, I can't do all that by myself." She sat down limply as if she were about to faint.

The ensign said, "We'll move you."

He did. Not only did he move us, but once we were tied up to the commercial wharf, he left a guard so that no one would steal anything off our deck. Or maybe the guard was watching us. When I woke the next morning, Rosie was sound asleep in her bunk. It took me a minute to recall my whereabouts. I put on shorts and went on deck. It all looked strange. We were tied alongside a fifty-foot fishing boat. An Arab on the boat nodded good morning, as if we had been there every morning for ten years. Putting the coffee on to perk, I sat back to watch the activity and wait for Rosie to tell me how in the devil she had got us there. When I heard her tale, I had to laugh. Woman power is sometimes strong.

Later, after a leisurely breakfast, I went to ask the boss of this wharf if we could stay there awhile. He held up two fingers and pointed to two days on the calendar. I was happy with that and went back to the boat for more sleep. We bought some bread and fruit at the customs-controlled gate and spent the rest of the time asleep. I hardly had enough energy to lift a coffee cup.

We had heard from the man who ran the water taxi that if we went out of this harbor and down the coast to the east two miles, there was another breakwater where there was a yacht club. I had tried to buy charts of the harbor, but had been unable to do so. It seemed impossible that no charts were available in one of the world's oldest ports.

The third day we motored over to the east harbor and entered with a boatload of police right behind us. I had to go through the police station and declare why we were there. Leaving the boat I told Rosie that if I didn't show up soon, just fly home. I was too tired to fight anymore. This time, however, it was easy. There was lots of passport showing and boat papers were needed, but after showing them I was allowed to return to the boat. After living in the freedom of America all my life, these police states made me nervous.

For two weeks I was too played out to even care that the boat needed a lot of repairs. The bug I had picked up outside of Cairo was still after me. When I was finally up to tearing into the boat, I found five planks broken on one side and four on the other. The toe rails, where they had put the slings before I had realized what was going on, were in shreds. These were the new rails I'd put on in Ceylon. It was enough to make a grown man cry, but instead I just cussed Arabs. The few Egyptians we met at the yacht club spent most of their time telling us how smart the Egyptians were and how they had won the war with Israel, and asking why we didn't stop giving aid to the Jews. As a guest at their club, I couldn't say much, but I had my own opinions.

After six weeks of hard labor, I had most of the topside repairs done as far as I could do them. Almost nothing in the way of good materials was available: no galvanized or bronze nails, bolts, pipe fittings, turnbuckles, or anything of that sort. Paint was of such a poor quality that it remained sticky for months. The mastic crumbled. But it was time to haul out and repaint the bottom. We were anxious to cross the Med before winter and, therefore, had to hurry things.

A small boat marine ways sat beside the yacht club. It was

busy hauling fishing boats all the time. The secretary of the yacht club told me about what they should charge. "If you have trouble, come and get me."

At the ways, I found an old gentleman sitting in a chair watching the work. I asked for the manager.

"I'm it," he said.

We discussed the job over the inevitable cup of tea and agreed on a price of thirty dollars. I knew this was ten dollars more than the local fishing boats paid, but I was anxious to get the job done. We set the date and time for high tide two days later.

I was on time. They were on time. An hour later we were high and dry on the ways. Ten minutes after that there was the damnedest screaming and ranting going on below me on the ground. An Arab was screaming at me to come down. Climbing down the ladder, I found a big lanky (and obnoxious) Arab flinging his arms around, pointing at me, the *Mustang*, and the water, jumping up and down all the while. I shrugged my shoulders in the universal sign, "I don't know."

A young man painting a sign on another boat came over. "This is the owner of the yard," he said. "He wants more money."

I pointed to the old gentleman still sitting in his chair and said, "No more money. I made a deal with the man."

Rosie was watching from the deck. In cases like this she always stood by with a pipe or a wrench, in case I had to defend myself. I pointed to the so-called owner and made a circle at my head, showing I thought he was crazy. He came at me. Rosie dropped the wrench over the side into my hand and I was ready for him. The sign painter and another grabbed him and pulled him away.

"I don't understand all this," I said. "What does he want now?"

The sign painter said, "Fifty dollars U.S."

I said, "Put the boat back into the water." I was cutting off my own nose so to speak, but I hated being pushed around.

The sign painter and the owner talked back and forth for a while and finally the painter said, "How about forty dollars?"

I finally agreed to that, although I knew I was being taken. I was getting to a point where I would pay almost anything to get out of Egypt. The club secretary had told me that everything had to be watched very carefully, so I hired two men to paint and I just watched the tools, paint, sandpaper, brushes, and whatnot. The next day at lunch I went up on deck to eat, shaking my head.

"What's the matter now?" Rosie asked.

"This is the damnedest place I've ever been," I replied. "I can be looking right at something and it disappears." It was a fact. Even with me watching, various items were stolen, one by one. One of the things gone was my claw hammer, a very necessary tool on the boat, so I sent Rosie uptown to buy another. She tramped all over the city and finally found an awkward tool like a father might buy a three-year-old for Christmas. For that she paid nine dollars U.S.

Two months after arriving in Alex we were in about as good a shape as we could get in that country. Our last night we decided to eat ashore before leaving for Turkey. We went ashore in our dinghy as usual, tied up at the yacht club dock, and went into the club for dinner. Two hours later, we started back to the *Mustang* and the dinghy was gone. It had been stolen from right under the light on the guarded dock. Right away a man comes down yelling he will take us out to our boat for five dollars. If I'd had a paddle, I would have hit him right over the head. We went back to the club and reported the loss. I could tell that the officials there thought we'd been careless, but a club boat took us out to our boat for one dollar. But it was a disaster. We could not leave without a dinghy. Since nothing is ready-made in Egypt, the next day I had to see about having a dinghy made. That was discouraging.

While we were waiting for the new dinghy, an Aussie on an English-made catamaran came into port from Greece. We became acquainted right off, as the Aussies say. One night we all went into the club for dinner, taking his dinghy. On the dock I said, "We'd better take the motor with us, and pull the dinghy up on the dock."

"No," he said. "I've had it two years and no one bothers it."

"Yes," Rosie said, "but how long have you been in Egypt?"

"Two days." Despite our comments, he would not take the motor off the boat, so we went up to the club for a leisurely dinner.

When we came out about nine, his motor was gone. After the Aussie reported his loss, the yacht club offered to pay half the cost of my new dinghy.

I thought this very decent of them, but declined. "You didn't invite me to your club," I said. "I came of my own free will and your club has offered us the use of facilities. We appreciate that. You don't owe me anything."

While we waited we stocked up, buying many things on the black market. On one street right downtown, black-market merchants sold openly. Items were stacked higher than your head. The cans were marked "Gift of the People of Denmark to the World Food Program," or "Gift of the People of Canada," or "Gift of the People of the United States." For these food-stuffs, Rosie paid as high as five dollars a can. I never saw a poor Egyptian with a can. The rich got richer. We were also told by a Greek freighter captain that an American boat loaded with foreign-aid wheat for Egypt was charged $1,200 a day in port charges while waiting to unload, and $300 a day while anchored out.

We only made one friend during seventy-five days in Egypt. There were many twenty- to forty-foot fishing boats in harbor. The fishermen were taken back and forth to shore by two or three rowboat taxis. One was rowed by a little kid eight or ten years old, who had the most engaging smile of any human I had ever met. That smile said, "Hello, how are you? I'm your friend"; all that one friendly person says to another.

His clothes were tattered patches on patches. Sometimes his shirt would have cloth over only one shoulder. We looked through our clothes and gave him all we could: jackets, shirts, T-shirts. Although it was often cold at night, we never saw him wear anything we gave him. He must have given them away, or sold them.

If he saw Rosie waiting on the yacht club dock for me, he might be twice as far away as I was, but he would row like mad to get there first to pick her up. Of course, he was paid, but he would have done it for nothing. He was just a sweet-faced lovable kid—and the slickest thief among an army of slick thieves. We didn't know it for a while.

I had let him know I would buy seashells, so he brought me a few each day. Most were not of good quality, but to help the little devil, I paid him a small amount and threw them over-board later. A few times he brought decent ones. I paid more for them. When he brought them, he'd remain on his boat and I on mine and we'd barter back and forth. When I bought good ones, I'd throw them on deck to clean later. It took a while for me to realize that they were disappearing. Now shells are like people—they all look a trifle different. About the third time the kid sold me the same shell, I caught on. Although to the best of my knowledge he had not been on our boat, somehow he was stealing the shells to sell back to me later. I jumped all over him with a lecture about honesty, etc., but he just grinned at me. To him life was a game of wits—his against the world.

The boat he ran was owned by an old man—a bent, shriv-eled, skinny, wrinkled, poor old man. The old fellow would often be in the boat. The kid would row by us and beg ciga-rettes for the old fellow. I had bought a few cartons of Amer-ican cigarettes in Saudi Arabia so that I could give a package as a gift now and then. One time the boy must have done some-thing to infuriate the old man. I saw the old fellow pick up a sharp-pointed anchor and take after the kid. Two fishermen intervened, saving the kid's life as far as I could see. The next day they were rowing around, friends again, the kid begging the old man's cigarettes. When we left for Turkey the old boy and the kid were the only ones to come over and wish us bon voyage.

37

Adrift in the Med

The second day out of Alexandria, a terrific storm hit us from the north. As our course to Turkey was almost due north, this put a stop to progress. I decided to heave to until things got better. For twenty-four hours we were a cork on a violent sea. Gad, how the wind howled and the boat pitched, rolled, and slammed around. Down below, all we could do was lie in our bunks and hang on.

At the end of those twenty-four hours, the wind and sea were still high, but the wind had abated somewhat, so I put up a bit of sail. In spite of everything the boat refused to answer the helm. It took another hour before it sank in to us that the rudder was broken. By then it was dark. With the tiller fastened down, I hung out over the transom with a flashlight until I could see the rudder flopping loose. The one-and-one-half-inch bronze rudder stock had broken.

I hated to tell Rosie. She got scared in storms and unusual situations. I knew we were not too well off. Having no rudder is about the worst thing that can happen to a boat—either at sea or close to land. When I told her, she said, "What are we going to do?"

I didn't know. I finally said, "Speaking for myself, I'm going to go below and go to sleep until morning. I can't do anything in the dark. We can't hit land before morning, and maybe by then it will have settled down some. Don't worry, we'll figure out something." I think she was slightly shocked, but she knew that one o'clock in the morning on a stormy night at sea was a bad time to think clearly, so she went below with me.

The next morning the sea had calmed down and I had

thought the thing over. It seemed to me I might construct a Mickey-Mouse rudder out of materials on board. I had a few pieces of plywood and our whisker pole was made of wood. I took two sheets of plywood about three by two feet, nailed them together, then nailed them to the whisker pole. I reinforced the whole thing, then attached it to the boom, and we were ready to give it a try. With a minimum of sail and the motor at slow, we brought the boat around to a northerly heading.

We were anxious to get a noon shot and were lucky we could. We fixed our position at about 130 miles north of Alexandria. After some discussion, we decided that if the jury-rigged rudder held, we would head back to Egypt. We were familiar with the port and the entrance. Since we had not been able to buy charts in Alexandria, we had only a very small scale chart of southern Turkey. I hated like hell to go back to Egypt. But we set a course, cautiously moved the rudder, and tried to come off the wind. The boat did not respond well, but it did respond. Slowly we came around.

There was tremendous strain on the rudder and I doubted it would hold all the way to Egypt. It was so hard to hold, Rosie could not handle it at all.

"I'm afraid it will never hold," I said just as the plywood broke off with a loud cracking and floated away. So much for that piece of hardware. With no helm, the boat came around straight into the wind. Nothing to do but take the jib down and figure the next move.

"First," I told Rosie, "go down and see where we will hit the shore if we drift straight downwind, if it stays from the same direction. Check the coastline to see if there are reefs and rocks. Check the depths along the coast." I knew it would be a bad coast because the prevailing wind was from the north and the big swells would be hitting it all the time.

I had decided to try to steer the boat with the sails. I had read the book *Once Is Enough*. Those people had done that for some nine hundred miles, as I recalled. I told Rosie that if they could do it, so could we. She looked skeptical, but she is a staunch mate in time of trouble.

When she came back up from checking the chart, she said, "At least the coastline is not littered with reefs. If we drift straight downwind, and it doesn't change, and nothing else goes wrong, we will approach the coast where there is a six-fathom shelf."

That didn't sound too bad. If we could get to that part, we surely could get the hook down before we were washed up on the beach and shipwrecked again.

For four hours we tried every combination of sails to try to get the boat headed downwind. Without any sails and crippled like we were, the boat wanted to either lie broadside to the wind or lie with the bow into the wind. Generally, with the sails up, it also wanted to point into the wind. But we had to come off the wind. Rosie finally did it. I had put up the big jib and scandalized it, let it loosen so it flopped in the wind. I had the mainsail reefed. I went below for a few minutes and when I came up, Rosie had backed the jib and slowly we fell off the wind and headed south. But it was touchy.

We were steering directly by the main sheet. If we were being pulled too far east, we hauled in a little to tighten the sail; if we were being pushed too far west, we let it out. With the slightest shift in the wind, or a stray wave, the one holding the sheet had to adjust. Since the boat responded slowly, we had to be careful not to overadjust. After the hassle we'd had coming off the wind, we certainly did not want to get back in that position. When we were on watch, we never let that main sheet out of our hands and watched the compass constantly. We didn't dare drop off to sleep for five seconds.

Sometime during the night, the wind shifted more to the west so it came more on our beam. In a way that was better, for the boat responded sooner, but we had to be more careful also not to come up into the wind. If the wind shifted more to the west, our system might not work at all. The wind held almost steady, however. Gradually, we crept closer to Alexandria at about forty miles a day. The third morning was overcast and cloudy. It was bad not to get a sun sight and fix our position. Time for a noon shot came and went. About three in the afternoon, we had to make the big decision. Should we continue as we were, trusting our dead reckoning, or should we stop at dark and drift?

About five in the afternoon, the skies suddenly cleared and we saw the hazy outline of the city ahead. A big freighter went across our bow a mile or so ahead. Rosie was all for shooting off some flares, but I would not let her. I explained, "We are not in distress now."

When she went below to make coffee, she was talking to herself and shaking her head. In another half hour we could see the buildings of Alexandria. I was still planning to anchor on the shelf. The only trouble was that if a storm came up while we were anchored, it would be mighty dangerous. I thought we were lucky to be this close. We could have missed it by fifty miles. Soon I could see the main minaret of Alexandria and I knew it was directly behind the entrance through the breakwater. Then I saw the lighthouse and we took a bearing on both that told us where we were.

I threw out the lead line. We were in fifty feet of water. Again, we had to make a decision: Should we throw out the hook and wait for help or attempt to go in?

We both saw the breakwater at the same time. In fact, the entrance was dead ahead. The waves hitting the breakwater threw water forty feet in the air. Because the water was shallow, we were doing a lot of rolling and that made it difficult to set an accurate course. Do we try it or don't we?

"It looks like we might be able to sail right through the entrance," I told Rosie. "Are you game?"

She is not one to make hasty decisions. I could almost see wheels going around in her head.

"Maybe," she said, finally, in a sort of whisper.

What we did not realize was that a strong current was running across the entrance from west to east. The closer we got the more it carried us past the entrance toward the east. We could only work upwind so much. I yelled at her to start the engine. The entrance was getting smaller and smaller because we were no longer approaching it from 90 degrees. Now it was too late to throw out the anchor. By the time we let it out, the boat would swing around and be right on the giant, jagged rocks of the breakwater. I hauled in on the main sheet all I dared and hollered at Rosie to gun the motor. "Hurry, Hurry!" We were no more than fifteen feet off the rocks. The water crashing on them sent spray onto the boat.

"Keith," Rosemary cried out, "I can see the bottom. We'll never make it!"

Rosie was pushing the throttle as far as it would go. Fearfully we watched the rocks. Suddenly the current let us go and we slid into the entrance almost crossways. We were in! My God, what a relief! I felt like a man given a reprieve from hanging.

Rosie was crying. "We made it! I can't believe it. We made it!"

We were so jubilant and cocky that we sailed right on into the harbor, made a 70-degree turn to starboard, and anchored in our old spot.

The police, immigration, and customs followed us right up to where we anchored, hollering continuously, just as though we weren't crippled. I ignored them. I dropped the hook and told Rosie to mix a drink. Finally, I looked at the pack of officials and asked what they wanted. I knew what they wanted, but to me they were small fry now. A man stepping out of a whale's mouth doesn't mind a fly buzzing around.

I told them we had lost the rudder. They did not believe me until I moved the tiller back and forth, showing them the rudder did not move. They left and told me to come to their various offices the next day.

The following day I went first to the shipyard to see about hauling the boat out. Since I was expecting a big hassle, it surprised me when the owner said, "We can haul you out in three days." The first evening we ate dinner in a hotel where we met two Greek skippers. One was off an American freighter and the other off a Greek ore carrier. They both spoke English well. One told us about the charges on the wheat shipment. Both skippers were very nice to us and gave us much-needed charts of the Med and a book of eastern Med sailing directions, better than gold as far as we were concerned.

When I got the rudder post off I found that a piece of bronze about ten by twelve inches had broken off the stock. The owner of the shipyard took me to a friend's welding shop. There they welded it twice and both times it broke before I could get it out of the shop. I was so damned mad I wanted to hid the welder over the head with it.

I had become acqauinted with a tall young Arab who appeared to be halfway sensible. When he heard of my problem, he led me on foot to a shop about two miles from the shipyard with me carrying the stock, which weighed at least thirty pounds. That welder appeared to know what he was doing and also guaranteed the job. We found out later an Egyptian guarantee isn't worth a darn when you are in the middle of the Atlantic.

One night, while the boat was out of the water, Rosie and I were asleep in our bunks. Rosie, a light sleeper, shook me awake and whispered, "Someone's on deck." Our bunks were directly under the forward hatch. I stood up, poking my head out of the hatch. I saw a big Arab on deck wearing the fez and burnoose they all wear and little thin sandals.

The anchor winch was right by that hatch. Its handle was made of three-quarter-inch pipe two feet long, flattened on one end to fit into the slotted winch opening. I grabbed that winch handle and took out after him. Rosie said I was yelling like a Comanche Indian. Indians yelled to scare their enemies. So did I. As I swung that handle around, occasionally I connected with him. We made two trips around the cabin. On the third trip around he made a big leap to the boat ahead of us, skirts flying. He was a good jumper because it must have been six or eight feet between boats. I stood on my bowsprit cursing him for a while, but it was dark and I'm not much of a jumper, so he disappeared. I chuckled to myself, "I guess I scared him anyway."

The next day I looked up from a job and he was coming toward me, another Arab with him. Picking up my hammer, I turned to face him. The one I had hit had a gash on his cheek. The other was better dressed and spoke to me in Harvard English. "This man says you tried to kill him last night with a knife."

"That is correct," I said. I had not realized he thought my pipe was a knife, but I saw no reason to ruin a good story. That would discourage others from coming around our boat. "He was on our boat. If you come on my boat, I will knife you, too."

He turned to the burnoose and said, "He says you were on his boat. He says he would knife me if I came on his boat."

Burnoose said, "Oh." Then he rattled on for about ten minutes in Arabic. Then the story was relayed to me. The young Arab was watchman on the boat ahead of ours. When he came up on the ways, the yard people had taken the ladder down from his boat and given it to us. So about midnight, when he was returning to his own boat, he had no way to get on it except by climbing on our boat to see if he could get to his.

I felt sort of foolish about it all, but we shook hands and I told him I was sorry. My friend John Gibbs, in Billings, has often said I am frequently wrong, but never in doubt. The next few days I saw that fellow everyplace I went. He would run a block to shake hands with me. He turned out to be a fellow I liked. I think he liked me, too.

Three weeks after the wild ride through the breakwater, we were going out again. We were late now to make the two thousand miles to Gibraltar before winter, so we gave up going to Turkey and headed for Rhodes instead. Rhodes is the easternmost island belonging to Greece. The Greek name for it is Rodos.

We were beating into the wind in stormy conditions the entire 350 miles, but it was worth it, for the island was a lovely spot. We marveled that 350 miles of water could make five hundred years of difference. The Greeks of Rodos were that far ahead of the Egyptians.

38

A Greek Island

We had not secured completely to the quay when two or three yachties came over to help and advise us. They told us that was not a good place to stay and more or less took it upon themselves to move us. Before I knew what was going on, we had been moved about three hundred feet to the other side of the harbor and were in among the other yachts. We were tied to the quay and could step off to the dock and walk thirty feet to one of many sidewalk cafés with brightly colored tables and umbrellas. A beautiful public market with beef, pork, ice cream, fresh produce, and bulk wine was just a few yards farther on. For the next week we gorged on salads, beef cooked on the hibachi, and ice cream.

There were a lot of yachts there: mostly West German and English with one American family on a tri. They had bought their boat in Europe and had come this far, where they bogged down trying to decide what to do. They did not think their tri could beat upwind to Gibraltar and cross the Atlantic, and they were considering shipping it home on a freighter. The other yachts were mostly charter yachts, but for us it was great fun to again be holding company with some other cruising people. It had been a long while.

Peter Losel of Anzingerstr, Germany, wanted to hear of the area around Singapore. He had been chartering in the Med for several years and was discouraged with the business. He said that when the rich Americans stopped coming, he starved to death. We thought the West Germans seemed richer than the Americans.

That was during the Greek-Turkish conflict in Cyprus and

the Greeks were mad at the Americans about it, but I never did find out what their reasoning was. There had been some demonstrations against Americans, and the port captain advised us to take our flag down, but I decided not to. It was pretty obvious we were Americans. We took our cycles off and made two excursions around the island. All the history made it interesting as we saw ruins dating back two thousand years.

After a week, we were off to Piraeus, the port for Athens. There was a large, well-protected harbor for yachts of which we were probably the smallest and scroungiest there. Piraeus was a typical Greek town with many small shops and sidewalk cafés. The Greeks go to these in the evening, order a fifteen-cent glass of cognac, and visit for two hours. I never saw an owner hinting that perhaps they should order more or leave. We had our favorite café where we could sip a little something and look out over the yacht harbor where there were over four hundred boats. Most were owned by the Germans, English, French, or Dutch and were berthed there the year round with the owners flying down for a few weeks a year. A few of the boats had crews on them and chartered when the owner was not there.

39

Bureaucrats—U.S. Style

The American embassy in Athens gave us an awful shock. Mail in Egypt had been impossible, and not knowing for sure where we were going from there, we had had our mail, including a necessary part for the pump, sent to us in care of the American embassy in Athens.

First thing after we arrived in port, Rosie headed out for the embassy in Athens to get the mail. We had been weeks without hearing a thing from home. The embassy was very impressive, a $5-million or $6-million building with the American flag flying from its flagpole. The lobby was large and ornate, and Rosie had a little trouble finding the receptionist. When she did, he was a Greek, reading a newspaper.

She stood by the desk for a few minutes while he paid no attention to her. Finally, he looked up and she said, "Can you tell me where I can pick up our mail?"

He looked puzzled. "Your mail?"

"Yes. We are on a sailboat over in Piraeus and we had our mail sent here."

"We don't handle mail."

"What do you mean, you don't handle mail? We had it sent here, you must have done something with it."

"We send it down to general delivery at the main post office."

Rosie was shocked. If the Greek postal service was like that in the United States, they would long since have sent our mail back.

"I can't believe it," she said. "We had some very important papers sent as well as an important boat part. Do you mean you just shuffled it off to general delivery?"

He stood up then. "Madam, do you realize how many American tourists we have in Athens in a year?"

Rosie said, "No, and I don't care how many. Every single one is an American taxpayer. Are you?"

A young marine was standing nearby and he came over. He was very polite. He said, "The post office is in the basement. You might try there before going to the downtown post office." Rosie thanked him, but she was getting good and mad. In the first place, she didn't particularly like going into an American embassy and having to discuss her problem with a Greek. Second, he was rude. A little less paper reading and a little more mail sorting would not have hurt him, she said.

In the basement she found the post office, but there was no mail for us. The man told her, "This is just for personnel of the embassy." Across from the post office was a little restaurant.

There was the pleasant smell of hamburgers cooking and a milk-shake sign advertising thick milk shakes. She went in and sat down. A lady came up right away. "May I see your card?"

"What card?" Rosie replied. "I do not have a card, only my passport."

"I'm sorry, we can't serve you unless you work for the government."

She got up and left. A Greek out in the embassy parking lot directed her to the main post office. When she found it, no one was behind the general-delivery window. After waiting a few minutes, Rosie asked the woman at the next window for mail. That woman did not speak English. Then she asked several other persons behind counters if she could get her mail from general delivery, but no one spoke English.

Finally, one girl went behind a wall and came out with a man who did speak English. He was quite unpleasant, almost hostile. Rosie wrote our names on a piece of paper and handed it to the man and asked if there was any mail. He looked and said something like "prin." It took her a minute to realize he meant "print." It dawned on her that Greeks use only print letters. They do not use longhand. Furthermore, it seemed there really wasn't a J in their alphabet. How could they read the address if they could not read longhand? He did not find but two letters in a corner. There was no boat part.

Rosie came back to the boat boiling mad, sat down, and wrote Henry Kissinger a letter suggesting that a few less useless employees and one person to sort mail might be of more use to Americans abroad than a $6-million building. She also pointed out that so far she had found out that employees had their own private café, their own theater showing American movies, their own radio station, recreation hall, classes in Greek, nursery, "and no doubt other benefits that I had not heard of. It seemed to me they could afford to spend money for someone to sort mail for American *taxpaying* tourists."

If Kissinger ever answered, she never got the letter. "It, no doubt, got lost in the Greek post office," Rosie said.

The next day I got the Hondas off and Rosie and I headed back to the embassy. I couldn't believe they could do this to us. I could see the flag flying a mile away. We parked in the lot with five big black limousines. Instantly two Greeks clapped their hands at me and made a shooing motion like they were shooing away a mangy dog. I finally figured they wanted me to move the bikes out of the parking lot into the street. I didn't mind moving the bike, but I sure as hell hated the fashion in which I was being told to move it. Being already on the fight, I stuck my face to within six inches of the attendant's and told him the next time he clapped his hands at me as he would at a stray dog, I was going to clap him right in the face. I didn't like being treated like trash.

So I was already good and mad when I walked into the lobby to find the Greek receptionist reading the newspaper. I said, "I want to talk to the consul."

"What is your business with him?"

"That is none of your business, but I am mad at you and everyone else around here. I intend to complain to someone in authority."

"You might try Room Two-oh-two." He made no effort to show me where the room was, so I turned and walked over to the marine corporal.

"Could you tell me where the consul's office is?" Taking me down the hall, he pointed to a room and said, "He should be in there, sir."

I went into that office, the door to which was open. The consul was not there, but in an adjoining office were about six young American fellows talking and laughing. I didn't have an appointment, so I waited patiently for a while, but it was obvious they were not engaged in any very important matter from the conversation I could hear, so again I was getting mad.

In about fifteen minutes, one broke away from the group.

"What can I do for you?"

"First of all, I want you to tell you I am mad. But if you find some of our important mail that was sent to this embassy, it will be doing something."

"Sit down," he said in a brusque tone.

"I'm not going to sit down. I can be madder on my feet."

"Sit down," he said again, pointing to a chair in front of me.

"I'm not going to sit down. I want you to find our mail or get it in writing why you won't." I knew I was being unreasonable, but so was he.

"You can't come in here and threaten me."

"Asking you to write a letter telling me why you won't do a job is a threat?"

I never got the letter. Hot words flew back and forth.

"We have too many tourists here to handle mail for them," he said.

"So why don't you get that fellow out front who is always reading a newspaper every time we come here, to do some mail handling? Not one tourist in ten is going to have his mail sent here. If you don't do that for Americans abroad, just what do you do? I've never had any help from one of you yet. You all live in a little diplomatic cocoon, a little too impressed with your own importance. This place costs millions to keep. Surely a little mail sorting isn't going to hurt any of you."

Of course, I was wasting my breath. It wasn't just the mail, although that was important to us. It was the attitude around the whole place, with the exception of the marine corporal out in front. They all acted as if we were trespassing on sacred ground.

We only got two or three letters the whole time we were there. Two years later we learned that most had been returned to the United States. The important boat part disappeared completely, for it was never returned to the factory and its absence caused us a lot of engine trouble later on, to say nothing of the fact that we had to pay for it. We also had to pay for a phone call to the United States to satisfy Rosie that everything was all right back home.

Despite the hassle with the embassy, we enjoyed ourselves in Athens. We took the Hondas on a trip inland. The olive tree farms on all the rocky hills, which somewhat resembled southern California, looked as though they could raise nothing. But they produced crop after crop of rich oil-bearing olives. An old farmer told us it took seven years for a new tree to bear its first olive and forty years for the tree to reach maturity. Every village had its olive-oil factory and we saw oil in all sizes of cans, bottles, barrels, and tanks.

Of course, we visited the Parthenon. You don't need to go in—just stand outside and be filled with awe. The ancients must have been masters of engineering to construct a building of such beauty with no jackhammers, sandblasting machines, or cranes. We were told the answer was slave labor and time. Someone had some brains to go with them.

Rosie was delighted to find a lot of American products on the shelves. On my end of the buying, I found that due to the fuel crisis, kerosene and cognac cost about the same—one dollar per gallon—in your own container.

On September 17 we left the harbor heading for the Corinth Canal, a short, water-level ditch three miles long. Going through it saves many miles. It cost us nineteen dollars. We compared it with the Panama Canal, which cost us twelve dollars for fifty miles, including raising and lowering the boat eighty-three feet.

In Corinth Bay, we moved into Itea, a lovely little harbor with pleasant officials who gave us immediate permission to take off the motorcycles. Our destination was Delphi, the center of education and religion centuries ago. Once again we could only look and marvel at the wonderful beauty of these architectural marvels. These were much higher up the mountains than the ruins of Athens. How and why did they build here? Every rock must have come up either on the back of a man or a burro.

That evening we ate ashore in Itea at a sidewalk café. Brandy was twenty-one cents and a thin beefsteak cooked in olive oil about eighty-five cents U.S.

We stopped at two more ports in the Corinth Bay before starting across the Ionian Sea between Greece and Italy. It was only three hundred miles and we planned to make it in two or three days. It took eleven.

40

Mediterranean Storm

A day and a half out of Greece, we hit a full-scale gale—winds of sixty knots, seas twenty feet high and more—coming straight from the boot of Italy, where we were headed. Foolishly, I tried bucking it for several hours, but I finally had to give that up, take the sails down, and go below.

We had at least one hundred miles of sea room. With the boat tossing, twisting, heaving, groaning, all we could do was wedge ourselves into a bunk and stay. When the action of the boat was so violent, a kind of lethargy overtook us, and it was an act of will to fix food, eat, or even go to the head. This sort of business terrified Rosie and I felt sorry for her. This is when she first began to maintain that the keel was loose. I pooh-poohed the idea, but she insisted that every time the boat rolled, she could hear this terrible thump down under us. I couldn't hear anything.

During the afternoon of the second day, I happened to look out the companionway and saw a freighter a short distance off. When I went up into the cockpit, I saw he was circling us. I waved to him, but he kept circling. He was probably trying to talk to us by radio. I was sure he was trying to ask if we needed help, but no voice could carry across the shrieking wind. Finally, I climbed as high on deck as I dared. Holding tight to the secured boom, I put my right arm out full-length and gave him the old thumbs-up sign.

The skipper was watching me through the binoculars, and after my sign he put down the glasses and waved. The man at the wheel straightened the ship out and they went on. It was lonesome out there after they disappeared into the storm and we were back to our own little world of pitching boat and screaming wind. I have to hand it to that fellow. He thought we were in need of assistance and he was ready to give it. I don't know how he would ever have got us aboard his ship, for even the freighter had been rolling and pitching, and a small boat would not have lasted ten minutes in those seas.

After three full days we woke to clear skies, sunshine, and no wind. We took our morning shot and when noon came we got a good position. We had drifted back east sixty-five miles. I knew it had been pounding us, but I had not realized it was that bad. In the next twenty-four hours there was flat calm, and as usual the engine refused to run. We made exactly eight miles. It was pleasant after the storm to get our clothes all dried out and enjoy the sunshine, but one day of just sitting is enough. The next day the wind came up right out of the Strait of Messina toward which we were headed. So for two more days, we worked against headwinds. The chart reported a strong current also coming out of the strait. Twice we approached the narrowest part, but with no wind or too much right on our nose, we would start going backward faster than forward. I don't know of anything more discouraging to a sailor. Two nights we looked at the light in the lighthouse on the southern point of Italy. With evening approaching on the third day, in desperation we decided to go up the east coast where the chart said something about marina or marino. We later found out *marino* means beach in Italian. I thought it meant a place to tie up a boat. We approached one cove that looked good, but was full of rocks. Meanwhile, the wind hauled off to the north and rose to about forty knots.

"We ought to go out to sea," I told Rosie. Her face took on a woebegone expression.

"Oh, Keith, I'm so tired and so are you. Let's try to find a place to anchor."

So we went another mile or two where the so-called marino was and found thirty feet of water within sight of the lights of a village. I threw out two anchors, one off each side of the bow. I'd never done that before and later I found out it was a bad idea. But that night I told Rosie, "I didn't know I could get so tired. If the anchor doesn't hold, we'll drag ashore. At least we can wade in." It was a rolly night, but we both slept.

The next morning Rosie was on deck when a small fishing boat came by. She gave a holler and it came alongside. In it were five brothers out of the nearby village. They had to go on then, but they said they would be back the next day to help us with the engine if I had not got it started by then.

There is an old saying among sailors that if you want a good night's sleep, just say to your wife, "I don't think the anchor is dug in too good." Then, you can hit the bunk and she will be up every fifteen minutes to look out. That means you don't have to. Rosie was already nervous, so I only commented, "Gee, I hope the anchor holds." Then, I turned in. We were anchored just off the village and a few lights were on all night.

At 3:00 A.M., Rosie was shaking and yelling at me. "We're dragging. We've dragged away from the village."

I stumbled sleepily up on deck in my long johns, looked toward shore, and sure enough, it was absolutely dark where the village should have been. There were lights farther down the coast, but not a glimmer toward the village. I tried to reason out what we should do now.

I knew there had been an outcropping of rocks downwind of us, jagged ones sticking out of the sea. There had been a stretch between those rocks and us with no houses onshore. The boat was still riding pretty smooth, so we weren't touching anything yet. I went forward and could see our two anchors out, but the lines were twisted together. I couldn't see how I would ever get both those anchors up at once the way the lines were twisted. I was damned sorry I had put two anchors out, but maybe they would grab before we hit the rocks. I peered intently into the darkness toward shore, looking for some landmark that I could remember. It was pitch-black, the wind was howling, and the waves were kicking us about. I climbed up on the vegetable box bolted to our deck and hung out in the shrouds, studying the shore. I thought I saw a whitewashed building of the type common in Greece and Italy. As I studied it intently, it seemed to me I recognized it. It was the little schoolhouse in the village. I was almost sure of that.

There had been a whitewashed church farther up the hill above the school. I studied the darkness, but decided that was the building for sure. The whole area was blacked out for some reason, but the longer I looked the more I could make out the faint outlines of buildings I recognized.

What a relief! We did not have to start swimming yet.

Early the next morning, the whole village turned out to help the fishermen out through the surf. When they came alongside, they told us about the power failure the night before. The one who spoke English told us, "It happens all the time around here."

They came aboard to help. One of the brothers had shoulders about three feet across. He took hold of the crank on our little two-cylinder and I pressed the starter button. The veins on his neck stood out and sweat rolled off him as he cranked that engine. The rpm's on the tachometer registered about right for the engine to fire and, by golly, it fired. I was sure glad to hear that.

Rosie started to cry with relief. The youngest brother put his arm around her to comfort her. We paid them what we could get them to take in dollar bills as we had no Italian lira. As I have said before, no matter what nationality, you cannot beat the commercial fishermen if you need help. Their town was named Bianca. They were anxious to leave, as they wanted to get back before the surf rose higher. They told us the surf was the least early in the morning and got steadily higher as the day wore on. We watched as, with the help of many villagers, they got ashore safely.

It took over an hour to get the anchors up, and a worse tangled mess I have never seen. But with the motor running, we didn't have to worry that without anchors we would drift down into the rocks or onto the beach.

When we again approached the Strait of Messina, we were able to slowly work on through with the motor at top speed and all sails up. At midnight we inched in behind the breakwater in the harbor of Reggio, Italy. The peace and quiet inside made it seem a different world.

With the motorcycles we rode around that end of Italy. Gasoline was two dollars U.S. a gallon and diesel one dollar a gallon. I needed kerosene for the stove but could not buy any since the government had confiscated every drop because Italians were burning it in their cars, since it was half the price of gasoline.

We desperately needed charts on to Gibraltar, so we decided to go to Napoli on the train. The train was European style: a little room for each party. A waiter came around with sandwiches, soft drinks, and wine for lunch.

In Naples the first large hotel we tried only had hot water from 6:00 P.M. to midnight. With everyone in that hotel trying to bathe in those short hours, I could guess how much hot water there would be. Two hotels later we found one with hot water all the time. I'll never take hot water for granted again. It will always be a luxury to be enjoyed to the utmost.

As we thumbed through the phone directory, because Rosie had forgotten to bring the name of the chart agency, I saw a listing for U.S. Sixth Fleet Air Support. Though it was 8:00 P.M., I called them. I apologized for calling after hours, but was informed they were on duty twenty-four hours a day. The operator called the duty officer who said, "Certainly, come out in the morning, and I'm sure we can help you." He gave us specific instructions on how to get there. We heaved a sigh of relief and went out to dinner.

At 6:00 A.M. we were up and at 7:00 A.M. we were at the gate. The duty officer came down to the gate to greet us. He apologized because the chart office did not open until eight, but in the meantime, we were welcome to go into the PX and eat breakfast. He would pick us up at eight and introduce us to the chart officer.

Two hours later we departed that air base with their good wishes, fourteen charts, and several new friends. On the way back to the hotel, Rosie said, "I didn't know there could be so much difference between people. Just look at the difference between those nice young, polite officers and enlisted men and that bunch of stuffed shirts at the embassy in Athens."

Our business completed, we took the train back to the *Mustang* that afternoon. In our compartment we met an old Italian and his wife. He told us that when he blew cigarette smoke in his wife's face, it made her sexy. She just smiled at him. They were about seventy years old.

The southern part of Italy was certainly pleasant, warm and balmy, with picturesque towers and castles, olive trees, and flowers. We left with a big supply of olives, which we ate as if we were eating peanuts. Our plan was to sail along the north coast of Sicily, then jump over to Sardinia. The Med was in one of its better moods. The sail down was a kettle of beer, as the Aussies say. We enjoyed watching Sicily go by so much, we decided to put into Palermo. It was a nice port, but dirty. With almost no tide there is nothing to wash these Mediterranean ports clean, no flushing action.

41

Waiting Out Another Med Storm

This may be hard to believe, but a second reason we put into Palermo was to buy bacon. We had not had any bacon for months. At breakfast we started talking about how we missed bacon. Soon we were worse than an alcoholic looking for a jug; we had a burning desire for bacon, bacon, bacon. At noon we decided to head into Palermo and buy bacon.

The city was full of butcher shops, but no bacon. They had meat, cheese, goat cheese, cream cheese, cow and burro cheese. They had olives, too, in bags, plastic, glass bottles, barrels, buckets, boxes, or your own container. We finally settled for five pounds of cheese and a gallon of olives. Really, cheese in scrambled eggs, especially dried scrambled eggs, is delicious.

Bread—the kind known as french bread in America—was the staple food in these parts. It seemed like everyone was either carrying two or three loaves under his arm or munching on one. It was also delicious. It was sometimes tough and always crusty, but a lunch of Italian wine, cheese, and bread was good fare.

Sadly sailing out of Palermo without the bacon, we set off for Sardinia. We had a little trouble finding the harbor and the city of Cagliari on the southeast end of the island. What mixed us up was one of those darned old stone lookout towers, which, according to the chart, was north of the city. When the tower appeared on the mountain, we decided we were too far north and turned south to get into the harbor. When the harbor did not show up when it should have, we did not know what to think. After taking several sun shots and crossing the lines, Rosie announced we were way too far south. I didn't believe her, but turned around just to humor her. Four hours later we sailed into the harbor.

We were amazed at these Mediterranean ports. Without exception, we were able to tie up alongside a wharf, or stern to. After anchoring for thirty thousand miles, we felt like royalty to be able to tie up. Every village and town had a breakwater. Many were started over a thousand years ago by fishermen to protect their boats. Both the Allies and the Nazis had a hand at improving them.

We would have liked to stay longer in Cagliari, but the weather was getting colder. Everyone advised us to get out before winter, for they said the Mediterranean was no place for a small boat in the winter. Our plan was to get to Gibraltar, and we had nearly a thousand miles to go.

Our chart showed little of the next port, only that it was shallow and care must be taken on entering. The Sailing Directions said, "For small craft only." Did that mean outboard, rowboats, or sailboats like ours? What's a small craft? One way to find out was to creep in with the lead line going all the time. This we did and must have been stirring up the bottom because we were down to six and a half feet. Perhaps the charts were vague because there was nothing there—no people, houses, buildings, or even goats. But there was a good, solid breakwater around a well-protected cove, a concrete wharf to tie to, and a sandy beach.

An Italian commercial fishing boat came in while we were there and tied up behind us. The skipper insisted we take two small skates. The skate is similar to a manta ray, practically all wings. The wings, according to the fisherman, were what you eat. I really did not want them, as we had seen many hanging on oriental boats and they did not appeal to me. The Orientals dried them to a crisp and considered them a delicacy.

I started to skin one with the fisherman watching. He took it out of my hands, threw it down on the dock, and in about fifteen minutes had it ready for the pan. He cut it into strips an inch wide, as long as the "wing," and skinned it later. It was one of the best fish we ever ate, very mild and white. The fisherman left and we enjoyed having the bay to ourselves.

We spent two days in this lovely, isolated little harbor, cooked steak on the hibachi, took a swim, and hiked up the hill to have a look at one of the old lookout towers. They were put together without mortar, yet had stood for hundreds of years. We thought of all the lonely hours men had spent there to watch the sea for approaching ships, friend or enemy. This day the sun shone hot and brilliantly and the sea was the famed royal blue.

October 19 we untied from the wharf and were off to a small island called Carolforte, thirty-two miles west. It was a good sail, but the water was getting a little rough by the time we slipped in behind the breakwater there. We planned to spend one night before making the six-hundred-mile jump to the Balearic Islands. We tied up about three in the afternoon, and as Rosie was filling in the log, she checked the barometer. We were getting ready for bed when she happened to look at it again. "Holy smoke, something must have gone wrong with this barometer." It had dropped two tenths of an inch in five hours. She tapped it gently and it went down a bit more.

By morning, the barometer had dropped nearly two inches from the previous afternoon. Still, the weather outside did not look too threatening. I decided we would wait one more day to see what developed. Like many Greek and Italian ports, Carolforte had a windbreaker as well as a breakwater. This one was about fifteen feet high.

By afternoon the wind had come up and by night it was blowing a gale. I went into the village and scrounged up three old tires and some planks. With our fenders, these helped keep the *Mustang* from surging up against the wharf. I also tied three extra lines on the boat. Allah must have had his arm around us for the next four days. The seas and wind beat against that wall until I thought it might tip over on us. About every ten minutes an extralarge sea would strike the wall and the wind would take off the top of the wave and send it cascading over the wall into the harbor fifteen feet downwind from us. We were continually drenched by a fine spray. The boat only huddled up to the wharf and wall a bit closer for protection, and there we sat.

We, for the most part, were huddled up to the stove in the cabin. Each afternoon we put on our oilskins and sweaters and walked up to the harbor master's office. In halting English, he would interpret the weather report for us. At the end, he would say, "No, don't go tomorrow either. Strong gale conditions, seas very rough." Rosie said it was the first time we'd had brains enough to stay in port during a storm. She had a short memory, as I could distinctly remember once when we were in port instead of out in the ocean. It was in Mexico.

A sailor is always worrying about something. Now, I was worrying about our dwindling supply of kerosene for the stove. With none available in Italy, our supply was down to ten days. If the storm kept up, we would have to burn brandy in the little one-burner alcohol stove we kept for emergencies. I had tried both brandy and cognac and they burned fine.

On the fifth day, the barometer rose, and in the morning, we went to the harbor master's office where he told us, "Gale moderating, seas moderate to rough." We waited until afternoon, then decided the wind had definitely gone down, the waves had stopped crashing over the sea wall, and the barometer was up, so we took off, feeling proud that we had outwitted that storm.

The Balearics were crowded, cold, and expensive. The yacht marina in Palma on the island of Mallorca charged eight-fifty a day to tie up one-quarter of a mile from the shower. It seemed all of Europe vacationed there. We met some Americans who had retired there a few years before because it was inexpensive, and now they were trying to figure out how to leave. It was a nice town, though, with broad tree-lined streets, sidewalk cafés, and good restaurants. Three days was all we could stand at eight-fifty a day. We had a very rough—and cold, cold, cold—overnight passage to Ibiza.

The Balearic Islands are about the same latitude as Denver and the winds seemed to come right off an iceberg. After several years in the tropics, we simply did not have enough clothes to get warm and resolved to buy some at the next port.

Once we reached the coast of Spain, however, the weather warmed a little, and though it was now November, we did not suffer so much from the cold. Besides, we were able to sail days and go into port every night. You don't get very far very fast doing that, but it is certainly pleasant. Torreviega, Cartagena, Aguilas, Almería, Matrial, Málaga, and José Banus all had breakwaters that we could get behind to tie up for the night. When the town looked interesting, we would stay a day or two, but Gibraltar was calling to us and we became just like an old workhorse going home.

All in all the Mediterranean proved to be a big disappointment to us. The Med had been the main reason we didn't take the route most boats making a circumnavigation of the world take—around the southern tip of Africa, northwest to the island of Saint Helena, from there more or less westward to somewhere in South America. A nice sail up past Aruba to the Windward and Leeward islands, and you are home.

Both of us had always wanted to see the Med, having heard of and about it for most of our lives. To me it sounded like Utopia. So, we choose the way up through the Red Sea into the Mediterranean.

Perhaps we were always comparing it to the South Pacific. Maye you can't leave paradise and ever be content again. It may have been the weather—which was terrible. Or, it may have been the feeling that if you weren't rich you weren't welcome.

Whatever the reason, the anticlimactic feeling about the Med stayed with us from Rodos all the way to the United States.

Another thing may also have begun. Having already succeeded in making it so far—and knowing all too well how suddenly things can go wrong—it is easy to focus on simply finishing the voyage rather than on enjoying the day-to-day events. Who wants to make it seven-eighths of the way around the world?

42

The Tale of a Pig

The last twenty-five miles into Gibraltar, neither of us took our eyes off the coast on our starboard side. Soon the great Rock of Gibraltar came into view. To us this was another milestone, as had been Panama, Tahiti, Australia, Singapore, and Egypt. At each one of these we only worked to get to the next one. To look ahead any further seemed foolish. Each seemed so far away we thought we might never make it. Rosie was sure we wouldn't. I, at times, had twinges of doubt, but never voiced it until we arrived. Milestones around the earth. I must admit there was a lump in my throat at our first good look at that old rock. It looked exactly like the pictures in our school books.

I dropped the anchor off the concrete wharf where all the other sailboats were, then had a bit of trouble backing into the narrow space between two English boats. I got a lot of advice from both of their crews, but no help. I finally managed to tie the stern lines to the concrete wharf. The Med was conquered, but it had not been easy. Since Gibraltar was a part of jolly old England, the officials were soon aboard. A fast, courteous shuffle of papers and we were in to stay as long as we cared to. They had not asked for cigarettes, whiskey, or tips. The last place like that had been Australia.

Gib was a joy. It's really not much of a place, something like three miles to south, less than that east to west, and fourteen hundred feet to the top. On Sundays everyone went for a drive. We were right in there with them on our cycles. They even had one-way streets. My first trip into town, naturally, I got on a one-way going wrong. About two blocks from the end, a bobby stopped me.

"I say, old chap, don't you know this is a one-way thoroughfare?"

It had just dawned on me, but I said, "No, I didn't know. I just got off a boat down in the harbor. I'll turn around and go back."

"Well now, that won't be necessary, my boy. Just carry on." The English have good manners.

Months ago Rosie had announced she was going home to see our kids for Christmas. I had tried several different tricks I had up my sleeve, but none of them was working. I put up signs saying, "Let's *not* go home for Christmas," and "I Like Gibraltar," "*Mustang* would be lonesome." My last try was "To heck with the kids." Nothing worked. Playing my hole card, I clearly showed her that a trip to Montana by plane would be instant bankruptcy. The next day a letter from her brother was in the post office with two tickets to Billings. I have never figured how they communicated without mail. He claimed he needed her to figure out his books, which had been fouled up by a crooked bookkeeper.

Rosie was like an old hen clucking among the chicks. Our youngest was twenty-eight years old and better off than we were. I don't know what happened, but I soon found myself on an airplane for London, New York, and Billings. As soon as I stepped off that plane, I knew why our relatives and friends wanted us to come home. They wanted me to shovel snow off their walks for two months.

After that, we needed to get back to the boat and rest up, but the boat needed work as usual: paint, cleaning, motor repair, sail repair, dinghy work, and new anchor chain. A boat always needs work, I think that is why they call them "she," but in this case, with the Atlantic ahead, nothing could be overlooked. Rosie still insisted the keel was loose, but I saw no signs of it when we hauled it out.

If you stay in a port long enough, something always happens to liven things up. Here it was Salty, a pig, who in some unknown way came ashore and took up residence in a cave. The authorities said there was no pig on Gib and if there was, it had not been cleared in. A pig would have to be cleared by the health authorities. The little local paper took up the challenge with pictures, letters, and phone calls. The immigration, health, and customs all said Salty must be removed at once. In no time there were Pro-Pig People and Anti-Pig People. The pros outweighed the antis.

Soon Salty had over three hundred pounds in his account at the bank—contributions mostly from pub patrons. If he had jumped ship and swam ashore, he had a right to asylum. Someone determined that Salty was not a male, but a female. Her name at once changed to Saltie. More money poured in for her defense. Soon the government backed off on their determination to eliminate Saltie.

Some of the headlines were:

SALTIE TIED UP WITH RED TAPE
GOVERNMENT SILENT ON SUBJECT OF PIG
FLEET GIFT FOR SALTIE'S DOWRY

Saltie's dowry benefited by nearly thirty pounds on Friday evening, when Petty Officer John Stanley of H.M.S. *Glamorgan* handed that amount into her fund.

TENTATIVE ARRANGEMENTS MADE OF SALTIE
SALTIE HAS DISAPPEARED

THE TALE OF A PIG

Saltie Is Found
New Home for Saltie Today

When we left Gib was giving serious consideration to getting a suitable mate for Saltie. I am sure they at least found her a home.

4 HEADED FOR HOME

43

Atlantic,
Here We Come

On March 1, 1975, we left with a feeling of having enjoyed it all and with many good friends behind. We planned a short 250-mile sail to Casablanca, Morocco. We had a weather report of twelve hours promising an east wind.

We had only a light wind and, against the current, were making only about one and a half knots. Ten hours later we were about fifteen miles west of Gibraltar when a hellish little storm hit us full blast from the west. By nine o'clock that night we were in the middle of a North Atlantic storm, with high winds and hailstones the size of marbles, which ricocheted up under our cockpit cover when they hit the deck. When the wind hauled around farther to the north, it put us on a lee shore, so we decided to go into Tangier. We didn't have a chart of the harbor, and it was night, but all hell was breaking loose on that ocean.

By 2:00 A.M. we had worked into the harbor and tied up to one of the main wharfs behind a big Yugoslavian freighter. I figured we could stay until morning when we could find a better place. The tides were high and the wharf fifteen feet above our heads, but I managed to tie to some tires hung on the wharf to protect the ships.

At 7:00 A.M., an armed guard told us we must move, now! He didn't care where, just move. A boy of about twelve watched the guard and when he left the boy indicated he would show us where to go. He came aboard and took us around a couple of wharfs to a small sailing club.

Tangier was a dirty city. The old town was walled and was

of white crumbling plaster with narrow streets, alleys, arched doorways and windows, and apartments all joined together. There were no yards, but occasionally there was a plant or two on a balcony.

Rosemary almost went crazy in the native bazaar where they had everything in the world for sale: beautifully colored rugs, brass platters, vases, leather goods, bolts of material. Every deal was a hassle. In their robes and burnooses, the Arabs stood around and haggled for hours. I think bargaining is their form of entertainment. We ended up buying a rug, which presented some problem of storage on the boat. I would not trust the Arabs to ship it.

A few days later we left a second time for Casablanca, now only two hundred miles away. We had an easy trip. Freighters were riding at anchor thick in front of the entrance to the harbor. What a miserable life that must be for the crews, waiting out in those roadsteads for their turn to pull into the wharfs to load or unload.

With our flea-size boat we sailed in among and around them into port and found somewhere to tie up. In this case, the Sailing Directions said the small boat harbor was back in the harbor until you could go no farther. It must have been over a mile to the end of the harbor, but there floated several sailboats.

We had been in Casablanca two hours when Rosie went to get a drink and could not get the pump to work. A pipe had broken between the tanks. We did not have a drop of water on board except our emergency water in plastic jugs on deck. We thought it lucky it had not broken in the Atlantic.

The Frenchmen in Casablanca were friendly and took us on rides into the country, to the public market, and to the giant bazaar. A French math teacher said his students often asked him if there wasn't an easy way to learn math. Only the rich go to school, and since they think they should not work, they also think they should not have to study. How can a man write out problems in arithmetic when his fingernails are so long he cannot hold a pencil?

Rosie said, "How can a country prosper when they consider

work degrading and noon hour lasts from twelve to five in the afternoon? It's no wonder they need help from someone else who is willing to work."

One day Rosie came home from the public market elated at finding some reasonably priced hamburger meat. "It was only two dollars a pound, compared to the four dollars I have been paying."

"This is great," I said. "Make sure you buy five pounds to have when we leave."

The next day she told me she had gone after more hamburger, but got quite a shock when she noticed that over some shops was a picture of a horse's head and over some was a picture of a cow's head. The two-dollar hamburger meat was from a "horse" shop.

"Should we eat the rest of that meat tonight?"

Since I am an old farm boy, I said, "Throw it out to the fish. I'm not so hungry that I have to eat an old friend."

44

Again Without a Rudder

On March 16 we cut close around the outer light at Casablanca, heading for the Canaries, six hundred miles away. It was a bright, sunshiny day with moderate seas and a twenty-knot warm wind out of the north. Forty-eight hours later we were once again tossing around. The winds had built up quite rapidly to gale force and there was nothing to do but take all sails down and put double lines on everything: boom, motorcycles, water drum, and anchors. I crawled around on deck to make sure all was secure. The barometer was down also, so this was not temporary. We had only been in the North Atlantic two weeks and already I hated it.

We lay ahull for three days, broadside to wind and waves. Most of the time I thought of all that nice sailing and weather in the South Pacific. Here the water was ice cold, so that about the only time we were warm was when we were bundled up in all our clothes under the blankets. The boat was leaking pretty badly again and Rosie was still talking about the keel being loose until I told her crossly to forget it.

"Even if it falls off, I can't do anything about it out here." I thought it was just her imagination.

Two days later I went on deck and things looked a little better. I decided I would start the motor and for a few hours just keep a heading toward the Canaries. I don't know why it continued to surprise me when the engine didn't start after riding out a storm. Yet, it never dawned on me that it wouldn't go until I pressed the starter button. *Clump*, and that was it. The wind was still blowing pretty strong, but I said, "To hell with it. I'm going forward to put up the small jib."

Rosie came on deck. I never went forward when it was rough unless she was in the cockpit so that she could see me if I fell overboard. I got the jib up, but we didn't seem to be doing too well. The sail kept flapping and cracking. Rosie was at the tiller, so I yelled at her to put the ship on course and stop messing around.

"I'm trying. Nothing happens."

"Let a real sailor at the tiller."

I took the tiller, but the *Mustang* continued acting very strangely. I took a quick glance at Rosie and I could tell by the stricken look on her face that she was thinking the same thing I was. We both dived out of the cockpit, lay on our bellies on deck, and looked overboard at the transom. The rudder was there. When the boat pitched with the stern up, one third of the rudder came out of the water.

"Work the tiller back and forth," I said. She did.

The rudder did not move.

If this trip hadn't done anything else for Rosie, it improved her vocabulary, in short, four-letter words anyway. I went forward to take the jib down again while we figured this one out. That damned Egyptian and his "guaranteed" welding job. Rosie was for going back to Alexandria and choking him.

She read and reread the Sailing Directions, charts, and any other information and came up with a conclusion as to where we could wind up. There was current down the African coast and the winds were northeasterly to southeasterly, making return to Casablanca impossible. It was three thousand miles to the South American coast where we would land on a lee shore if we just drifted. Our destination of the Canaries was directly downwind as the wind was blowing now. The question was whether we could sail this tub until we could swim ashore on the Canaries. If we got within swimming distance, what then? We would have to decide that when and if we got there.

Once again we started trying combinations of sails. We could not use the same arrangement we had in the Med because then we had the wind quartering our stern or on the beam. Now our destination lay directly downwind, and we could not afford to miss our destination, for then we would have the whole Atlantic to cross. As before, the big problem was to get the boat to come off the wind and headed the right direction. To get the boat to fall off, I put up a jib and a staysail, something like a small jib fitted inside the other, only in this case we let them both fill from the stern. I backed and sheeted them in until I thought something would give way. The boat came off the wind, and when the bow came to within 40 degrees of our desired course, I loosened the staysail a little. We began to sail 40 degrees off course but in the general direction of the Canaries.

We took our sights and found we were 350 miles from the harbor of Grand Canary, for which we had a detailed chart. The boat hung right on to that course. With the next morning shots, we could see we would have to change course, so we worked and worked to tack so that we could go 40 degrees on the other side of our course. We had to tighten the sheets until the wind caught the sails from the other side, then loosen them just enough so that the boat did not turn too far. We were not tacking in the sense that we were bringing our bow into the wind, but rather the stern. It was better in a way than our other experience because once we were on course we didn't have to handle the sheets, but just check the compass every ten minutes or so. In that fashion, we made about fifty miles a day on course, crossing our course line every twenty-four hours.

I kept out of Rosie's way the first few days. I don't hear too well, but I still caught snatches of her thinking out loud. The Arabs caught it for days. The boat came in for plenty. The builder of the boat got a working over. And the architect, according to her, wasn't fit to live anywhere but Siberia. It would serve the Russians right.

I made one attempt to fix the rudder so that we could turn the boat a little if necessity arose. I put the bos'un's chair over the stern. Tying on a safety harness, I went over the stern with a six-inch, deep-throated C-clamp. My plan was to attach the C-clamp on the trailing edge of the rudder. Then with two three-eighth-inch lines on the clamp coming up on each side of the boat, through a pulley, and tied to the tiller, I thought it might give us one good turn in an emergency.

But as I hung in the bos'un's chair, I was like a pendulum and swung back and forth wtih every roll, knocking first against the boat and then dunking into the icy water. I could not hang on and still use both hands to do the job. I finally managed to get the clamp on, not too securely, and had to get back up on the boat, for I was shivering violently. I went in once more and tried to tighten it, but I did not have much faith in the arrangement.

After seven days with no rudder, we sighted one island. We were still headed for Las Palmas on Grand Canary. Of course, the bad part was in approaching that lee shore. Anchoring outside the harbor would be impossible, for it was far too deep— no shelf as in Egypt.

The Sailing Directions said there were many fishing craft in the area, so many that a good watch should be kept day and night. I decided Rosie should dig out the Spanish-English dictionary and prepare a letter saying something like this in Spanish:

We are the sailing vessel *Mustang*. We have no rudder and
no lights. Could you send a towboat to help us enter the
harbor? Our boat is orange colored and thirty-two feet
long. Our weight is ten tons. Please give this letter to the
port captain by radio or note. Thank you. Keith Jones,
Skipper.

Rosie wanted to add one more line, but I would not let her.
It was "No brains, either."

We planned to give this to one of the many fishing boats that
were supposed to be in the area. I planned to wave my arms
and holler to attract their attention and, perhaps, they would
come alongside. We saw three small freighters, a lot of air-
planes, another island, and two whales heading north, but no
fishing boats. Tacking and maneuvering to stay upwind of the
harbor, it seemed as if we were all over that end of the
Atlantic.

"Any other time we would be hard pressed to avoid hitting
them," Rosie observed. The current heading south was strong
in this area, and it soon became clear we would be carried past
the entrance, so we had to try to sail into the harbor. Perhaps
closer in we would meet a boat.

It was nerve-racking business. We were sailing more or less
down the row of rocks called a breakwater so that we would be
sure to see the end of it. When we spotted the entrance and
had to make a right-angle turn, we hauled on our ropes to the
rudder. Fortunately it held and we were just congratulating
ourselves when damned if another row of jagged rocks didn't
show up right in front of us—another breakwater. It was not
on the chart. Could we be in the wrong port? By then the wind
had petered out to almost nothing, but we were able to turn
and go down this second breakwater and head inside of that,
once more using the ropes. But one was hung up, and in my
haste, I gave it a hard tug and must have dislodged the clamp.
We tacked at least twenty times trying to work on inside. We
were in the middle of about fifty boats, mostly fishing boats
and a few sailboats. There were big three-hundred-foot trawl-
ers from many countries swinging at anchor. We almost hit
two of them.

"Why weren't those buggers out fishing?" I asked Rosie. "Lazy bunch of bums."

In forty feet of water by the lead line, we finally threw out the anchor. The wind had died completely and there wasn't more than fifteen more minutes of daylight. This was a three-rum day. A three-rum anchor drink. Our nerves were so frazzled, I thought Rosie would jump right into the bay and swim for the airport.

I asked, "How do you feel about flying home tomorrow?"

As I was rowing ashore the next day, I stopped to talk to an English couple on a sailboat. He said, "We watched you come in last evening. That's a good-looking boat you have there."

"Thanks, but we had a broken rudder." He had probably been sitting in the cockpit with a drink in his hand. He could have come and helped.

"We couldn't tell there was anything wrong," he said.

I didn't say anything more, but I wondered what kind of sailor he must have thought I was to have damned near hit that big trawler. On better acquaintance he turned out to be a rather nice sort of bloke. I'm sure he would have helped had he known we needed it.

The only two marine ways in town were busy. Most of those fishing boats at anchor needed work and were waiting to be hauled. The man at one told me he could take me in four days.

"How much?" I asked.

He never batted an eyelid. "Five hundred dollars."

I knew he was giving me the old American discount, so I told him I'd think it over. Seventy dollars would have been a big price. I thought to myself, I'm getting tired of being a foreigner, and the minority at that. I'm also tired of the "American discount."

As I walked up and down the waterfront, I saw a concrete wall with a high board fence in front with a locked gate. A sign said, "Club de Nautic Motor." Taking this to mean a motorboat club, I assumed we were in the sailboat club. I went back to the *Mustang* and rowed over to the club to find the manager. He spoke no English, but I got through to him what I wanted. He gave me permission to lean our boat against the club wall for three days for ten dollars a day. Back at the *Mustang* again I tore the diesel apart to see why it would not run. I thought if Rosie could run the engine slow, I could row ahead in the dinghy and put our bow around to guide it into that spot next to the wall.

The problem with the diesel was water entering the exhaust during the storm. With water on the pistons, the starter would not turn the motor over. The next day I got it running and determined to fix that exhaust differently after we got the rudder repaired.

We moved over to the wall the next day. There was only six feet of tide, so I was wading around in the water taking the rudder off. It was evident that the rudder had broken in the same place—the weld. That Arab welder was lucky he wasn't in hearing distance.

I took the rudder to a machine shop and they told me they couldn't do it until the following day. Then I would need another day at low tide to get it back on. When I got back to the *Mustang*, the manager of the club came up and started talking ninety miles an hour in Spanish. I could not understand him, but I could tell by his actions that he wanted me to move the boat. Right then and there I made up my mind that if they moved me, it was going to be by force.

Finally, I said, *"Uno momento"* (one moment). Leaving him there waving his arms, I got a Swiss fellow who spoke English and Spanish. He had offered to help if I needed it. Back inside the motor club I found the manager and my Swiss friend asked him what the problem was. In a flurry of Spanish and motions, the manager said I had to move. He said I was in the road. The Swiss reminded him that he had told me I could stay three days. Well, now he had decidedly differently.

The Swiss turned to me and said, "What he really wants is more money."

I told the Swiss our bargain.

"Well, he has heard how much the marine ways was going to charge, so he probably has decided he agreed too cheaply. These people's word is worth nothing."

"How much does he want?"

The Swiss turned back to the manager and talked some. Then he turned back to me. "Fifteen dollars."

"Tell him I will give him a full quart of bourbon." The Swiss passed that information on and the manager agreed and the deal was made on that basis. The bourbon had cost me two dollars in Gib and we don't drink the stuff. Two days later I had the rudder back on the *Mustang*.

We had a sailmaker stitching the sails. He gave us a day when he would be through. Two weeks later he got them done. The commodore of the yacht club had told me to bring our chronometer into the club desk and he would see that it was repaired. We took it in the second day we were there. Two weeks later, when we were getting ready to leave, I saw him and asked if it was done. He had never touched it and, in fact, had obviously forgotten all about it. No one could even find our hundred-dollar timepiece. Just the day before we left they finally found it, unrepaired, so we had to leave with an inaccurate timepiece to navigate the Atlantic.

There was a big supermarket in Las Palmas. Rosie went crazy buying canned food and dried things for our Atlantic crossing. I must have made twenty trips on the Honda carrying provisions. The dollar rate of exchange went down every day, so paying a dollar fifty for a pound of dried beans seemed like a terrible price, but Rosie said, "We have to eat, so I just close my mind to the prices."

The English couple left to go back to Gibraltar. They were gone three days and sailed back in to anchor in their old spot. They said it was just too rough out there, beating upwind and up-current. Later they made arrangements to ship their boat on the deck of a freighter. Our Swiss friend told us of a little port called Puerto Rico on the other side of the island that he said always had beautiful sunny weather, so on the sixteenth of April we sailed out of Las Palmas for an uneventful trip to the port of Puerto Rico. It was lovely and, as the Swiss said, warm and sunshiny. It was also full of European yachts and condominiums.

We met a very nice Dane there, Jorgen Gronlund, photographer to the queen, who had a calendar-publishing business and a sailboat in Denmark. He was kind enough to invite us to his apartment for a bath. People, God bless them, always offered us baths. Is it possible we were encrusted with salt and had BO?

45

Rosie Heard It, All Right

Out of Puerto Rico, we were bound for the Cape Verdes Islands, nine hundred miles away. We had fair winds, but right behind us, which made that boat roll like a fat old lady. Rosie again complained about hearing a *thump* every time the boat rolled. I dismissed it, but she became more insistent that something was amiss. Since I am about half deaf, I lead a more peaceful life than someone with acute hearing like Rosie's. The wind screaming in the rigging, the rudder flopping back and forth when it was broken, a loose halyard flapping against the aluminum mast didn't bother me a bit. But they bugged Rosie and the dear girl then bugs me. Naturally, I turn the complaints off as long as possible, but since she is an insistent girl as well as a dear one, she made me settle down to find this *thump, thump.*

Down in the cabin, I took up the floorboards, and putting my best ear to the keel bolts, I could definitely hear a *thump, thump* with every roll of the boat. That was bad tidings coming from that area. I went back to the cockpit where she was on the tiller and tried to tell her that I thought it was a whale scratching his back on our keel. Ḥaving been married to me as long as she has, she can tell in a minute when I'm lying and she only said, "What do we do now?"

How or why she expects me to come up with instant solutions to life's daily problems, I can't figure out. But she does. I said, "Well, all I can think of is that we will not push it and hope it hangs on another five hundred miles." I did not mention that also that morning I had discovered oil in the bilge and

noted that while we were running the motor to charge the batteries we were using oil at a very fast rate. The worst part
about that was that if we didn't charge the batteries, we
couldn't use the autopilot, which meant someone on the tiller
twenty-four hours a day.

I have found the easiest approach to a problem like this is to
do nothing. If you are not drowning, why swim? So, we took it
slow and easy the rest of the way and eleven days after leaving
Puerto Rico, we sailed into the harbor at Mindelo, São Vicente.

As we entered the harbor, I had the motor turning over
slowly, but once we were through the entrance, there was a
forty-knot wind blowing straight at us. I could not figure out
where it came from. Rosie put the engine in gear and I ran
forward to bring down the sails. We were among boats and
ships of all descriptions. Give me the open ocean anytime.
These crowded harbors with rocks, wharfs, ships, and beaches
all around only get you into trouble. As soon as the sails were
down, we turned broadside and began drifting downwind.

"Speed up the motor," I shouted, trying to make myself
heard above the howling wind. She did, but we still were out
of control. Hastily, I put the sails up again and we worked
forward upwind among the boats. It was hard to tack back and
forth between the boats, so I lowered the sails again so that we
could motor into position. Back we go! Rosie wasn't doing anything right. I went back to the tiller to do this thing right. Flub-
bing up in front of a bunch of sailors is embarrassing.

"I'll take this thing up to the anchorage."

"Go ahead," she screamed at me, "if you think you're so
smart."

We still drifted downwind sideways. The devil himself must
have a hold of us, I thought. I couldn't believe it. We were
heading straight for a trawler. Nothing to do but put up the
sails again. Rosie observed that no doubt the propeller had
fallen off, or the keel.

"Yeah, sure! You're just a regular mechanic now, aren't
you?"

Since I didn't have time to give her a course in diesel me-
chanics, I rushed forward for the umpteenth time and raised
the sails. My arms felt like they had pulled out of their sockets.

Haul that halyard. Pull that sheet. Untangle that damn knot in the sheet. Take this boat quickly. Can't you see we are about to strike that dumb tug?

At last we worked to the only open spot in the harbor and dropped the hook. It didn't hold and we were dragging astern. I rigged up another anchor and threw it overboard. With the second anchor out, we seemed to be holding.

Rosie went below to fix an anchor drink. I zeroed in on several points ashore to determine if we were dragging. There was an old derelict aft of us. I decided that if we dragged again I would tie to him until morning.

Being a slow thinker is no picnic. It took me a night of puzzling to figure out the problem. Since there was no place in this port to haul out, I was hoping I could solve it. Next morning, I went down into the engine room. It was a space where, unless I sat with my head bowed at all times, I came up with five bumps on it. With the engine troubleshooting book in one hand, I took off the transmission cover and tightened the clutch. Any damn fool should have known the clutch was slipping. Turning bolt B three quarters of a turn to the right did it.

With the cover back on and only two bumps in my head, I came on deck and started the motor. It was the clutch all right. We bounded forward like a greyhound at the races. That proved the clutch worked. Slackening up on the anchor lines when we bounded forward must have pulled the anchors loose, however, as I could never get them to hold again in that spot.

Saying "to hell with this," I decided to go over and tie to the wharf and see what the harbor master had to say about that. The motor worked fine, at least it pushed us in the right direction, but it was using oil about as fast as I could pour it in.

We tied up between two small sailing freighters and I took our papers to the port captain's office. He was Portuguese and treated me with all politeness. Later, Rosie was below straightening up and I was trying to get the deck in some sort of order when I heard a voice saying something in English. When I looked up, there stood on the dock a big—I mean like 260 pounds—blond, smiling Viking.

"Aello, aello," he said.

"Hello," I replied.

"Var you cum from?"

I told him the Canaries and invited him aboard for coffee. He was another good-natured, big Swede out to take a look at the world. Over coffee, I asked him if he ever had had any experience with a Swedish Albin diesel.

"I can take vun apart and put it together blindfolded. Do you have vun? Vat's the problem?"

I told him that all the oil was going into the bilge as fast as I poured it into the crankcase.

He said, "I have look."

I weigh 160 and that engine room seemed cramped to me, but somehow he slid his 260 pounds into it to have a look. Coming back on deck, he hollered to someone on the boat he was from. Three minutes later a young Frenchman arrived with a wrench. Carl, the Swede, introduced him and he came aboard smiling. Carl took the wrench, squeezed through the engine-room hatch, and in five minutes said, "Let's try engine."

I started it up and ran it for a half hour while we drank coffee and talked. When I checked the oil level, it had not leaked a drop.

"That engine just needed to hear some Swedish," Rosie told him.

"*Ja.* It takes a Svede to talk to Svedish motor."

As it was about lunchtime, Rosie invited them both to lunch: newly baked french bread bought that morning in town; cheese, cold cuts, and meat bought in Las Palmas; and Heineken beer from Holland. The Frenchman grinned broadly and the Swede drank beer. All the beer they had was Portuguese and this was like home to them.

During lunch we found out they were off a small salvage boat. It was a converted Dutch canal barge. The Swede was the diver and the Frenchman his tender.

Rosie asked, "Since you are a diver, could we hire you to go down and look at our keel bolts? We think they are loose."

"*Ja,* I do that."

After lunch they left and returned shortly with knife, mask, tanks, and a steel brush. They climbed down to our boat and the Frenchman helped the diver on with the tanks and gear. Over the side he went, backward. Bubbles came up from under the *Mustang* up and down the length of the keel. He would come up every so often asking for a big hammer, or a big pry bar.

Another half hour went by. He came up huffing and puffing, handed his tanks to us on deck, and climbed up our boarding ladder. I was surprised it stood the strain. Water drained off his great body. Blowing and snorting he panted and sucked in great gulps of air. I laughed at his showmanship. For Rosie and future lunches aboard, he really put on a great show. I appreciated it, too. He was really something. In less than two hours he had fixed our engine and diagnosed the trouble with our keel. Wiping down with the three towels Rosie produced, he reminded me of a great old bull sea lion we had seen in the Galápagos: clumsy on land, but graceful in the water, big, strong, no neck. All the Swede needed was a moustache and a tusk or two.

"*Ja*, she is loose, the keel. I can push with hand."

He and I went below and lifted the floorboards to look closely at the nuts on the keel bolts. To me they looked rusty and dirty. I was positive we would never be able to move them. According to his measurements underwater, they would have to be taken up at least two threads before they would begin to tighten. We all discussed the problem. If the bolts, even one of them, broke off, there would be nothing to do but haul out somehow, take the keel from underneath, and insert a new bolt. After looking at some of the repair jobs on the local boats close to us, that looked like planned disaster.

Carl stood up and said, "Ve go." They went. Late in the day he came back to measure the outside dimensions of the one-and-one-quarter-inch nuts. "I make wrench," he said and left again. Before he got away, we invited him and any of his buddies for drinks that evening.

He said, "Ve cum."

The crew of that salvage boat was a great source of entertainment. The skipper was Belgian; the woman cook was Indonesian; a partner was Dutch; Carl was the Swede; and his line tender, French. Their only common language was English. If the Frenchman and the Dutchman were talking it was usually in French, but if the Dutchman was talking to the Belgian, it was in Dutch. So it went. We always envied the Europeans their use of many languages.

The next morning Carl and his helper were on board to tighten the keel bolts. They had made a socket wrench five feet long to fit our bolts, all from bits and pieces of scrap from the pile on their boat. Most of it had been brought up from the deep while they were salvaging machinery off sunken craft. The wrench even had a movable handle. It was a surprise to me when each bolt turned on its threads without difficulty. In about four hours, our keel was tight again. The forward bolts only took up one thread, but the after bolts required as many as three full threads. When the tightening was complete, they gave me the wrench.

What this amounted to was that in about forty-eight hours, Carl fixed our engine, fixed our keel, and brought Rosemary's spirits up 1,000 percent. For all this they would take no pay. We took the whole crew into town several times for dinner and gave them all some bottles of our duty-free liquor from Gibraltar.

Carl wrote in our guest book: "Thank you for rum, bourbon, whiskey, and everything. I will send you the bill from my doctor at the alcoholic clinic."

We were invited to their boat several times. It was an interesting habitat for a group of young "goers." The main table was made of planks put together six by six on top of their scrap-iron bin. Bunks and gear were everywhere. A few chickens were in a pen close by. The young, rather pretty Indonesian cook slept with the Belgian skipper in the wheelhouse. The head was a small house suspended over the stern. Their main food was cheese and french bread. They were thinking of eating the chickens. "We've had those damned chickens for two months now and they haven't laid an egg."

We later heard from Carl that the day after the islands gained their independence from Portugal, the salvage boat was run out by gunfire. They had been diving on a wreck just offshore, with full permission of the new authorities, when about thirty soldiers appeared on the beach and began firing. The skipper pulled Carl out at once and they departed for Dakar, Senegal, with bullets singing overhead and glancing off the steel hull. They were a great bunch and we were more than lucky that they happened to be there when we were.

May 4, 1975, found us leaving the Verde Islands for Barbados on the other side of the Atlantic. If the old tub would just hold together, we just might make it around the world. We had just 3,550 miles before we would be crossing our own longitude line: 2,050 to Barbados, then another 1,500 to 75 degrees west, 23 degrees north. Until this day it had never seemed so close.

46

The Home Stretch

We had the wind right on our tail. Sailing straight downwind is difficult, but home was over the horizon and we did not want to spend too much time going north and south. It was rough and rolly the whole time.

When I was at the helm one day, Rosie watched the compass a bit and said, "Don't you know a straight line is the shortest distance between two points?"

"I, too, took geometry in school. What I did not take was a course in sailing a sailboat straight downwind with thirty-knot winds and high following seas." That put her in her place.

We continued rolling the sails under on both sides about every five minutes. Nineteen days and we were rounding the island of Barbados, as always just at dark. The yacht anchorage was just a roadstead in the lee of the island and we crept in among the yachts after dark. But it was great. We had the big Atlantic behind us.

The next day we saw that getting ashore would be a problem, with breakers two or three feet high most of the time. We raised anchor and went about a mile farther into a short, deep bay called the Careenage. It was a creeklike narrow harbor for small inter-island freighters and a good spot from our viewpoint. We tied up alongside one of those freighters. Everyone was black and spoke good English and was friendly. We felt safe to leave the boat. First order of business was to go ashore by climbing over various items of cargo and find a hotel with an ample supply of hot water. We rented a room at a small local hotel for two days and each took at least five hot baths. So much salt came off me that my skin felt odd.

We still had fifteen hundred miles to go, but we felt the trip was almost over. Our greatest concern was now to make this last jump to the States without losing the boat. We were almost home, but the hurricane season was almost upon us, and there were still some nasty sailing grounds indicated on the chart—lots of reefs, currents, and tides.

The ninety-five miles from Barbados to Bequia was an overnight jump. We spent ten days in this quiet, well-protected harbor, shell hunting, snorkeling, and visiting with other people on yachts, mostly Americans. It was like a vacation. There was a sailmaker to repair our badly worn sails and we sold one of our motorcycles. Going up through the Windward Islands, anchoring every night, was easy sailing. One of our favorite places was little, isolated Cumberland Bay, where the natives take a stern line ashore after you have dropped your bow anchor. They tie it to a palm tree. Here we got a concert by a local steel-drum band. The water was crystal clear, and after a swim to shore, there was a placid little creek with a deep pool for a freshwater bath. Fifty feet later it tumbled into the Caribbean. Rosie found out our propeller was loose, so we stayed three days, diving down, pulling the cotter pin, unscrewing the nut, and putting another washer on so that the nut would tighten up against the prop. It was such an idyllic spot, we were glad of an excuse to stay.

From there we went up through the Leeward Islands—Martinique, Guadeloupe, historic Antigua, and English Harbor. There we met Bill Gilson, a former Billings weatherman who had taught us to navigate, for a fun reunion.

I could not get over the habit of taking on water at every opportunity. Here we were with water available every thirty to one hundred miles, but I still filled every gallon jug and teapot when we left port. Rosie said I was a waterholic. I may have been a waterholic, but she was a foodaholic. She couldn't stop taking on provisions for three months ahead. Habits are hard to break.

In Fort-de-France, while trailing the dinghy, we caught its painter in our prop, which required another diving session to cut it away. Saint Eustatius, Saint Martin, St. Barthélemy, Saba were all good spots, but we had to push, for in July the hurricane season begins in earnest, and already it was June.

Saint Thomas was our first American territory for many moons. It was great—American supermarkets, American money, no language barrier, and if we felt like complaining, we could do it loud and clear. Two of our daughters and their husbands met us for a two-week cruise. Rosie was clucking around like an old mother hen with some of her brood. There we met another Dane, a professor at the University in Puerto Rico. We cruised with him and his family while our children were with us, meeting in Lime Juice Bay, Hurricane Harbor, and other delightful little bays.

Around the World

After they all left came the big decision. Should we keep sailing the Bahamas during hurricane season or should we hole up some safe place for four months? I was in favor of moving on. I thought it was time we got home and started refurbishing our bank account. Inflation had eaten a big hole in our very modest income. Rosie wanted to wait.

"We've come this far. Why take a chance now on running into a hurricane? I don't think the poor old *Mustang* could weather a hurricane."

"Of course it could. But, I don't think we will have to. The weather reports are excellent and in English. They track these hurricanes from miles out to sea."

"So, what good does that do us?"

"Well, if one is headed in our direction, we will just duck into some harbor and wait."

"But what if there isn't a harbor?"

"We'll never be too far from land. We'll go through and mark all the hurricane holes between here and Florida, so we'll know where we can duck into. Then, if one heads our way, we will just sail into one of the harbors we've marked and stay put."

"I don't know. You make it sound so easy, but that's about the time our motor will quit or something."

So the argument went. But, as we discussed this, we kept moving from port to port: east coast of Puerto Rico, south coast of Puerto Rico, Dominican Republic, Haiti, moving west all the time. July came and went. August came and went. We were still working west, one port at a time.

From my diary:

September 2, 1975. Fort Liberté, Haiti. Well, we have been in Haiti or close to it for three days and have run aground three times. The bottoms are covered with sea grass and shoal rapidly. The last time, two hours ago, we were approaching a broken-down dock and two hundred yards out we grounded. Took two hours to get off with the anchor and winch, and putting the boom out and sitting on it, and running the engine in reverse. This town is dirt poor. We are trying to get the weather forecast, but the radio is acting up. Rosie gets so mad when she can't hear the forecast, she slams pans and pots around. I told her today that the day we got to Florida, I would give her a hammer and let her bust the radio into little pieces.

September 3. Cap Haitien. We came in yesterday at 1500 hours through a poorly marked channel and tied up to a wharf. Passed the place where Columbus is reported to have shipwrecked one of his boats. How he got around these parts at all is a mystery. The town is very poor. Rosie is buying a lot of wood carvings.

At Cap Haitien, I said to Rosie, "We can't stop here. We only have six hundred miles to go."

"Well, I don't know why not. Hurricane season will be over in a couple of months. We can go then."

"If we get a good weather report tonight, let's leave in the morning. What do you say?"

"Ummmm. Maybe."

Lucky me. The report came in loud and clear and good news. So on September 9, we left for Great Inagua in the Bahamas, 111 miles away. From there on up to Staniel Cay, we had good weather, good sailing, and beautiful anchorages with clear water and sandy beaches. On that leg, we crossed our own longitude line. We had gone around the world! But on that day, September 15, we were so busy looking for some much-needed landmarks on the Exumas that we hardly had time to celebrate.

At Staniel Cay, we got the word that a hurricane was headed in our direction. It was a long way out yet, but we were right in its path. Staniel Cay was not a hurricane hole, offering only partial protection. Two or three other boats were there also and we all got together and talked over what to do. Some of us went out in a small motorboat and tried to find a better place to anchor, but the best places were too shallow for me to get into with our six-and-one-half foot draft. At last I decided I would go offshore, put out my heaviest anchor, put on a life preserver, and turn on the engine. I told Rosie she could stay onshore.

"Well, after all this, I guess we don't want to do that. We might as well go together. Ha, ha."

The hurricane was then in Puerto Rico and had caused a lot of damage. The next morning it was in Hispaniola. It had changed course somewhat and now should miss us by fifty miles or so. I pointed out that had we stayed in Puerto Rico or Haiti, we would have been right in its path. By the following day we were no longer in its path, for it took off over Cuba and into the Gulf of Mexico.

We left in company with Emily and Jack Donnelly on the *St. Paulie Girl* and had a perfect sail to Allans Cay and Nassau, twenty-knot breezes and smooth seas. We did not stay long in Nassau, for at fifteen dollars a day to tie to the wharf, it was too expensive.

September 26 we were heading across the Gulf Stream to Fort Lauderdale and the good old United States. That Gulf Stream heads north at the rate of from two to four knots. It was a beautiful day for motoring, not a ripple, not a breath of air. Twenty miles out of Fort Lauderdale the motor quit.

"I can't believe it," Rosie said. "Something's got to happen right up to the last minute. I suppose now we'll get carried to New York City before the wind comes up."

It took me two hours to locate and fix the trouble. By then we were nearly past the Lauderdale breakwater. We chugged along, bucking the current, until nine o'clock that night. That last port, we just had to enter at night. No use breaking our record now.

We tied up to the customs dock and just had to congratulate ourselves. No fanfare, but it felt good to be home. We arrived with three months' provisions and enough water to last fifty days. Whoopee!

48

After the Trip

We lay alongside the customs dock, which was plainly marked. A sign said that after hours and weekends we must go to the public phone on the dock and call customs. Overtime would be charged on weekends.

A most congenial fellów came out about ten o'clock the next morning. He should have been good-natured: It was Sunday, and we had to pay twenty-five dollars for overtime, which would go straight to him.

It didn't matter. All we wanted was to be free to roam the streets, to walk into a good American restaurant. What we would order had been decided the night before while we were sitting on deck watching the lights of the city come on. It would be steak, a large one please; baked potato also—they are almost unheard of in any foreign country—and a tossed green salad with plenty of blue cheese dressing on it.

Customs cleared us in about fifteen minutes, filling out the necessary papers and giving a cursory examination, which took about fifteen seconds. Then a quick handshake to welcome us back to the States.

Rosemary then went to the phone and called Jack and Emily Donnelly, the couple we had met in the Bahamas. They came out immediately with a bottle of wine to drink to our safe return. Piling into their car, the first place Rosie wanted to visit was a supermarket. When she walked into that large store, which was crammed with all the goodies of life, I thought she was going to carry the whole place back to the boat. There was nothing to do but restrain her. We all kept telling her, "You can come back tomorrow. We're not leaving this port for some far-off place." She couldn't get used to the fact that there would be another supermarket just around the next corner.

That evening we all went out for dinner. It was certainly a pleasure to buy four big steaks. What joy to eat grain-fed beef done to a turn. We all wanted them done differently; they were all perfectly cooked.

The next morning Emily piloted us up the New River to the New River Marina where a spot was found for us and arrangements made to haul out the next day. That was operating a bit fast for me, but it was that day or wait five days until they had another opening in their schedule. So, two days after returning to the States, we were lifted out and setting on dry land. I couldn't believe it. Here we were with a scraper in one hand and a wire brush in the other. No rest for the wicked. We hadn't hauled out since leaning against that concrete wall in the Canary Islands; the bottom was a bit cruddy but not too bad.

We had made the decision to sell the boat, move ashore, and try to get our wits about us while adapting to the new environment in which we found ourselves. In the last few days we had been informed of and had learned about this nasty inflation. We had realized that for the last couple years our dollars didn't go as far as they had before. We had blamed it on the rate of exchange.

It seemed a bit odd not to be going to another strange port. Now all at once things had changed. It seemed rather shocking and perplexing to us. Maybe good, maybe bad.

It took ten days of scraping, sanding, and painting to put the boat into salable condition, "cosmetically" as the boat salesmen say.

The yard put us back into the water about five o'clock one evening. We had a "for sale" sign ready to put on the stern as we were laying stern to the shore in our new slip. By noon the next day I was dickering with a fellow who was interested. He said he would go home and think about it, so we were somewhat surprised when at eight o'clock the next morning he was back to take us to his bank to transfer our asking price to us.

Things were moving too fast for this poor old sheepherder from Montana. It would put us out of our home of several years, right out on the street so to speak. Never one to turn down money, I, of course, took the check, cashed it, and started an account in that bank for us. He gave us two days to vacate the boat, as he was anxious to go over to the Bahamas on some deal he had going.

There we were; we didn't even have a suitcase, didn't have a car, didn't know where we were going nor what we were going to do. I felt about the same as I had when my dad had broken my plate that day when I was seventeen years old and told me that I had better think about leaving home, soon, today in fact. It is an odd feeling to suddenly be homeless.

The people in the slip next to us were leaving for Panama in a couple of days. The captain of the boat told me that he had an old Cadillac for sale. He had also been eyeing that big ninety-pound anchor I had bought back in the Cape Verde Islands.

We talked a bit, and pretty soon Rosie and I owned a car. He owned that anchor and a fifty-dollar bill I had had in my pocket. He had to use the car one more day to haul in supplies for the trip south. That meant that we would have to vacate the boat on the following day and be ready to move out to somewhere. We had decided to head west at least, probably go to San Diego where we had joined a yacht club and had liked the city. On the way south we had considered locating there upon our return to the United States.

We decided to unload the boat making two piles out on the dock behind us: one pile to sell or give away, the other pile to go into the Cadillac. This worked okay except that the pile for the Cadillac was larger than the inside of it. It took about six hours to sell or give away everything we couldn't carry. Very few items went into the garbage cans. When we pulled out of that marina the rear bumper was almost on the ground.

After a five-day trip to San Diego we found a motel while we looked things over. San Diego didn't look quite the same then as it had before. There was a lot more traffic, more freeways, and more people. They were all driving ninety miles an hour on and off the freeway right downtown. We decided to go up to Billings, Montana, where we were better acquainted and there weren't so many people. It seemed that the old car was riding lower than ever. Ten more pounds of air in the tires and we were headed north.

49

Epilogue

To the people in Wyoming or Montana there are four directions besides north, south, east, or west. They are down south, out west, back east, or up north. The twelve hundred miles from San Diego to Billings is really up north.

In the old Cadillac it was a three-day trip, but the car made it in good shape. Driving a car gives a man time to think, and the farther we drove the more it seemed we were doing the right thing by going back to our old home. We knew most of the people there. We knew the bankers and they knew us. It seemed that we should have everything going for us to make another start.

Our oldest daughter had invited us to stay with her family. Even her husband had invited us. They had two children aged five and seven.

We certainly did appreciate them asking us in, but after two days it was easy to see that three days would be enough of that.

"Rosie," I said, "call up that real estate friend of yours. It's about time we bought a house, I think."

He picked us up the next morning to go house hunting. We liked the first one we looked at, so I made an offer to the owner, which he accepted. The house was pretty much of a wreck. We moved in, working on one room at a time—at first living in one room. It was good therapy for us. A person can't be thinking about sailing while he is fighting loose plaster and squeaky floors.

We had no sooner become settled than that same agent came

by and said, "Keith, I think I have another house you can buy right now and make some money on it." We laid down the tools to take a look at the house—and bought it that day. All of this was, of course, on borrowed money.

I only bought the houses that I figured I could restore in thirty days or so of hard work. I would get an FHA loan on the property and rent it after fixing it up. Usually we would rent it long enough to make any profit on it come under the capital gains provisions in the income tax laws.

Sometimes, though, someone would come in while I was working and tell me they wanted to buy it. I have always been one to think that a dollar in the pocket was worth two on paper, so, if their offer was right, we sold right there and then.

Rose was kept busy picking all the colors and the carpets and wallpaper. We put on lots of wallpaper. It covers a multitude of sins.

We turned out a finished house about every month. By this time I had a college boy helping me. In the next two years we bought twenty-three houses and sold all of them except the one we were living in, one other house, and a threeplex.

After a short time we could easily tell that this life was a bit restrictive after wandering around the world for six and a half years.

One day at breakfast I asked Rosie, "By any chance are you getting tired of this life, all work and not much play?" "Yes," she said, "I am." Talking it over a bit more we decided to call our Ft. Lauderdale friends and ask them to send us some want ads out of the newspapers on used boats for sale.

At the time we were thinking along the lines of a motor sailor. After receiving the paper for a week or ten days there was an ad in it for a thirty-eight-foot twin-diesel power boat that had a price we could afford. We called the number and the old fellow told me that the boat needed some work and that he would come down two thousand dollars if we were interested.

Our van was all packed for a trip to the mountains that coming weekend, so we just turned it around and headed toward Port Salerno, Florida. Four days later we drove into the owner's yard. He took us out on a demonstration ride and hit some coral and rocks going out through the opening into the Atlantic. After turning around, we crippled back to his dock. He was pretty discouraged then, so I made him a low offer, which he accepted. The next day he and I took the boat over to the marina to haul out. The props were badly bent but the shafts had not been damaged.

We left the boat in dry storage so that Rosie and I could head back to Montana to settle the ragged ends of our business.

After returning to Billings we decided to really fix the boat up first class so we could live on it in the winters and spend the summers in Montana. It took four months to sell a couple more houses, find someone to manage what we hadn't sold, and buy some things for the boat that I shipped down to the yard in Port Salerno. I was lucky enough to find, in a junkyard in Billings, a little potbellied stove. We later bolted the stove down in the galley area.

I worked hard on the boat for thirty days: took out the old stove and refrigerator, the settees in the lounge, the old lino-leum.

Rosie picked out some wallpaper for the galley and carpet for the whole boat. The *Mustang III* looked first class when we put her back in the water. To us, the boat seemed large, having almost twice as much room as *Mustang II*.

Mustang III practically gives us a free ride: no putting up the sails, no tacking to get up a channel. With two 100-HP diesels it will turn on, or in, a space its own length. Easy living.

Now we had a home in Florida. What did we do? We imme-diately left Florida, having decided to take a run up to New York City to see one of our daughters. Traveling up the Intra-coastal waterway is a beautiful trip. Rosie said, "This is just how I like to cruise. I can always swim ashore." Since we an-chored or were in a marina every night we had no need for night watches.

We left Port Salerno the sixth day of June 1978 and arrived in New York on July 12. We pulled into a marina at Twenty-third Street on the East River. It was crowded, but after I told the manager that I would sure like to stay there a few days to visit our daughter on Manhattan Island, he found room for us. New York is not all concrete canyons and uncaring people.

We had heard a lot about the New York barge canal and

decided to find the charts for the Hudson, the canal, and the Great Lakes, and then sail up the Hudson, into the canal at Albany via the Mohawk river. I had read about this stretch of water all my life, and could hardly believe we were actually traveling its full length by boat. We were told that George Washington helped survey some of that project.

We made our way across the Great Lakes to Chicago, down the Illinois river, and on down the Mississippi, finally returning to Florida.

Florida is close to heaven in the winter months; it's wonderful to be out by the swimming pool or cooking dinner outside in the evening.

We never go any place by car if it can possibly be reached by boat. We do fly or drive up to Montana each summer, where we keep a fifteen-foot sailboat on a lake near Helena.

More trips are in the planning stage. As they say here, "You can get to any place from Florida."

Often people ask me whether I would like to take another trip around the world. I would like to, but there are so many interesting places in our part of the world that it could occupy a lifetime.

Rosie often says, "For one million dollars I would not willingly again put foot on a small boat that was departing to sail across the Pacific, Indian, or Atlantic Ocean."

She means it, too. Try as I might, I just can't seem to convince her that we had a delightful, practically trouble-free six years—the best six years of my life.

It May Rain

e cloudiness Monday
w showers or thunder
Cooler Monday with
of 65 and the low of 40
will be cloudy and cool
weather, vitals page 8

The Billings Gazette

84th Year—No. 45　　　　Billings, Montana, Monday Morning, June 16, 1969　　　　10c

Billings Couple to Live a Dream

By ROSS CARLETTA
Gazette Staff Writer

going to take quite a bit to
o with these Jones.

h and Rosemary Jones,
. 30th St., are going to do
millions of Americans
ove to do if only they had
rage.

r 10 years of planning,
g. studying and learning
e almost through building
-foot, two - masted, sea -
ketch which will be their
to the kind of freedom
everyone would like to

very nail and screw and
put into place by Jones

this is almost incident
ctual feat of the craf
ction.

gh Jones and his w
ut the project casua
e obviously proud
d that their drea
oming true.

Jones brushes of
mments by sayin
o one would think

ars ago Jones bu
t barn in the ba
ly to house the
s construction.

then on it was nothing
an hard work. Jones is
vice in building boats.
uilt many, but none this

INISHED product will
, they estimate, about
To buy such a ship,
s, would cost about

ans alone cost $150,
purchased from a ship
Edwin Monk, of Seat-

ans were originally
1942 for a Canadian.
an was killed in World
r giving Monk a retai-
were only five sets of
lable. Jones is one of

y there is a great deal

have — a slow, five - year voyage
arou the world.

It　　　　　　　10 years to
com
have
hav
the
qu
lo
tr
w
v

As one
home the two masts can
protruding from the barn.

"The mizzen was man - han-
dled to the top of the barn and
dropped through the hole in the
roof," Jones explains.

The larger main mast
into place with t
friends and a hydr
et owned by the N
Service, which jus
be working in the
when Jones needed

THE MAST was
the bucket's help a
through the other h
roof and lowered into
Many of the fixture
galley and head were p
fr m marine supply co
in Portland and Seattle.

The Jones have their
tion equipment and wit

Jones seems to be a firm be-
liever that "you can't take it
with you."

ile up money and then
to enjoy

which w
bowsprit. The hea
the Jones are particularly
is being carv

Needless to say Jones has
help in this monumental feat.

HE IS learning the art
science of navigation from
1001 Rimrock Ro
constar

Rosemary Jones takes a break from construction work on "Mustang" to dream about the
voyage which lies ahead of her and her husband, Keith. The 36-foot ketch will be ready
for transportation to Seattle July 28.

Dreaming?

Billings Landlubbers Have Their Troubles

SEATTLE (AP) — After 10
years of leisure-time labor on a
36-foot ketch, Keith Jones of
Billings, finally lowered the
craft into the salty sea near Seattle only to see it promptly
to sink.

afloat in a sling, the water
for the Mustang what Monta
humidity couldn't — sw
the seams — and she
ready to brave her new en
ment.

A few weeks ago the J
set out along the Pacifi
toward a final destina
They sailed to